IMAGES
of America

ABILENE

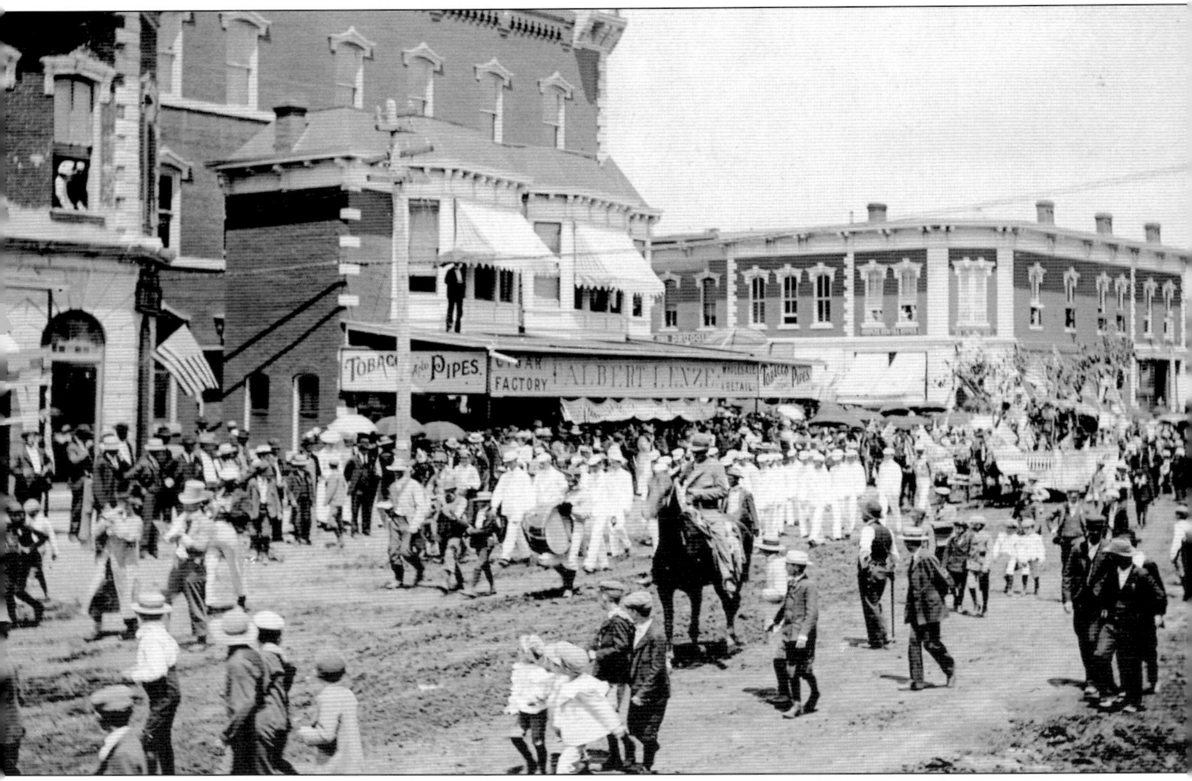

Busy and bustling, Abilene in the 1890s was full of parades, civic celebrations, and entrepreneurship. The essence of this bustling town is captured with the displays and collections of the Heritage Center of Dickinson County. The historical museum houses exhibits depicting life on the Plains during the American pioneer movement and westward expansion periods. Visitors can learn about Plains Indians, prairie settlers, and Abilene businessmen and businesswomen. The center also houses the Museum of Independent Telephony, which traces the development of the telephone industry. Outdoor exhibits include a fully restored 1901 C.W. Parker Carousel and a pioneer community made from actual buildings moved to the site from various communities. Visitors can see an outhouse, barn, blacksmith shop, telephone office, and general store. (Courtesy Heritage Center of Dickinson County.)

On the Cover: Sand Springs Bottling Company was established in 1908 and provided the citizens of Abilene with mineral water, carbonated drinks, root beer, and ginger ale. The proud manufacturers claimed that the water pumped in from the Sand Springs was 99 percent pure and full of health. (Courtesy Heritage Center of Dickinson County.)

IMAGES
of America

ABILENE

Stephanie Bearce and the
Dickinson County Historical Society

ARCADIA
PUBLISHING

ISBN 978-0-7385-9053-0

Published by Arcadia Publishing
Charleston, South Carolina

Printed in the United States of America

Library of Congress Control Number: 2011940522

For all general information, please contact Arcadia Publishing:
Telephone 843-853-2070
Fax 843-853-0044
E-mail sales@arcadiapublishing.com
For customer service and orders:
Toll-Free 1-888-313-2665

Visit us on the Internet at www.arcadiapublishing.com

To all my friends and family who live in the great state of Kansas.

Contents

Acknowledgments 6

Introduction 7

1. Rails and Trails 9

2. Prairie and People 23

3. Fairs, Festivals, and Fun 41

4. Boom Years 63

5. Parker's Carousels 87

6. Defying Disaster 93

7. Politics and Presidents 107

ACKNOWLEDGMENTS

As a Kansas schoolchild, I have fond memories of field trips to Abilene. We toured President Eisenhower's home and library. We had fun visiting Old Abilene Town, watching the reenactments of local gunfights and learning about the heritage of our great state. It has been a true pleasure to research the history of such a vibrant community. My deepest thanks to the staff of the Heritage Center of Dickinson County, who allowed me full access to their archives and patiently answered my questions. A special thanks to Jeff Sheets for all the work he does in developing programs to educate adults and children about the history of Abilene and the Chisholm Trail. Any factual errors in this book are entirely my responsibility. I have tried to give an overview of the early history of Abilene using the photographs available from the Heritage Center. The information in this book is archival and concentrates on the first 100 years of Abilene history. Thank you to my patient husband, Darrell, and my supportive family. Also, a big thank you to my parents, who taught me about the joy of history and the quest for knowledge. All photographs in this book are courtesy of the Heritage Center of Dickinson County.

INTRODUCTION

Timothy Hersey was the first settler to stake a claim in the area that is now known as Abilene, Kansas. He built a log cabin on Mud Creek in 1856 and was joined by his family the next year. The Hersey family was one of a handful of settlers who lived in the area platted as Dickinson County. Homesteaders were slow in recognizing the value of the upland prairies. Most pioneers made their homes close to creeks and streams and considered other land to be worthless grassland, but Hersey took a plow to the sod and was one of the first settlers in the area to prove the value of the rich prairie soil.

The 1862 Homestead Act signed into law by Abraham Lincoln made 160 acres of land available to anyone willing to live on the land for five years, build a home, and raise crops. More families moved into the area, and it became apparent to Kansas officials that a county seat should be named. Hersey and his neighbor C.H. Thompson saw the advantage of having the county seat located by their land, so part of the Thompson land was surveyed and laid out into town lots, and a few log cabins were hastily constructed. Hersey's wife, Eliza, was given the task of naming the town and decided on Abilene, referencing Luke 3:1 in the Bible. The newly built Abilene was put into the competition for county seat and won.

The growth of Abilene was rather slow until the arrival of the Kansas Pacific Railway in 1866. Settlers could ride in fast-moving railcars rather than the slow-moving horse and wagon. Supplies could be shipped to farmers, and in turn they could market their grain and animals in the city. One of the settlers who arrived by rail was Joseph McCoy. This young entrepreneur saw the advantage of the location of Abilene on the rail line directly north of Texas. Due to the Civil War, Northern cities had a shortage of beef, and lack of rail lines in Texas left ranchers with no market. McCoy lobbied the cattlemen of Texas to drive their herds up the Chisholm Trail to Abilene. From there, the cattle could be shipped out to city markets. The ranchers, McCoy, and Abilene would all profit. McCoy's plan was a success, and from 1867 to 1871 three million head of cattle were driven to Abilene, making it the first of the Western cow towns.

Payday came at the end of the cattle trail, and money flowed through the hands of cowboys like whiskey at a party. Gambling, alcohol, gunfights, and prostitutes all became a part of life in Abilene. The town fathers tried to tame the streets by bringing in lawmen such as Tom "Bear River" Smith and Wild Bill Hickok, but neither of these famous marshals was successful. The townspeople became extremely frustrated and requested that McCoy move his cattle operations to another site. Only when the cowboys left town did Abilene become a "civilized" city.

Boom time for Abilene came with the plowing of the prairie. The thick prairie sod proved to be fertile for crops, and farmers started planting corn, wheat, and sorghum. Cattle grazed the prairie. Train cars carried crops to market and settlers to Abilene. By the 1890s, Abilene offered its citizens a fire department, gas works, streetlights, and three railroad lines. The Union Pacific Railroad was joined by the Sate Fe and Rock Island Railroads. The three railroads built the north-south feeder lines to the major east-west rails, providing excellent transportation opportunities for the citizens of Abilene and surrounding communities. Small factories and manufacturing plants were established. Mills and cream stations sprang up and began servicing the agricultural community. Chelson Brown opened his independent telephone company.

Growth did not come without pain. Drought was a constant threat. At one point, the neighboring town of Solomon contracted with Rock Island to have its "rainmaking car" visit the city. The residents paid the sum of $200 only to find that the rain car was a sham. Tornadoes ripped through farms and towns, causing damage to property and crops. Grasshopper infestations devoured crops and ruined the livelihood of some homesteaders. Each year, a few less hearty souls would pack their bags and board the train to go "back East." Plains farming was only for those who could endure both boom and bust.

Despite drought, tornado, and pestilence, some businesses thrived. C.W. Parker started his amusement company in Abilene in the 1890s. An intuitive mechanic, Parker learned about amusement games by first repairing and then running a mechanical shooting gallery. He purchased and refurbished a used carousel before deciding that he could build a better one himself. From the humble beginnings of a workshop in Abilene, Parker grew his company to be America's largest manufacturer of amusement devices. In amusement-park circles, C.W. Parker was known as the "King of the Carnival."

World politics interrupted life in Abilene during "The Great War." In May of 1917, it was announced that Dickinson County had to provide 250 men for the war. Young men between the ages of 21 and 30 trained in Abilene and were shipped out on August 4. Company H from Abilene saw combat in France, and casualties were heavy. They returned home to Abilene in April 1919.

One famous hometown boy was Dwight D. Eisenhower. A young man who loved books and sports, Eisenhower played both baseball and football for Abilene High School. After graduation, he worked at the local creamery until he received an appointment to West Point. During World War II, Eisenhower became a household name when he served as the supreme commander of the allied forces in Europe. He was named a five-star general, and his war strategies were critical to the allied victory. He was elected as president of the United States and served his country in this role from 1953 to 1961. Eisenhower always considered Abilene his hometown. He selected it as the site of his presidential library and museum. His gravesite is also in Abilene next to his beloved wife, Maime, and their son, David.

Abilene's rich agricultural heritage lives on today. Farms and ranches produce hundreds of thousands of bushels of food and pounds of meat for the American economy. Visitors still marvel at the beautiful Victorian-era homes and buildings, and thousands of visitors flock to the museum to learn why the world not only respected but also liked Ike.

One

Rails and Trails

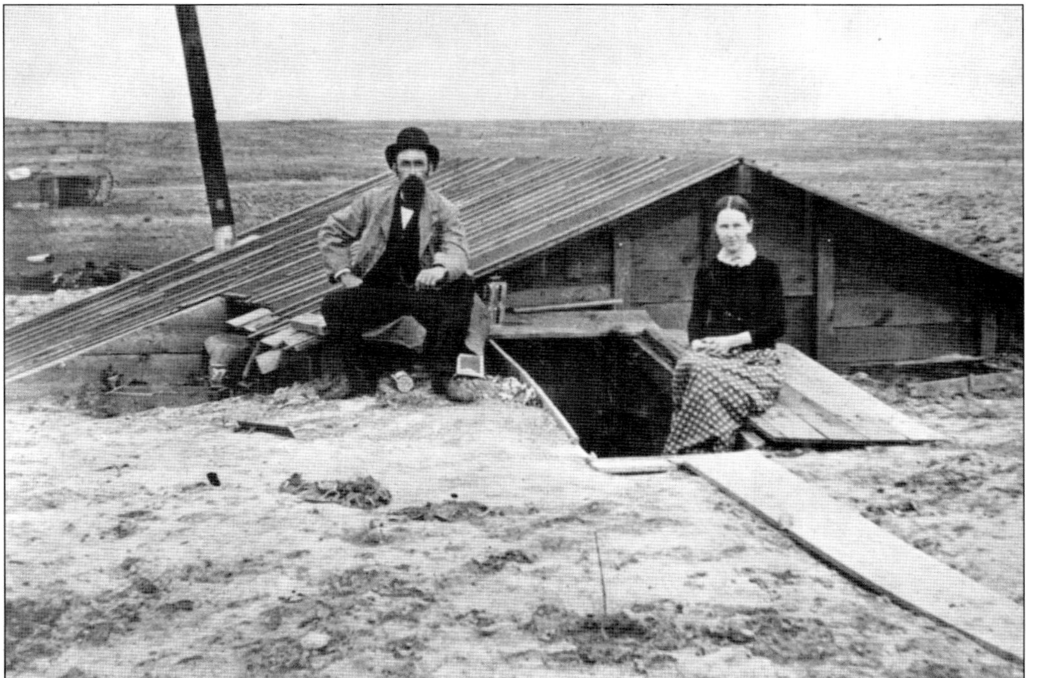

Settlers on the Abilene prairie solved the problem of lumber scarcity by digging down. Dugouts protected settlers from harsh wind and snowstorms, but they were small and dirty homes. Pioneer wives had to constantly watch for snakes in the house.

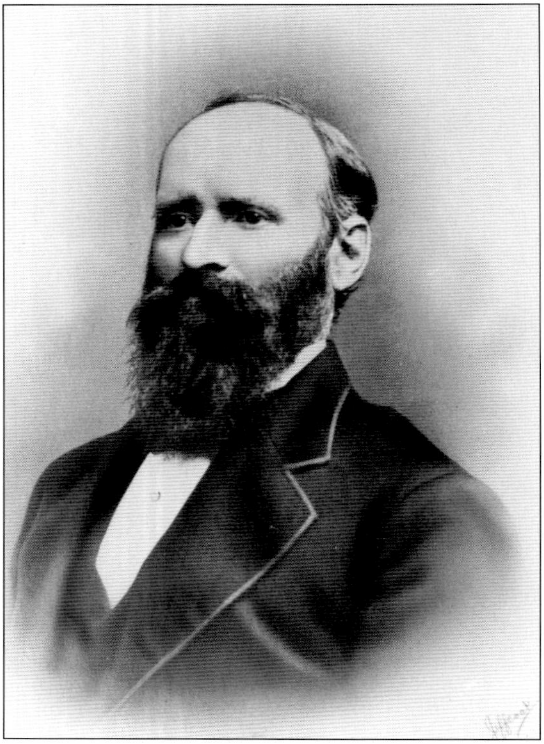

Timothy Hersey was the farsighted pioneer who envisioned a county seat where only grass stood. He saw the potential for the prairie to produce crops and was the first in the area to break the sod.

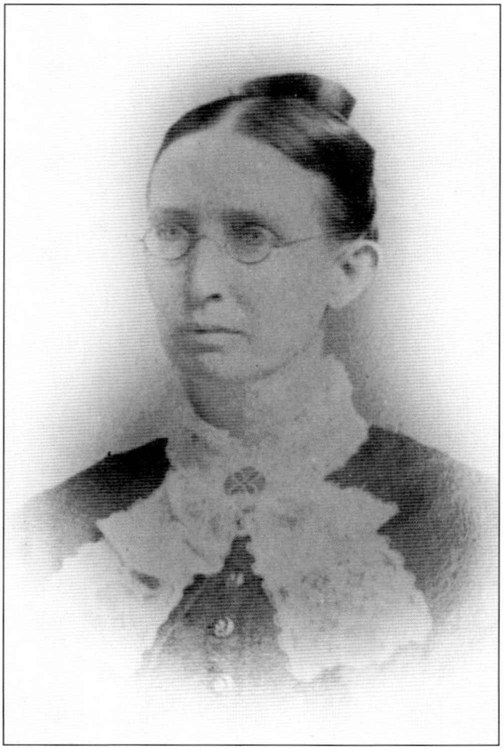

Eliza Hersey christened the town of Abilene with a name taken from a passage in the Bible. The name means "city on the plains."

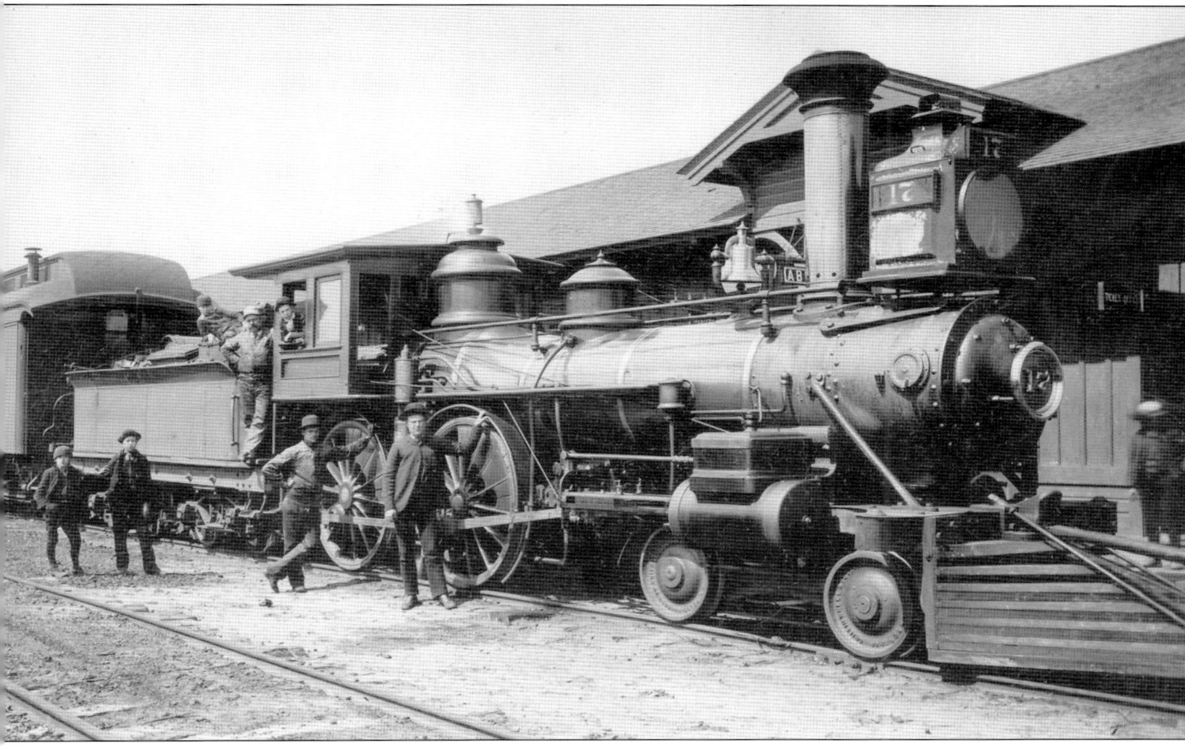

On March 15, 1867, the first Kansas Pacific train rolled into the newly built Abilene Depot. With its arrival came more settlers and the ability to ship and receive goods to the East.

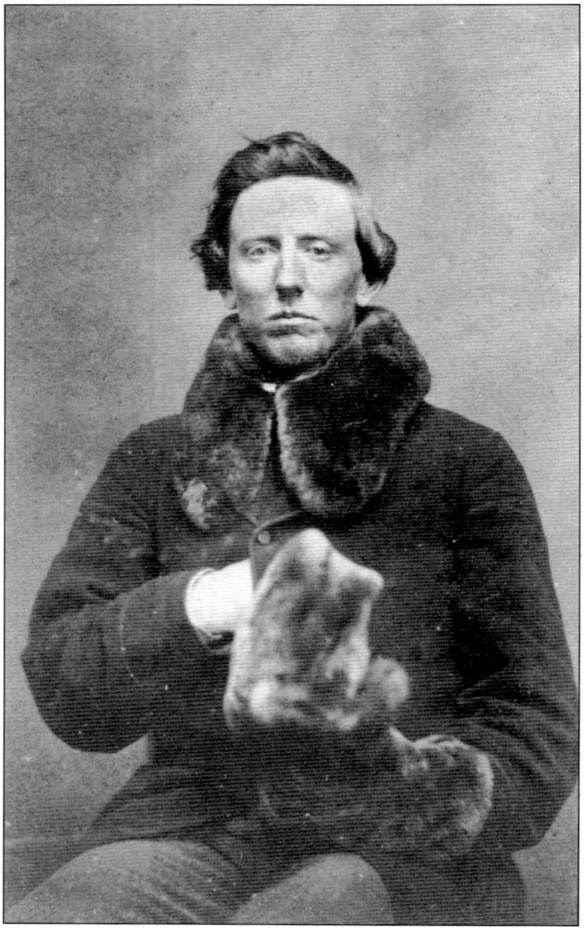

Joseph G. McCoy saw opportunity and profit in Abilene. After the Civil War, beef was scarce in the North, and cattle were sold for the premium price of $40 a head. In Texas, however, cattle were plentiful and selling for a mere $4 per animal. By driving cattle up the Chisholm Trail to Abilene, the animals could be shipped out by railcar to the East and everyone would profit.

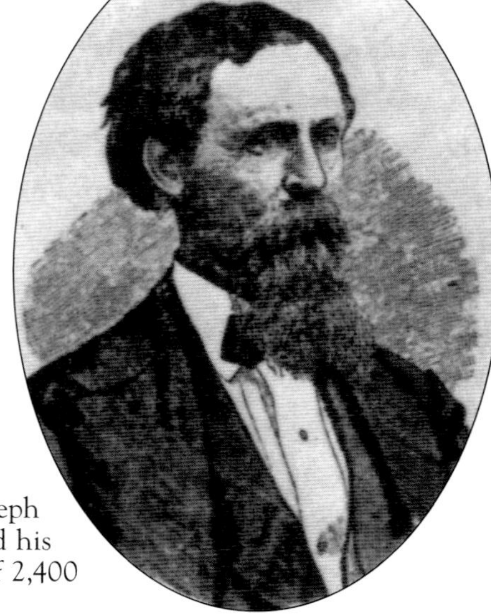

O.W. Wheeler was the first cattleman to answer Joseph McCoy's call to a cattle drive. In 1867, Wheeler and his partners used the Chisholm Trail to bring a herd of 2,400 steers from Texas to Abilene, Kansas.

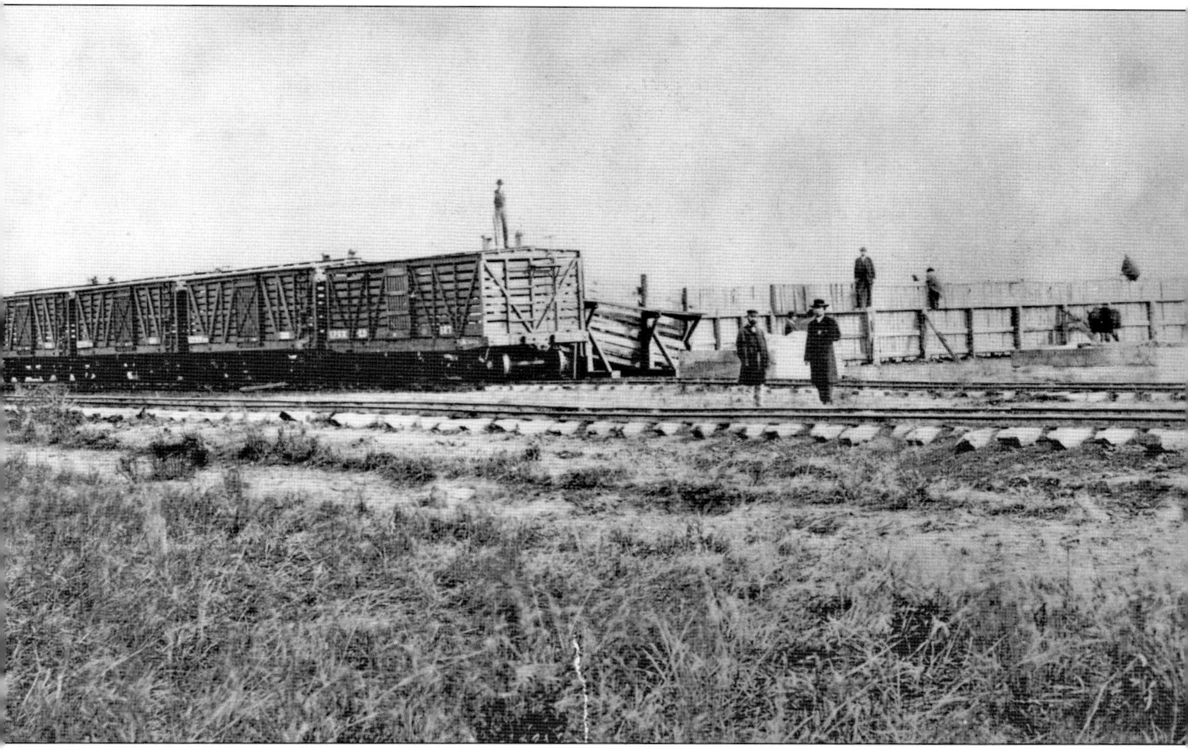

Joseph G. McCoy and other cattlemen stand by stock cars ready to be loaded with cattle in Abilene.

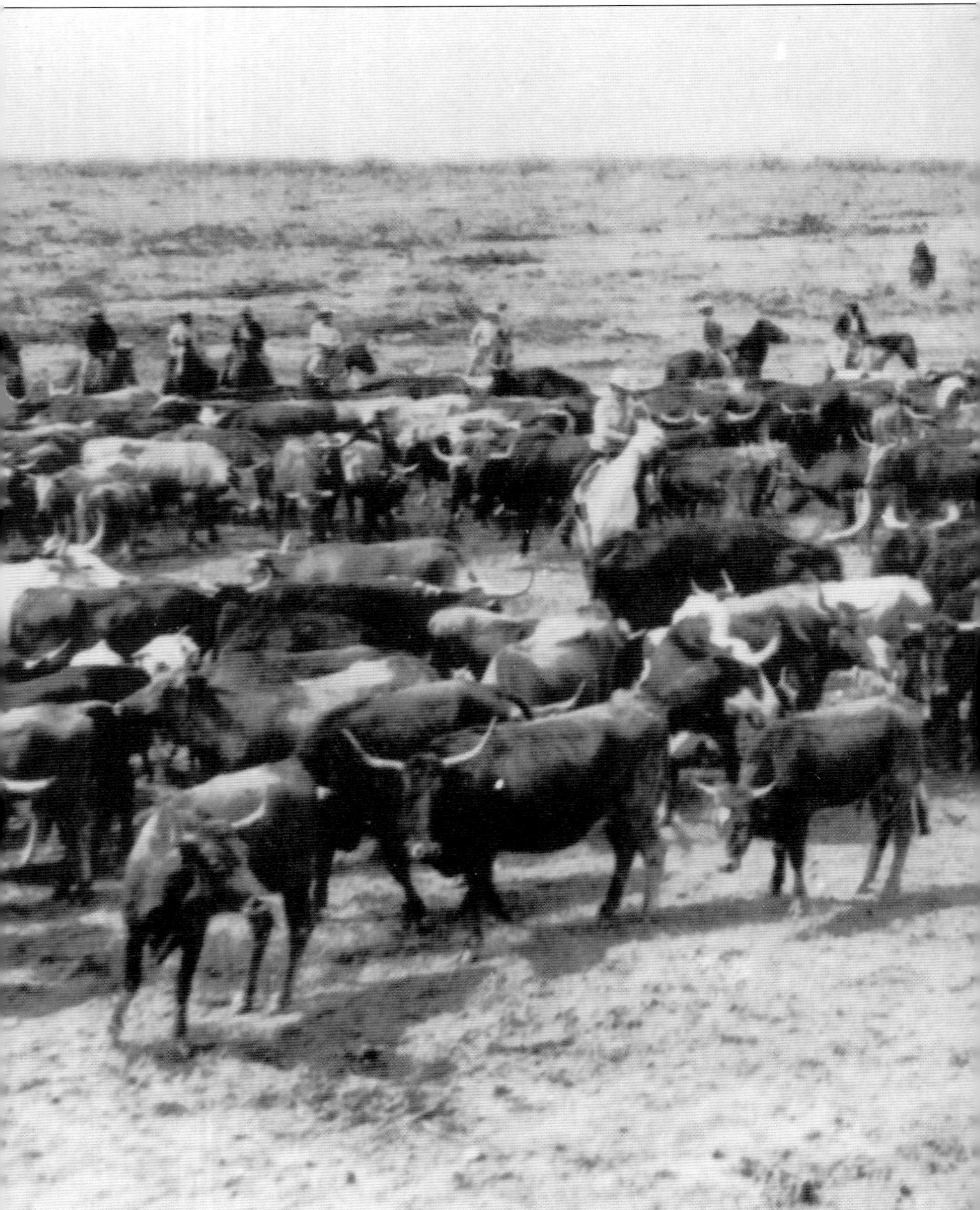

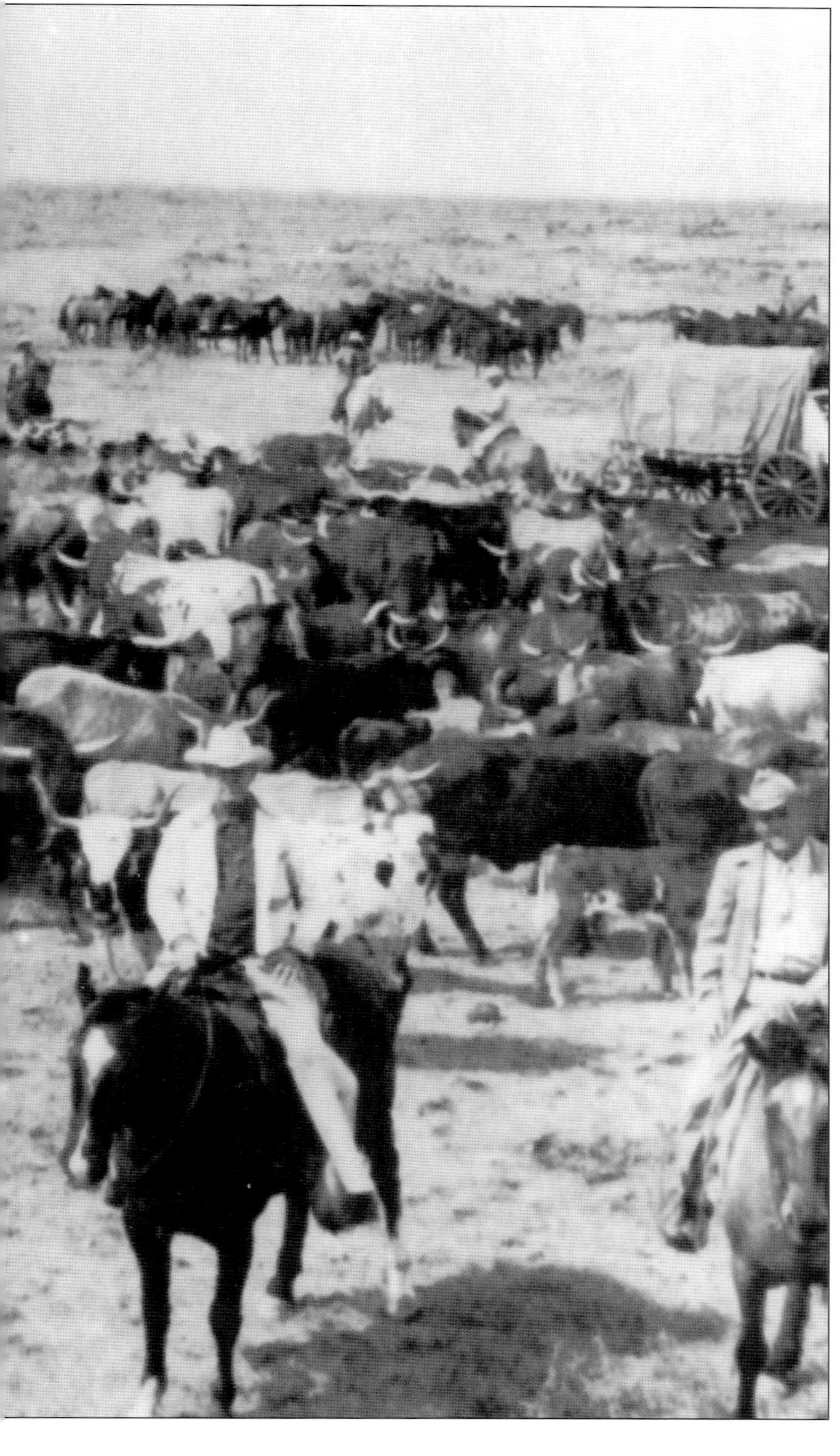

The Texas cattle were a hearty breed and actually gained weight on the trail. Herding was slow to keep cattle from stampeding, so there was plenty of time to graze on the rich prairie grass.

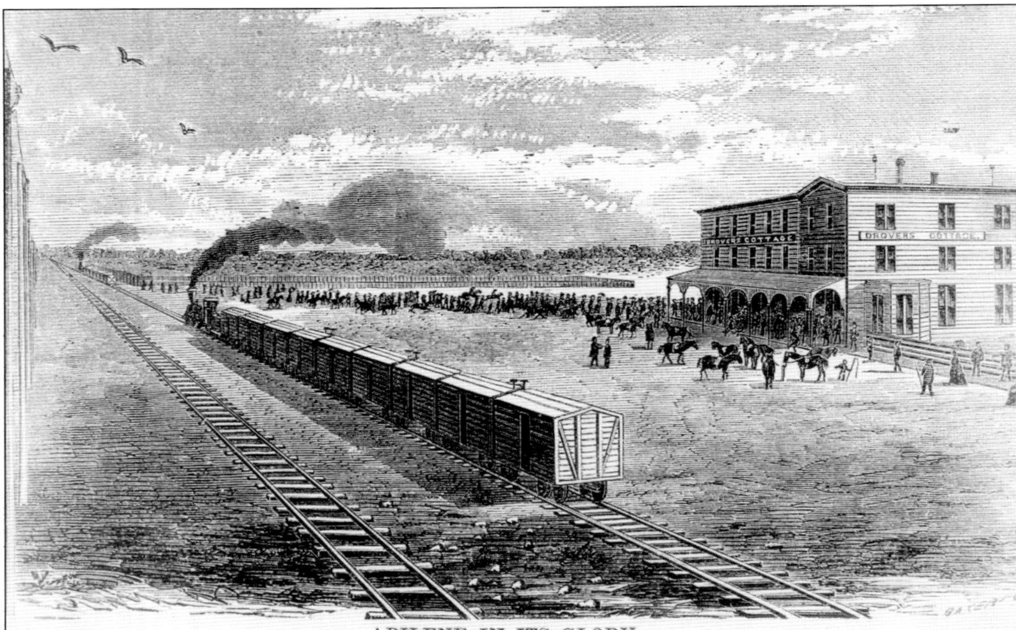

ABILENE IN ITS GLORY·

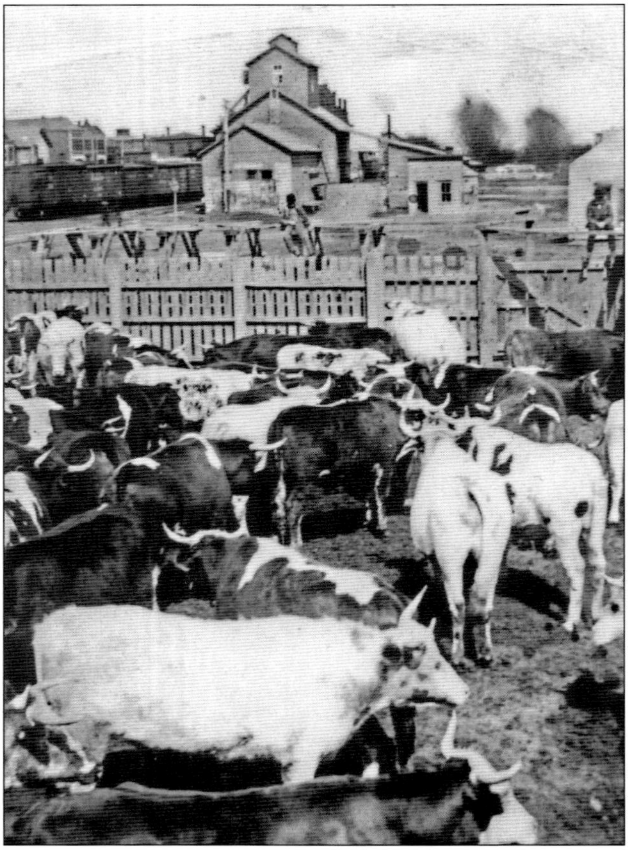

By 1868, Joseph McCoy had built a stockyard, a hotel named Drovers Cottage, and a bank. Abilene had officially become a cow town.

Cattle were held in Abilene stockyards until they were shipped out on railcars. From 1867 to 1871, over a million head of cattle were driven up the Chisholm Trail to Abilene.

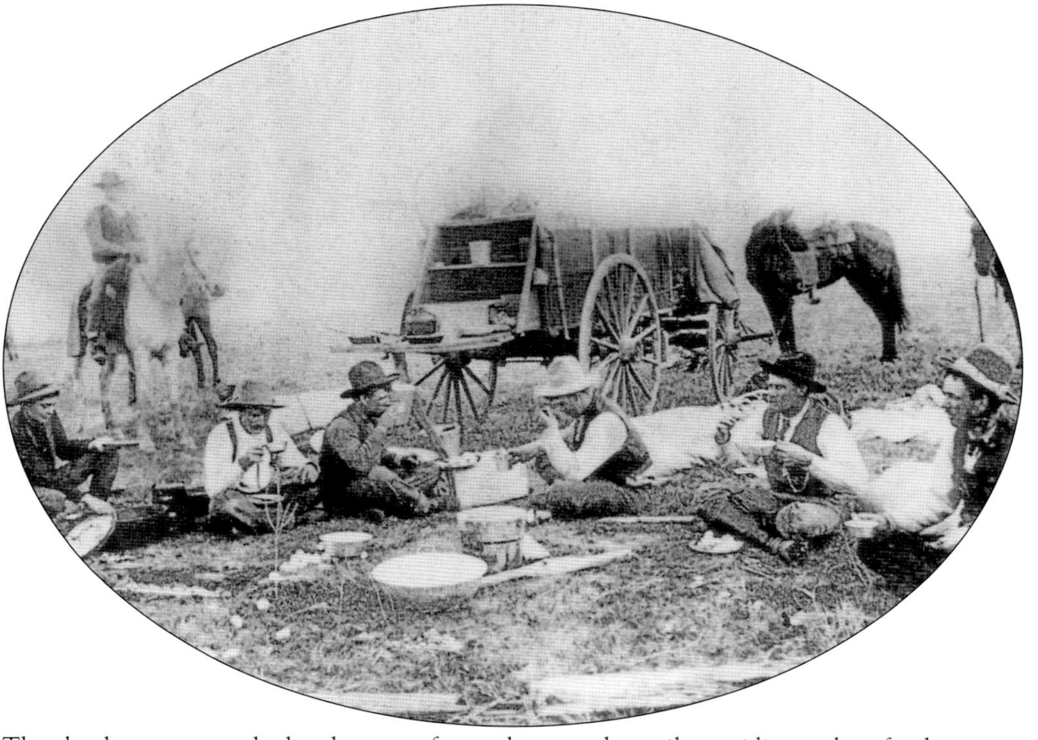

The chuck wagon was the headquarters for cowboys on the trail, providing a place for drovers to rest. Pictured outside Abilene, these cowboys are enjoying a cup of coffee before beginning the final drive into town.

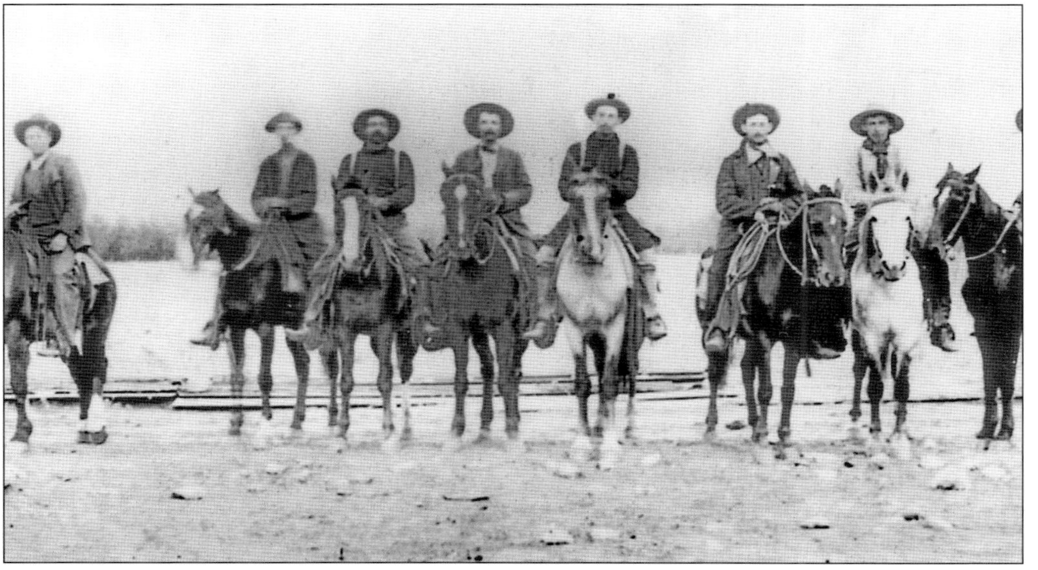

Drovers (cowboys that herded cattle) were the backbone of the Abilene cattle industry. After months on the trail, they arrived in Abilene, received their pay, and were ready to have some fun. Unfortunately, the fun sometimes turned violent. Gunfights, saloon brawls, and skirmishes at brothels became a part of life in Abilene.

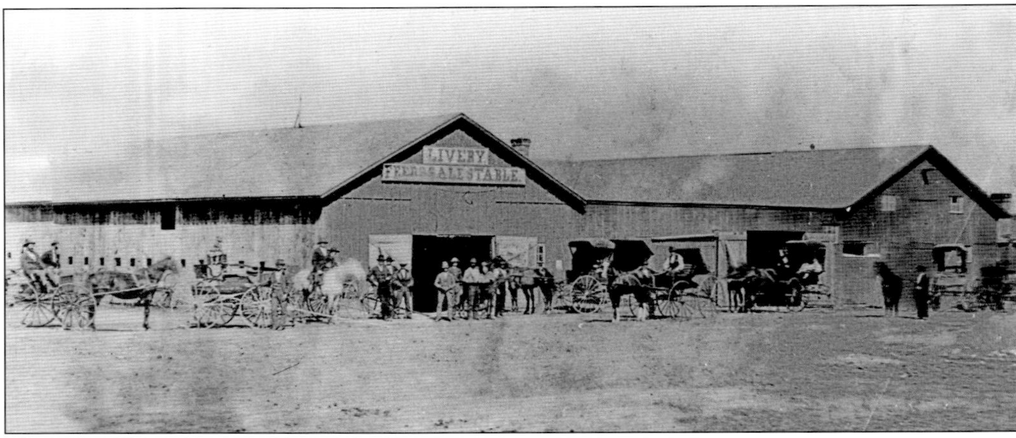

These twin livery stables, built in 1868, were located in Abilene between Second and Third Streets and just east of Spruce Street. They were operated by Ed Gaylord and used by Joseph G. McCoy.

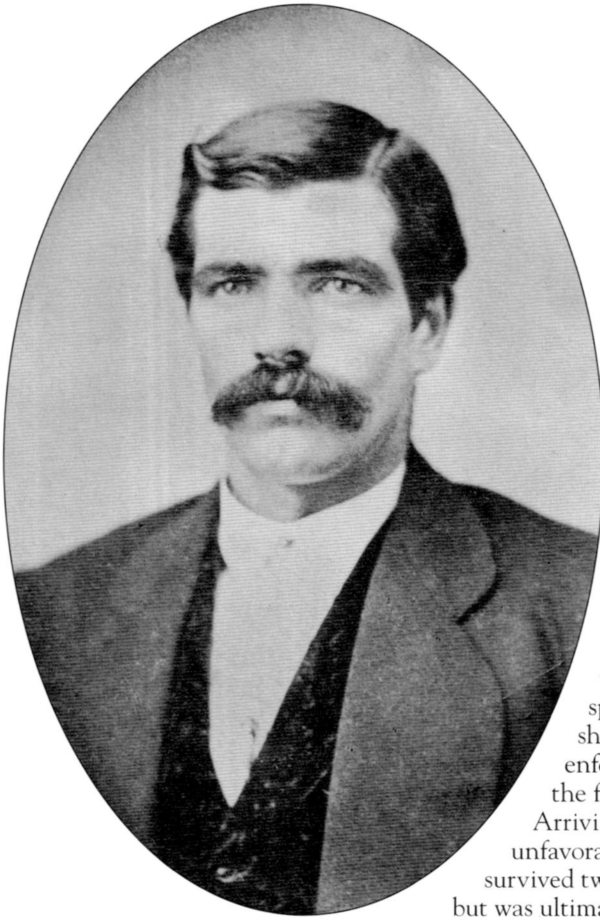

Payday for the cowboys came at the end of the trail, and Abilene provided many ways for a young cowhand to spend his cash. Gambling, brothels, and shooting caused the citizens' outcry for law enforcement. Tom "Bear River" Smith was the first man to become the town's marshal. Arriving in late 1869, he implemented a highly unfavorable "no guns in town limit" rule. Smith survived two assassination attempts in two months but was ultimately murdered in November 1870.

James Butler Hickok, otherwise known as "Wild Bill" Hickok, was hired as sheriff of Abilene in April 1871. Town residents hoped that this well-known quick draw would be able to keep peace and order in the village.

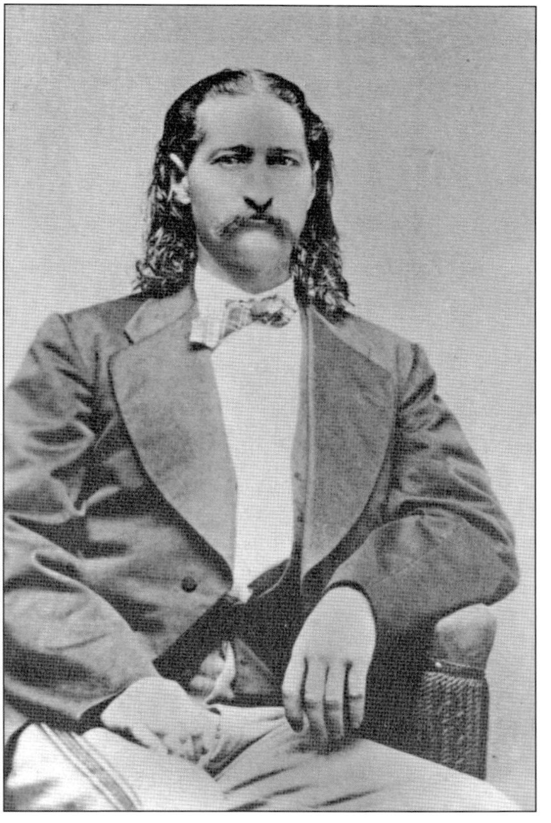

Bill Hickok was presented this watch in October 1871, but two months later he was dismissed as sheriff after accidentally shooting and killing his deputy. Hickok had an ongoing dispute with saloon owner Phil Coe. On October 5, 1871, Hickok was attempting to stop a street brawl when Coe fired two shots into the crowd. Hickok ordered him to be arrested. Coe explained that he was shooting at a stray dog and then turned his gun on Hickok. Coe took two shots at Wild Bill, and Bill then fired a shot a Coe, killing him. Hickok's friend, former deputy Mike Williams, came running to help, and Bill mistakenly thought he was an attacker. Hickok shot and killed Williams—it haunted him the rest of his life.

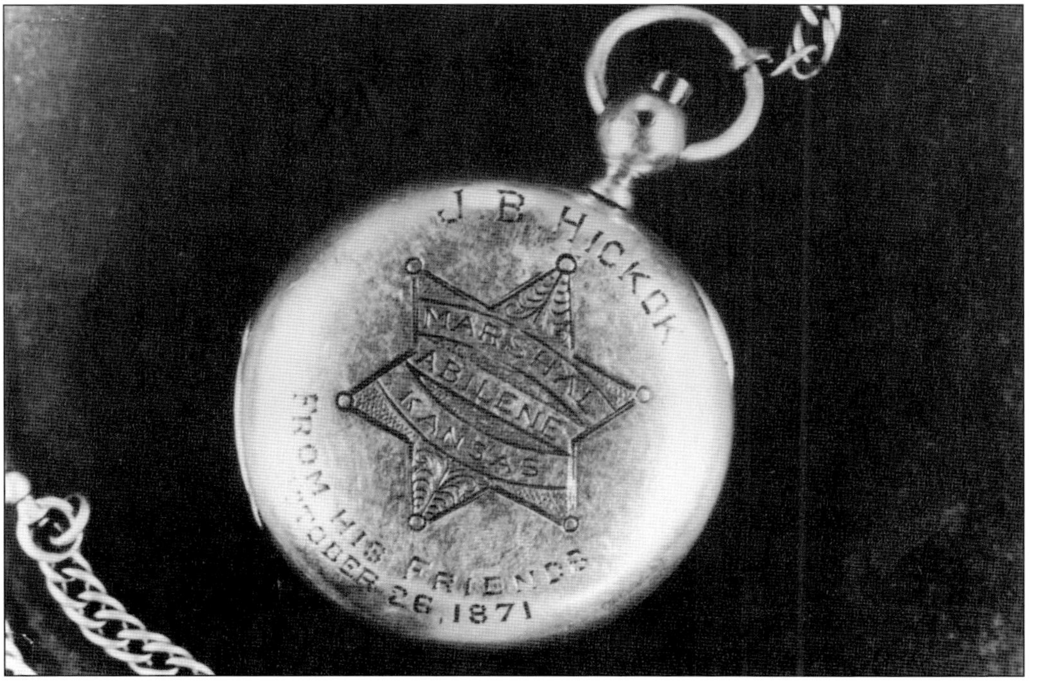

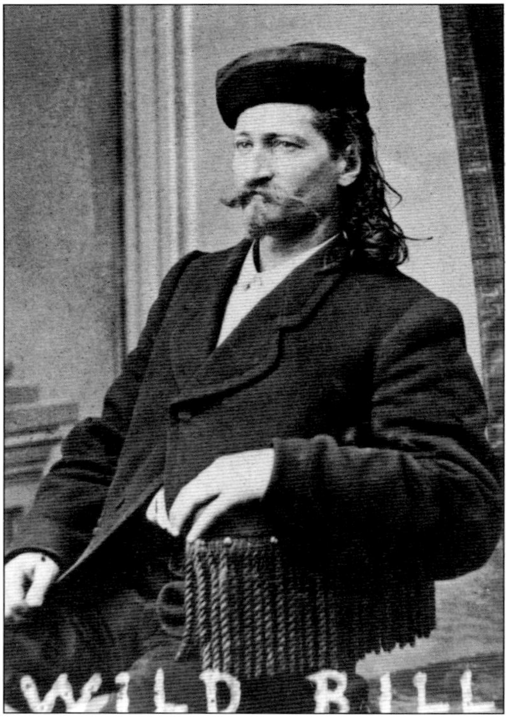

Hickok was killed only five years after leaving Abilene. He was playing poker in the city of Deadwood in the Black Hills of Dakota Territory when a buffalo hunter named John McCall shot him in the back. Hickok died while playing his favorite game.

Ramon Rucus, an expert rider and roper, served as a drover on the Chisholm Trail in 1870 and 1871. After his days on the trail, he homesteaded land south of Abilene. His son became the Dickinson County representative to the Kansas Legislature.

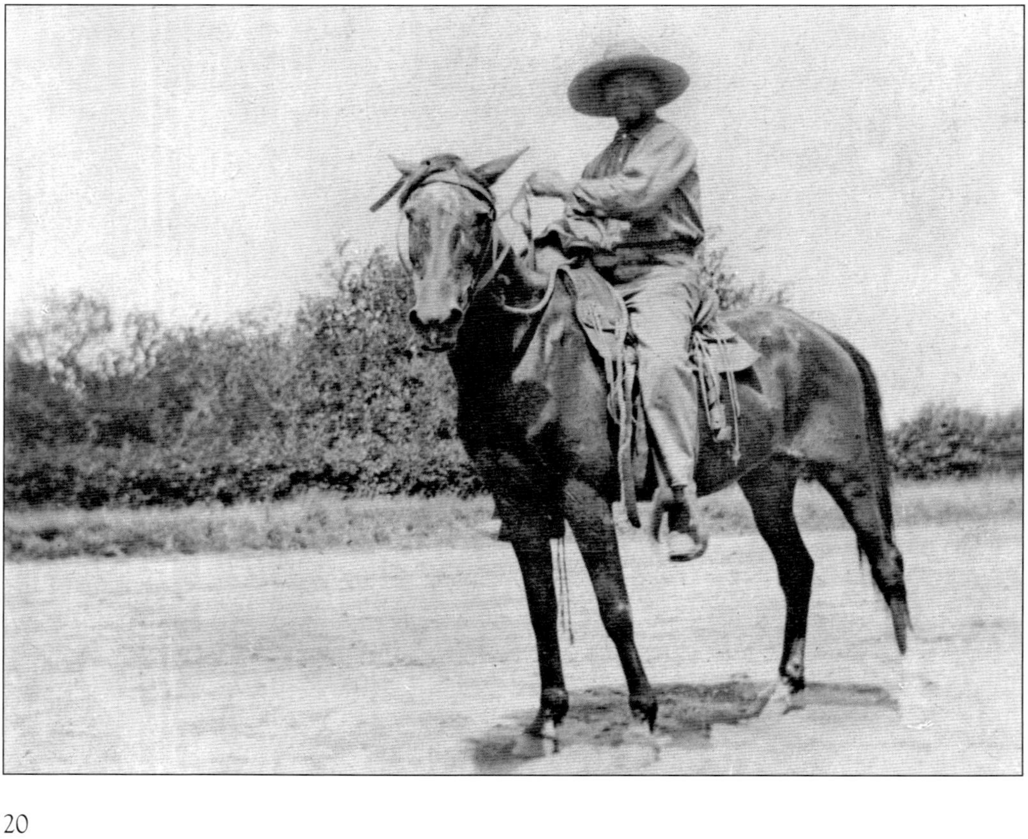

In this photograph, taken after the cattle-drive era, are Joseph McCoy (seated) alongside his brother James McCoy. After leaving the cattle-trail business, Joseph went on to serve as a representative to Congress for the Territory of Oklahoma. He wrote a memoir of his cattle days entitled *Historic Sketches of the Cattle Trade of the West and Southwest*. It was published in 1874.

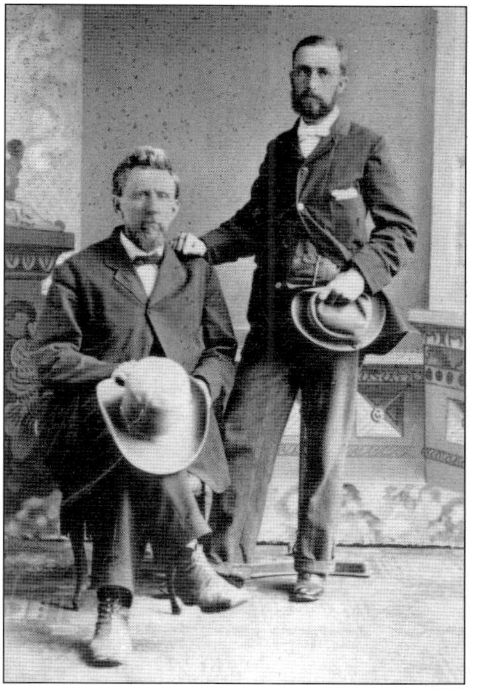

In the fall of 1871, the last of the cattle herds was driven to Abilene. Residents were tired of hosting the wild cowboys, their fights, and saloons. Joseph McCoy honored the requests of the residents. The stockyards of the Chisholm Trail were moved to Ellsworth, Kansas, and Abilene began a new life as an agricultural center.

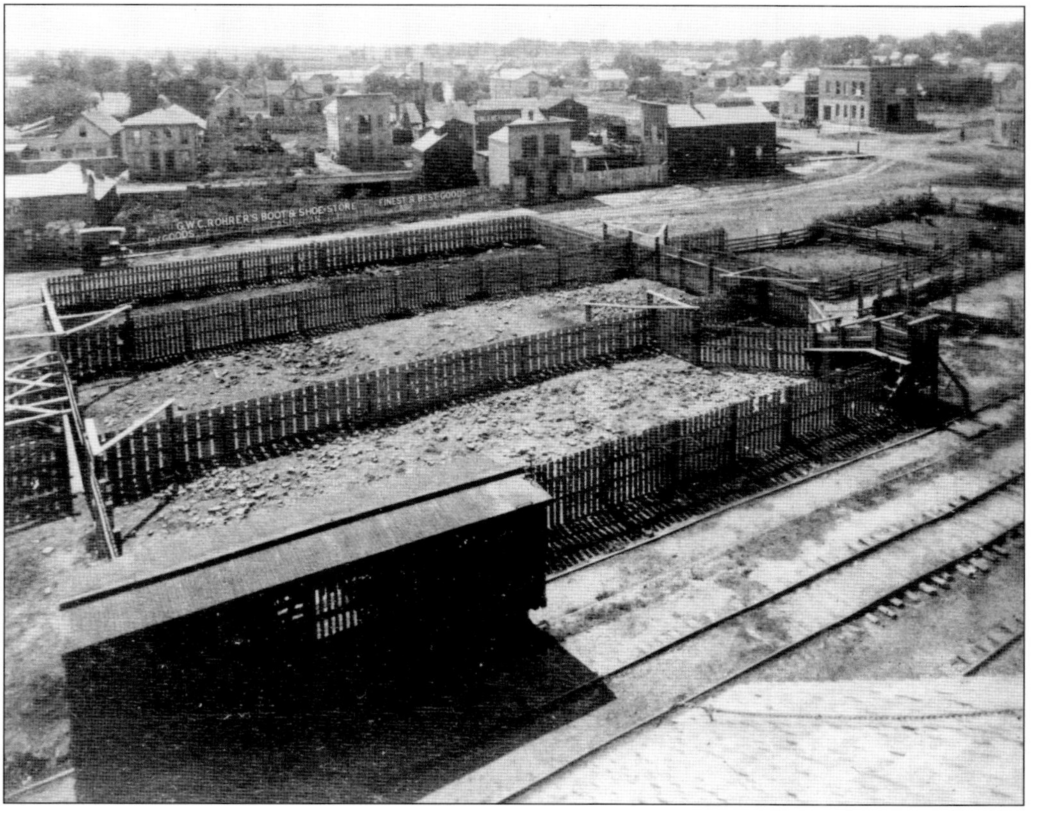

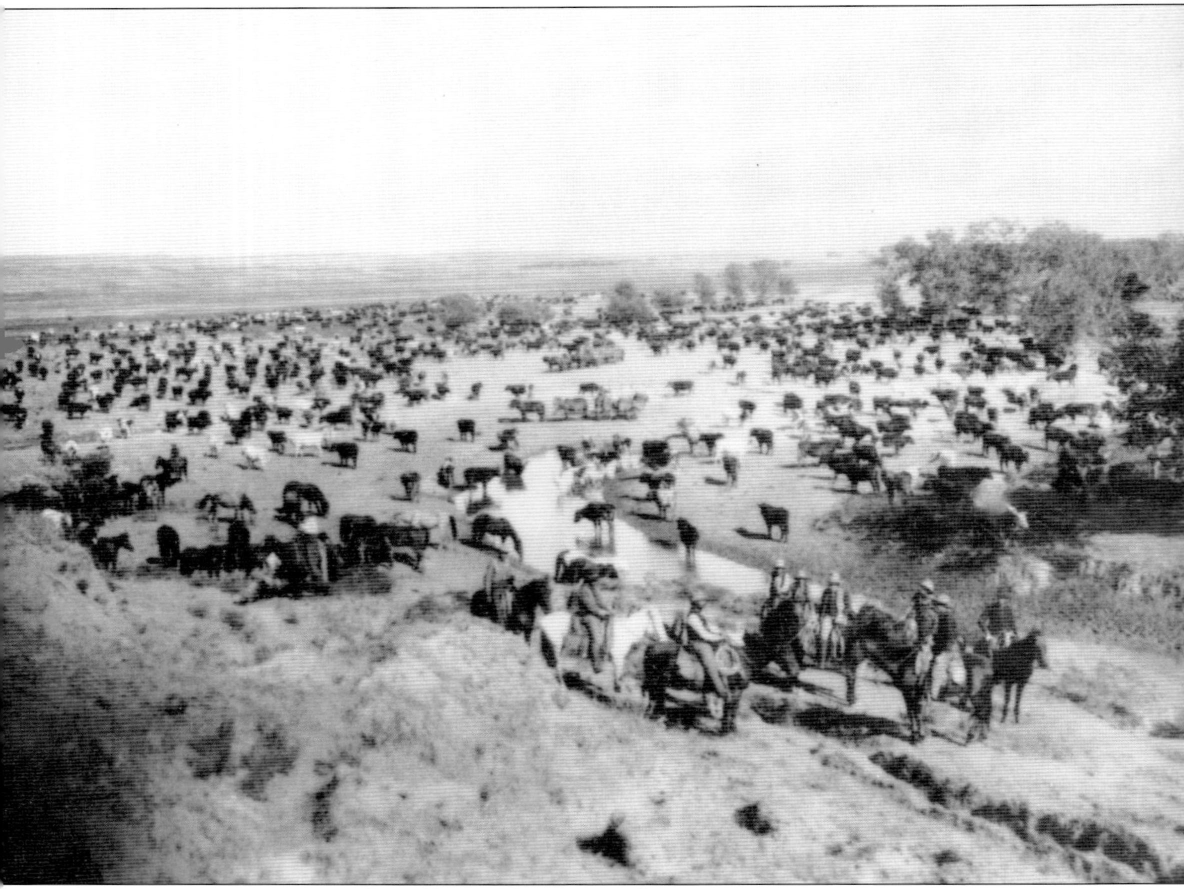

From 1867 to 1872, about 1.5 million cattle were moved up the Chisholm Trail from Texas to Abilene.

Two

PRAIRIE AND PEOPLE

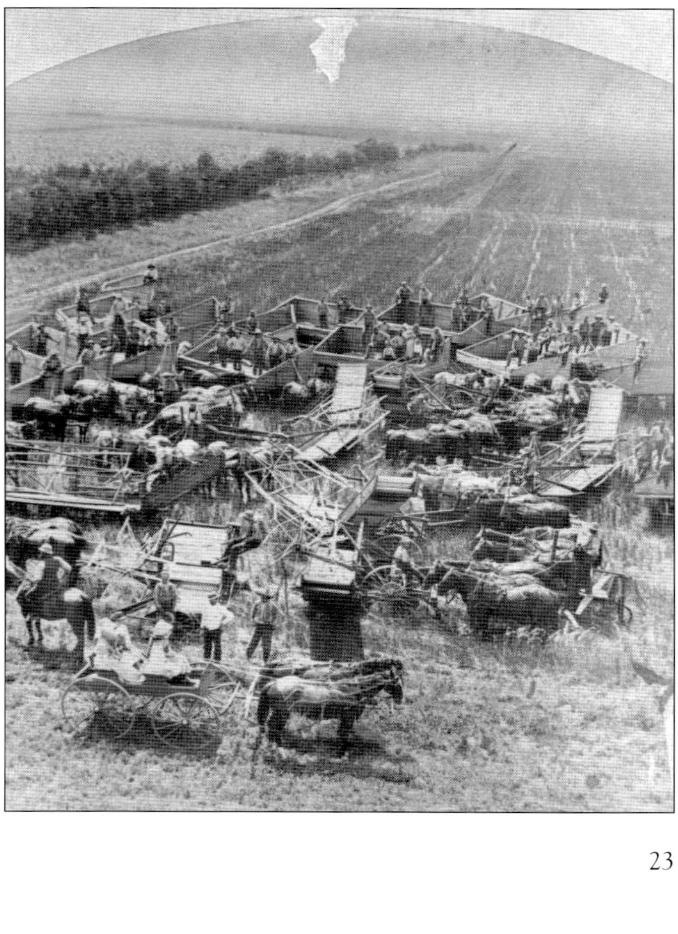

The fall of 1871 saw the end of the cattle drives to Abilene. The success of winter wheat crops were bringing farmers to the area, but farmers and drovers had a natural conflict of interest. Farmers wanted to raise crops on the upland prairie, while the Drovers wanted to graze their cattle in the same area. Cattle trampled crops and caused significant financial damage, and the farmers were outraged. Laws were eventually enacted to protect a farmer's right to protect his own land.

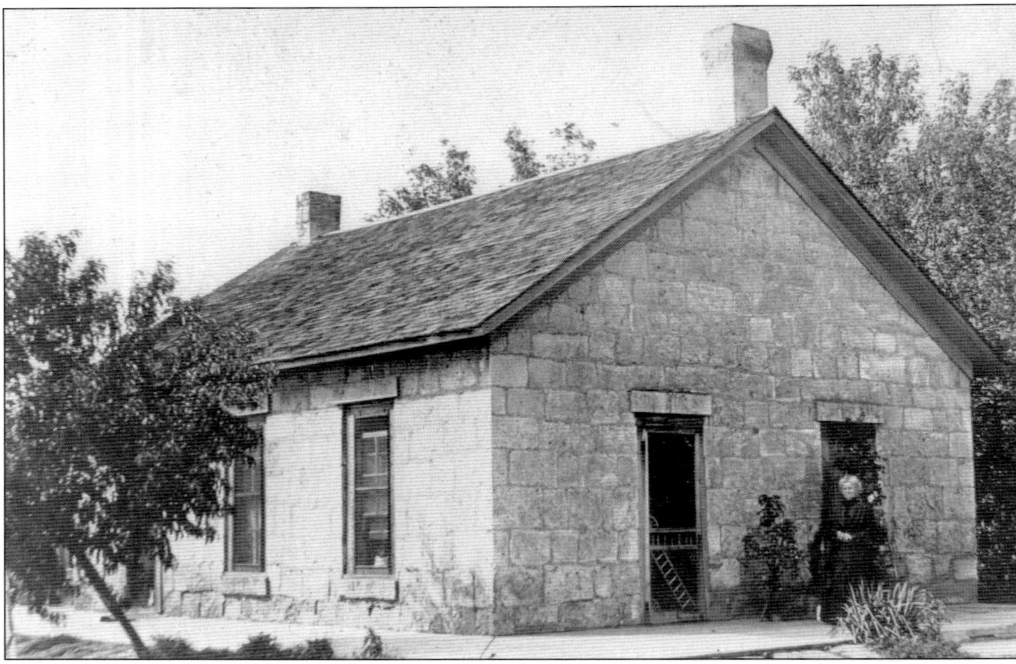

The first school in Abilene, built in 1869, was located in the area that is now the southwest corner of Second and Mulberry Streets. This one-room schoolhouse provided a basic education for all Abilene children who were of school age, sparing them from farmwork.

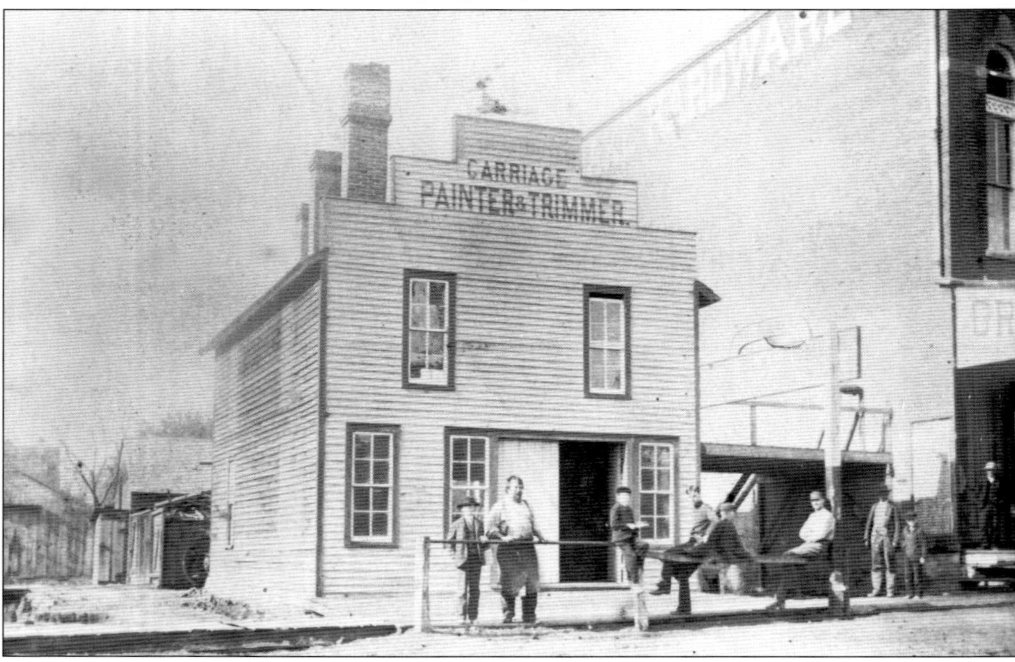

The increase in population provided the opportunity for enterprising citizens to establish businesses in Abilene. Residents required everything from farm tools and hardware to nicely detailed carriages and wagons.

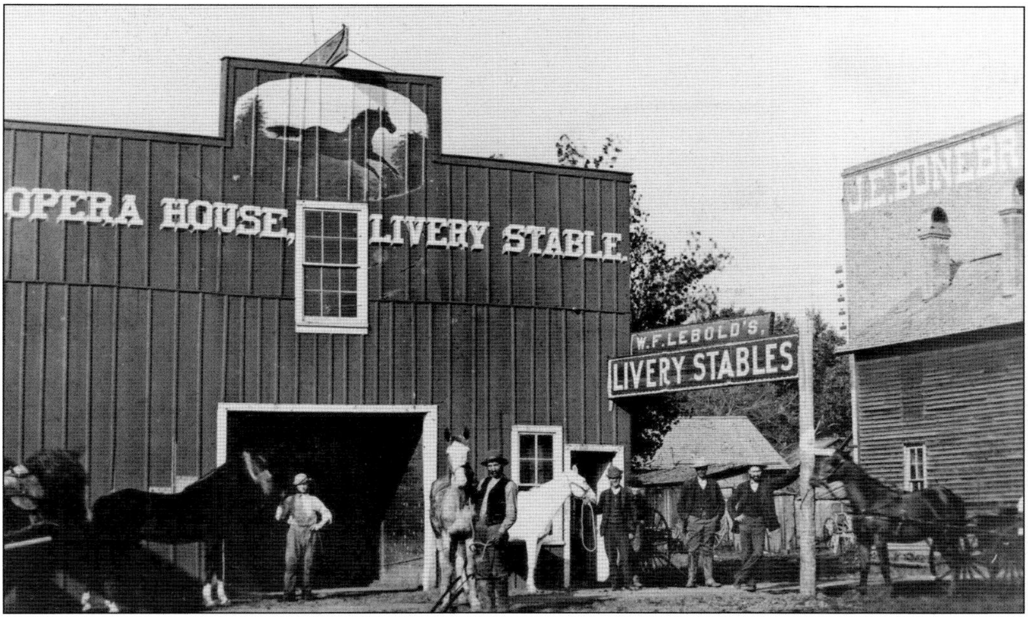

During the 1880s, the Opera Livery Stable provided a stable and boarding for horses owned by local townspeople and visitors.

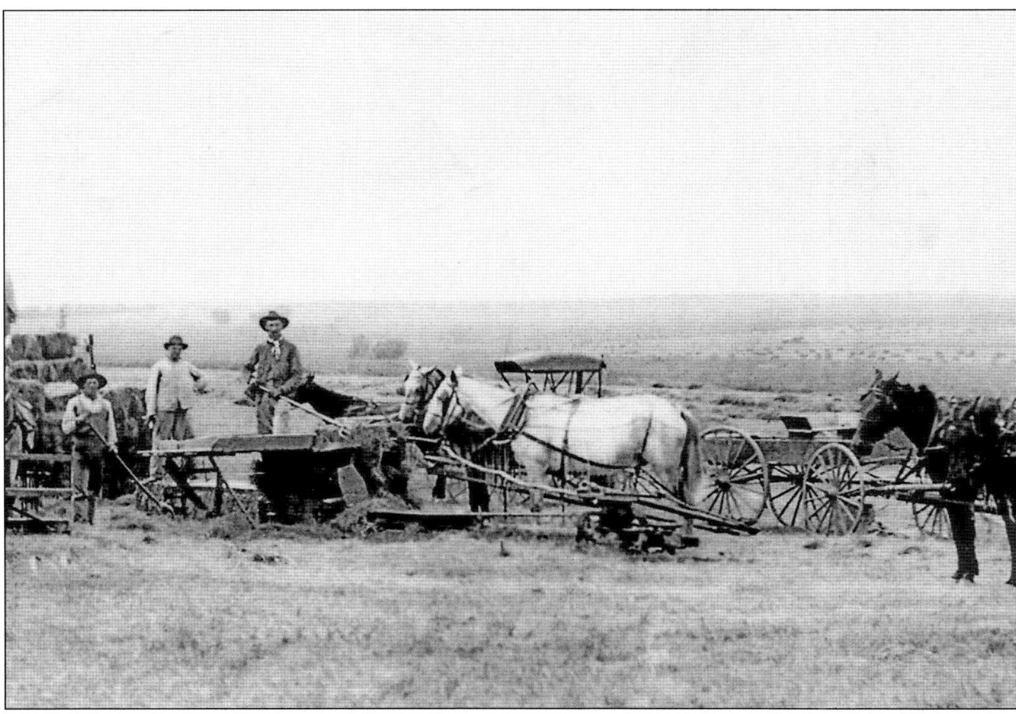

The prairie grass around Abilene provided an abundant supply of hay. This horse-drawn farm equipment dates from the 1880s.

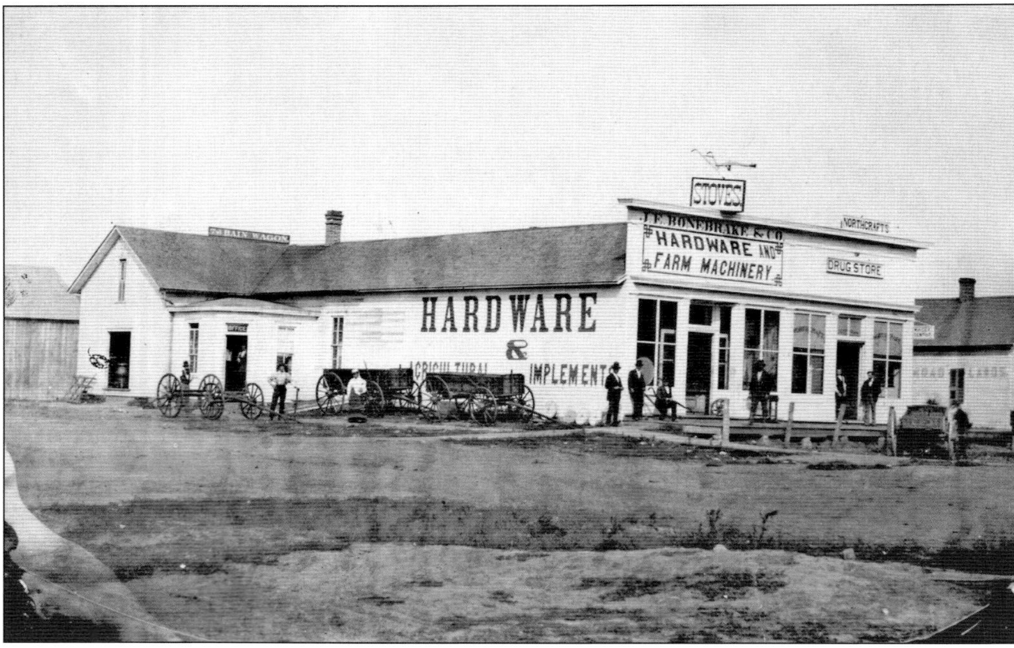

Bonebrake and Company provided Abilene farmers with everything from penny nails and hammers to wagon wheels and steel-blade plows. Ever the innovator, Bonebrake owned the first telephone in Abilene, which linked the store to the Bonebrake home.

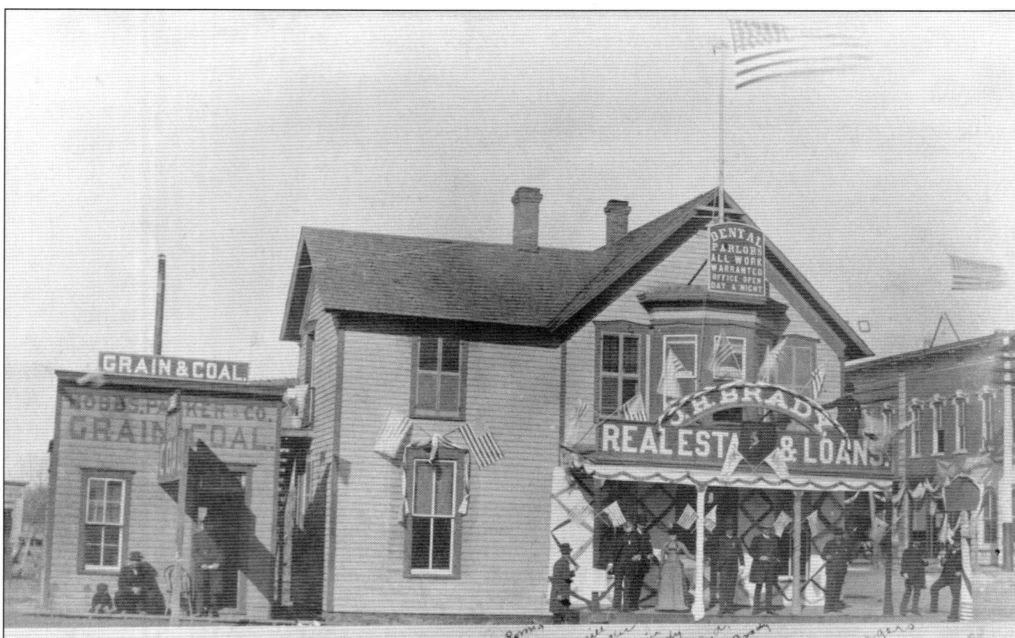

The Brady Real Estate office was a landmark in Abilene for over 25 years. Located at the north end of the Union Pacific Railroad tracks, real estate and loan services were available to settlers fresh off trains from the East.

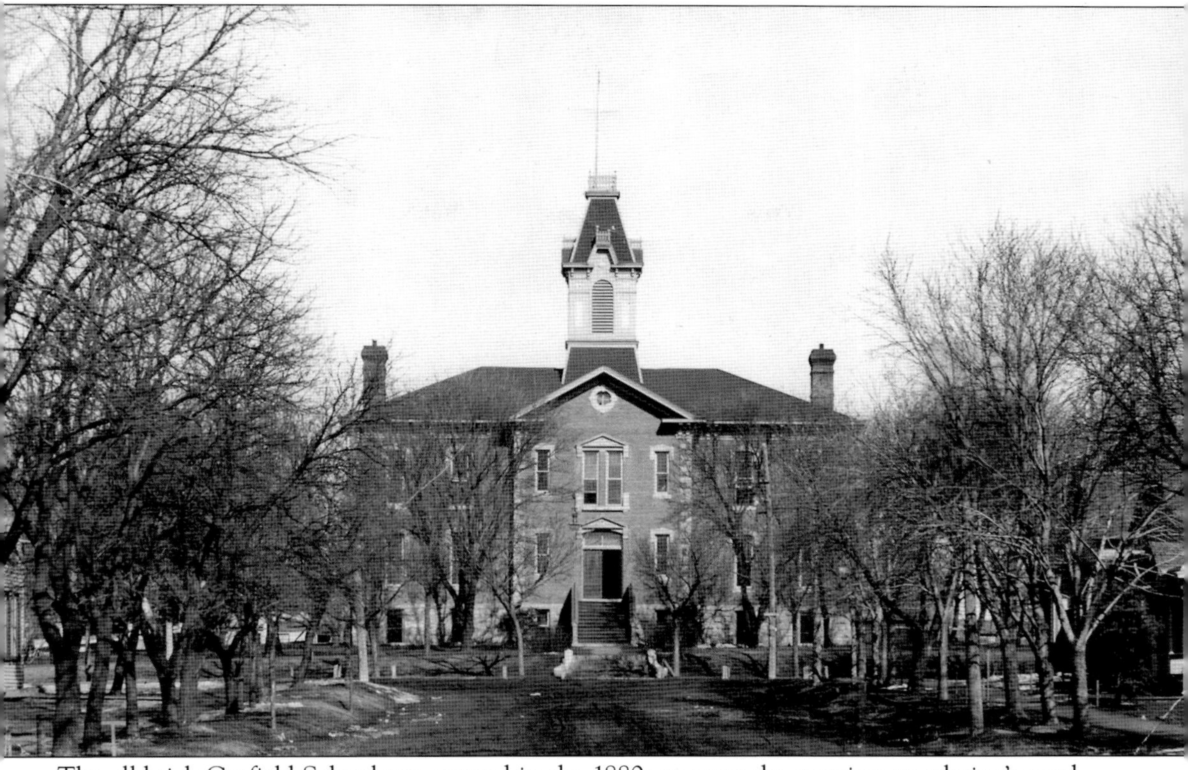

The all-brick Garfield School was erected in the 1880s to meet the growing population's need for education. Children in first through eighth grade attended classes in the building, while high school classes were held in city hall.

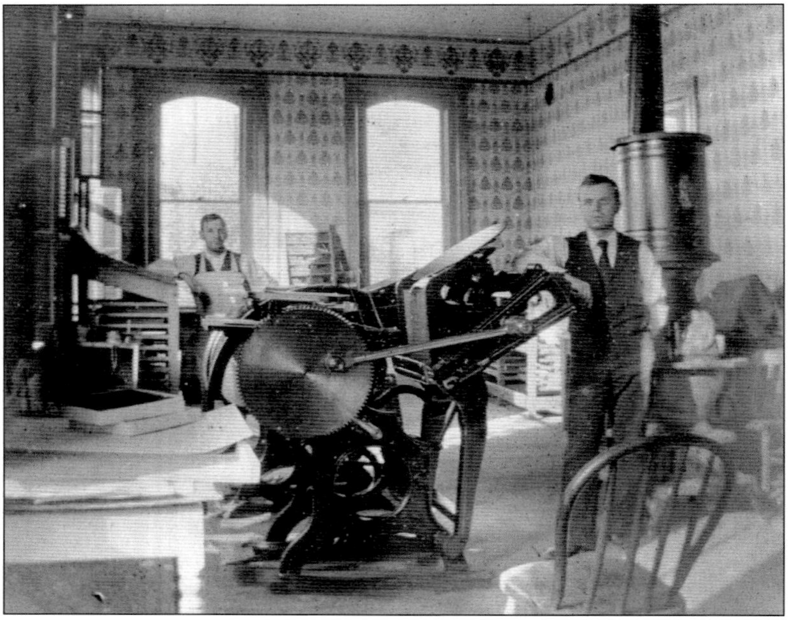

With the increase in population came the demand for newspapers, advertising, and various other printing services. This photograph shows Shandinger Printing Company during the 1890s.

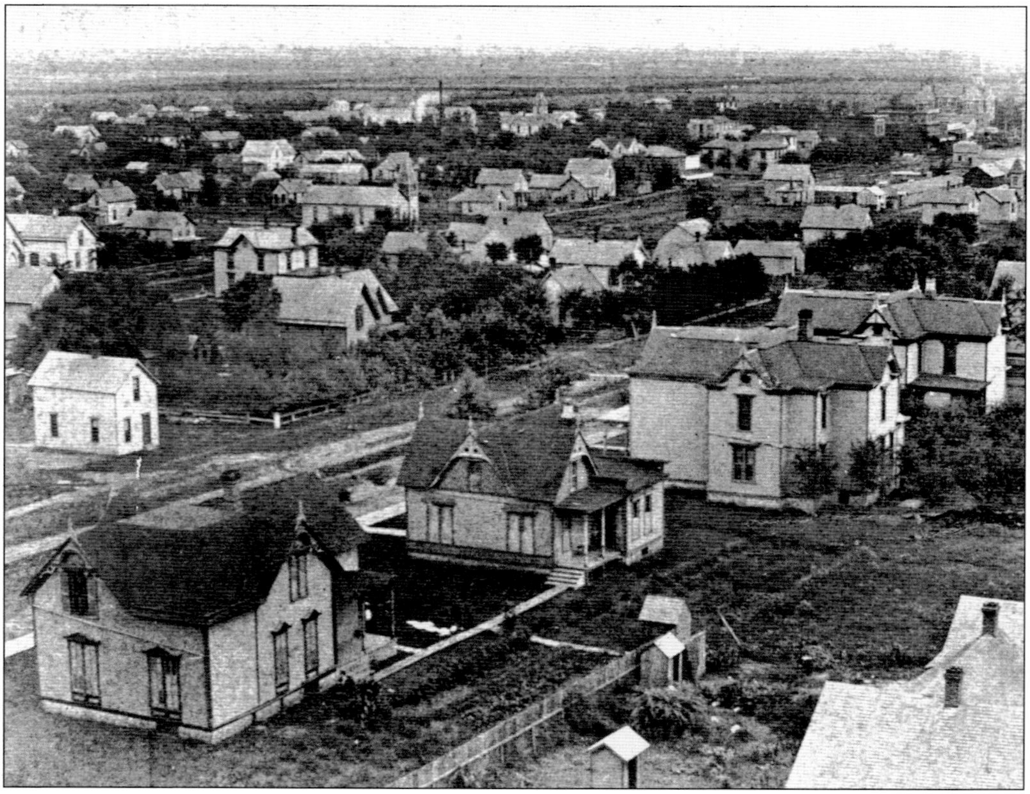

This 1882 view of Abilene was captured from the top of Garfield School. Facing south, the background in the image illustrates the rapid growth of family residences. In the foreground is the back of the hardware store and the Continental Hotel.

Like many Western towns, Abilene had dirt streets that often turned to mud, but modern boardwalks kept the ladies' skirts off the streets. Newly installed electric lines provided modern light to businesses and some homes.

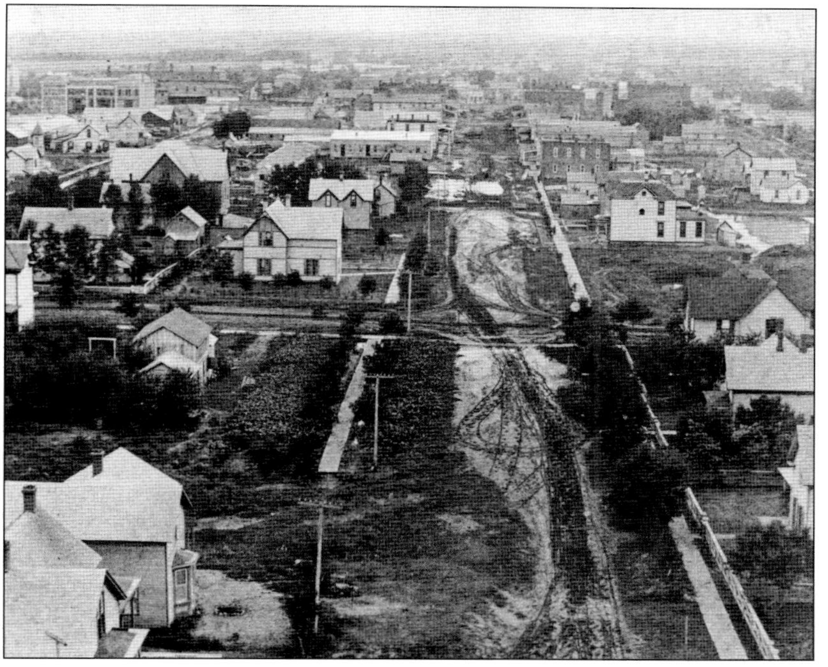

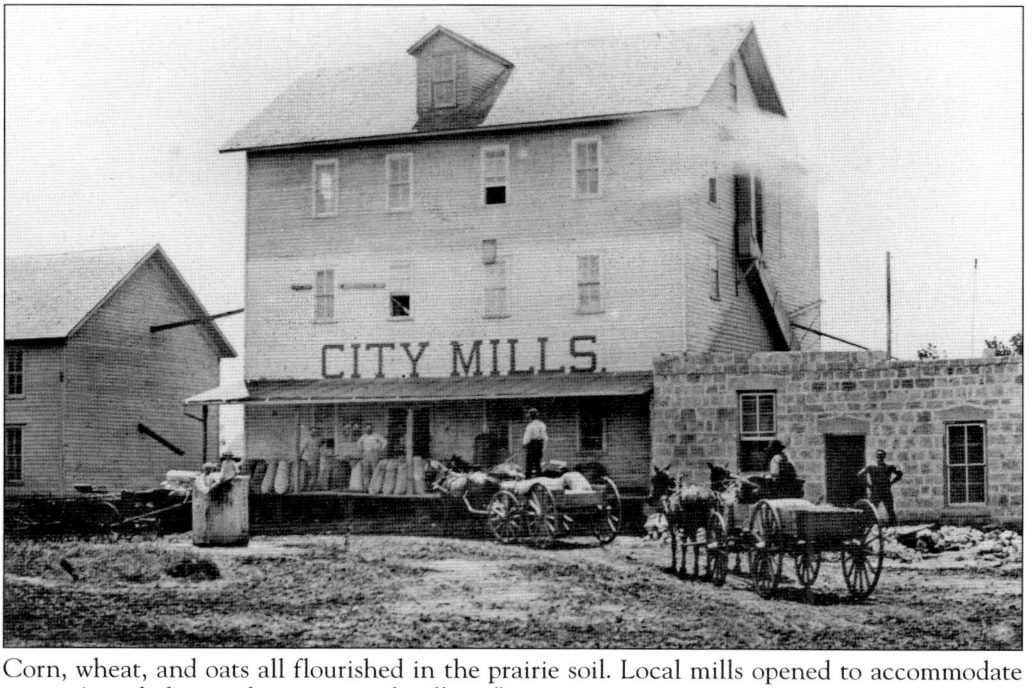

Corn, wheat, and oats all flourished in the prairie soil. Local mills opened to accommodate citizens' needs for grinding grain and milling flour.

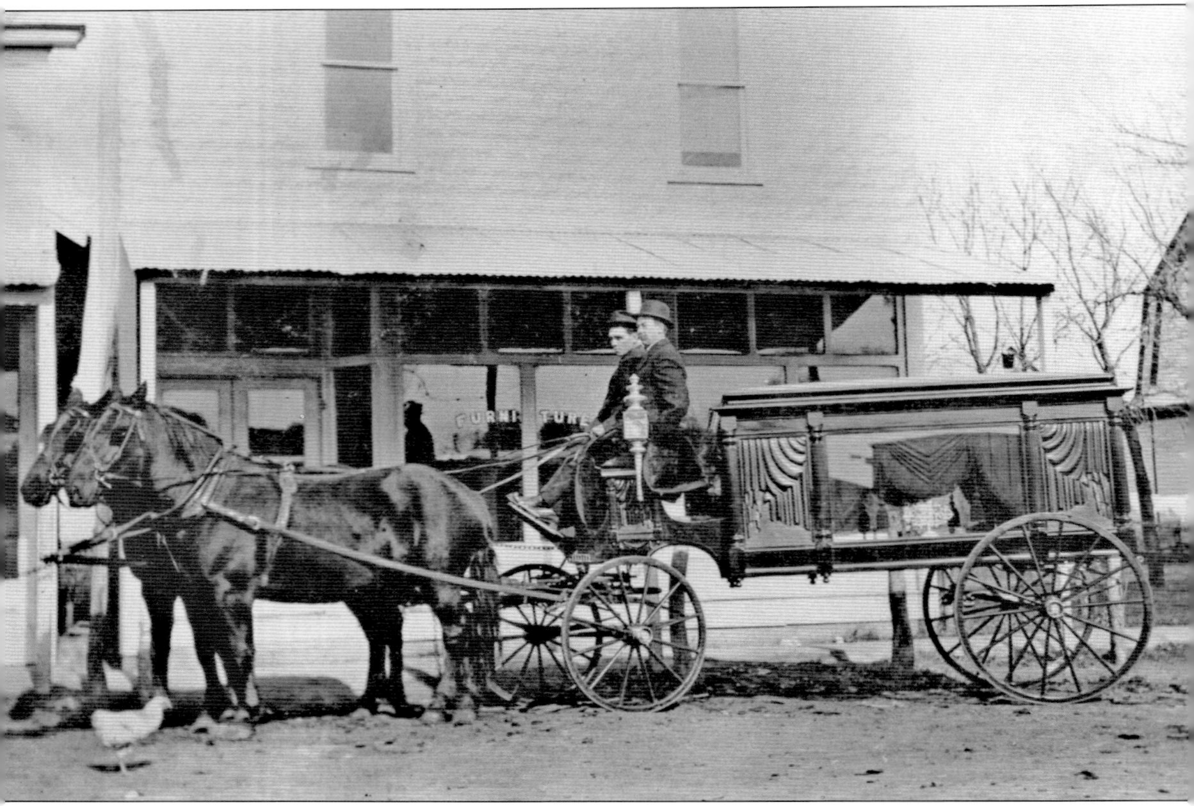

Undertaking was one of the oldest businesses in Abilene. W.H. Eicholtz & Co. was established in 1869 during the height of the cow-town era. In the newly civilized Abilene, funerals became more proper and dignified.

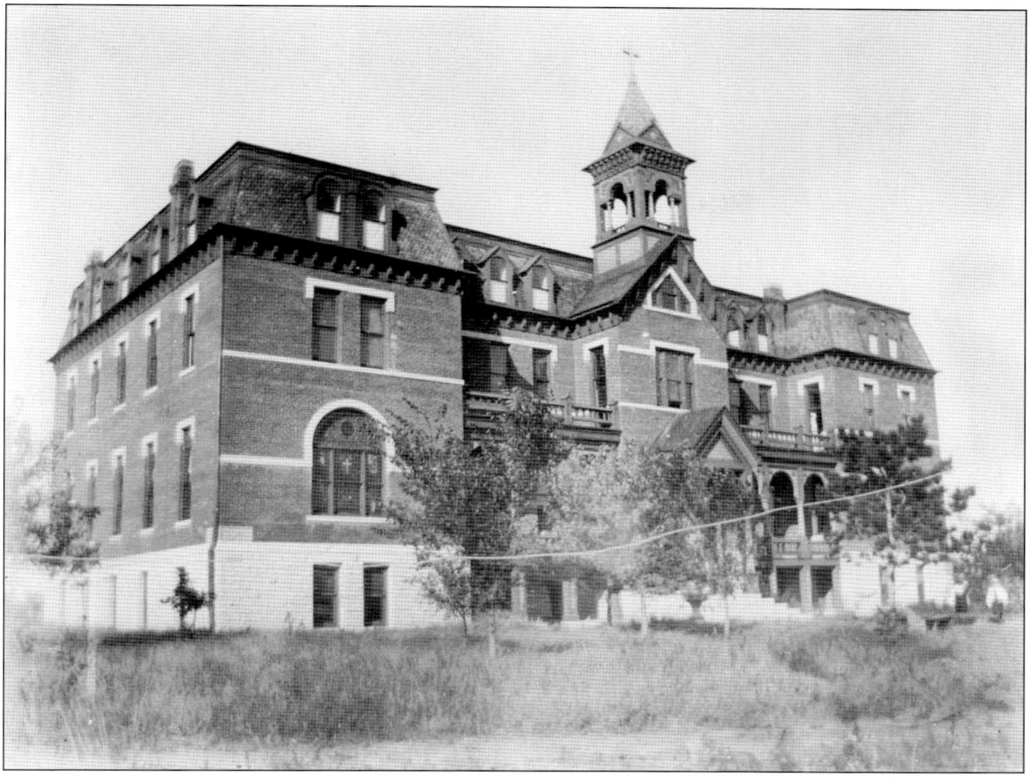

Care for widows and orphans became a priority and a civic duty for the residents of Abilene. Constructed as St. Joseph's College in 1887, the building was converted to an orphanage in 1915.

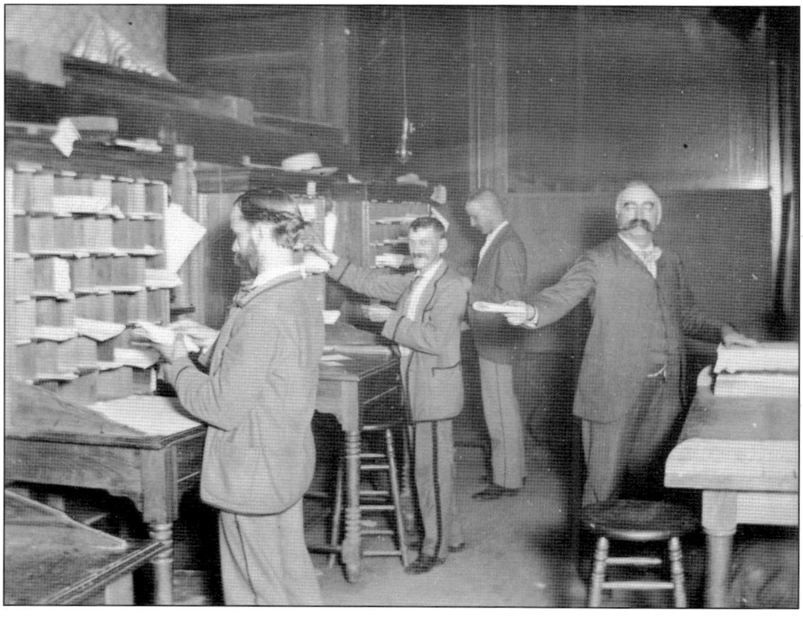

The Abilene Post Office was a center of activity, providing news and information from relatives back in the East. In this 1880s photograph, post office workers sort letters into the appropriate boxes.

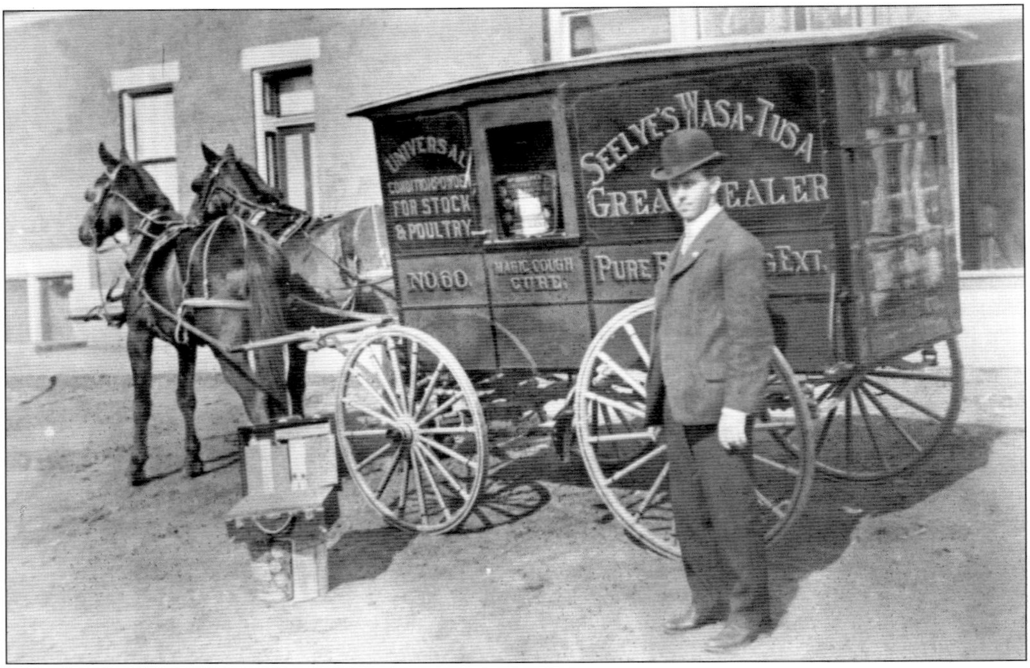

The Seelye Patent Medicine Factory was founded in 1890. More than 100 products were manufactured in Abilene and sold in a 14-state area throughout the Midwest. One of the best-known medicines was Wasa-Tusa, a "universal conditioner" for stock and poultry, and Ner-Vena and Fro-Zona were popular cure-alls as well. Most of these types of medicines contained a high percentage of alcohol.

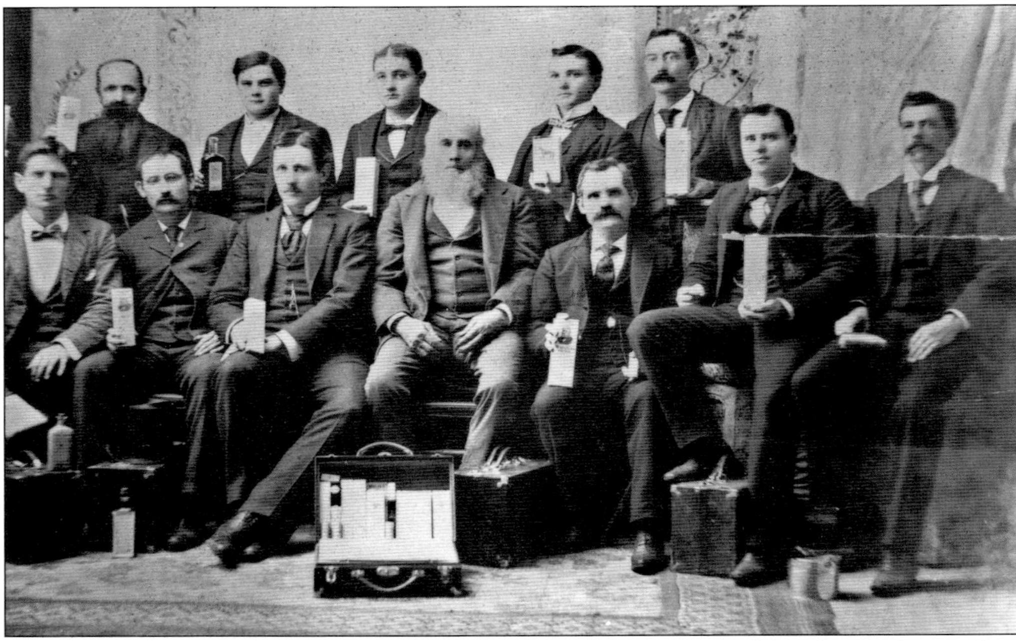

Traveling salesmen were the backbone of the Seelye enterprise. They sold medicines door to door, covering hundreds of miles of rough dirt roads on horseback and in wagons.

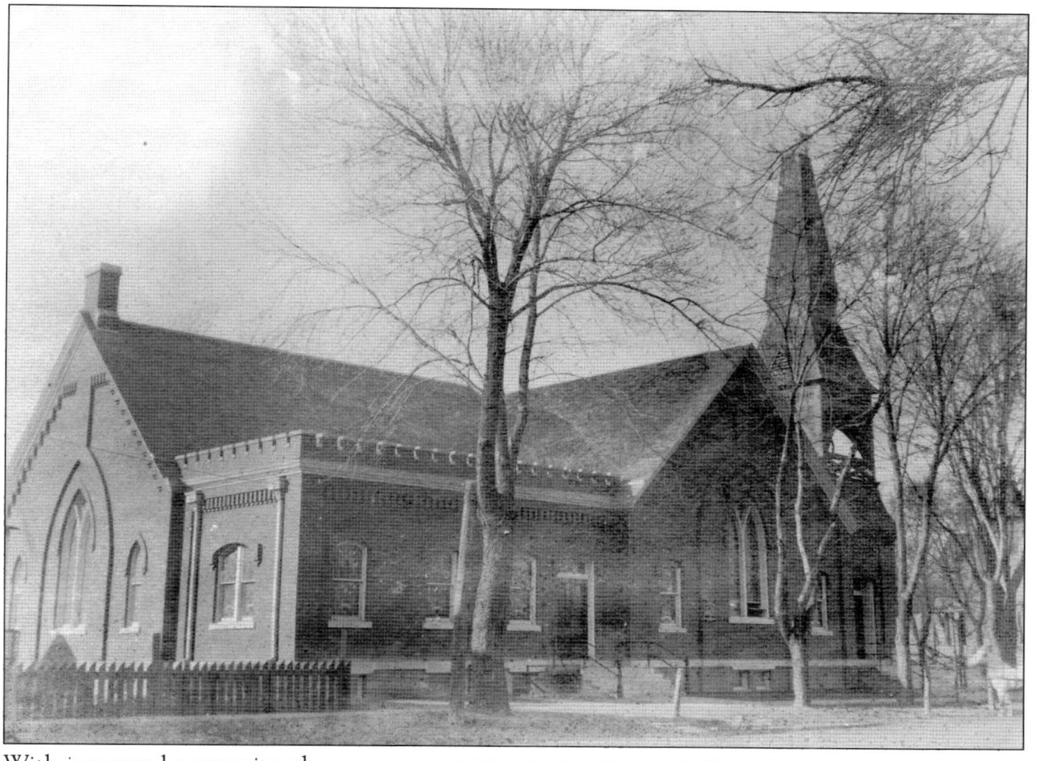

With increased prosperity, the citizens of Abilene were able to build significant structures to house their religious and civic organizations. The Trinity Lutheran congregation built their church in 1870.

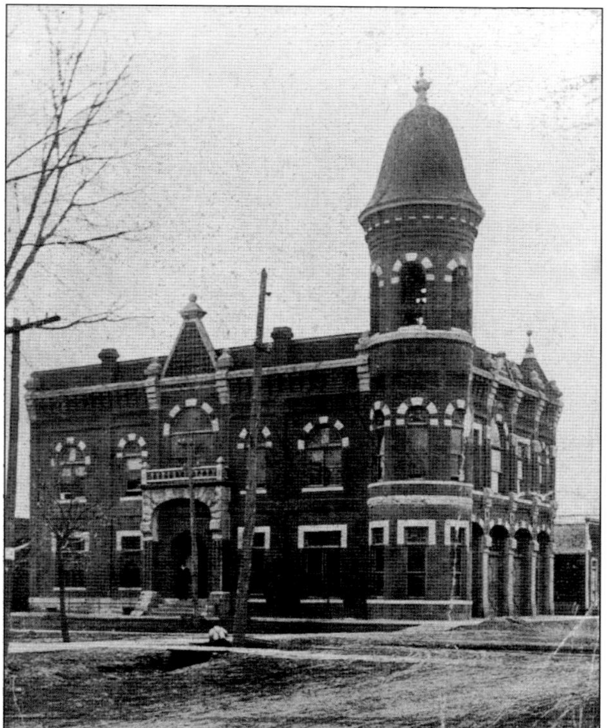

The sturdy city hall building was the pride of Abilene. It not only housed city offices but also served as the location for high school classes from 1876 to 1907.

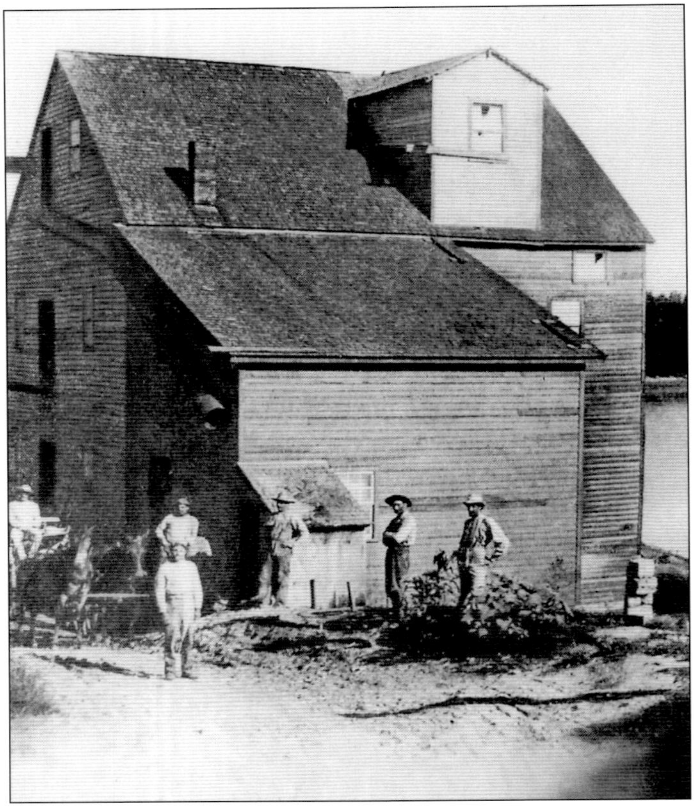

This gristmill located on the Smokey Hill River, just south of Abilene, was used by area farmers to grind feed and flour. It eventually became the site of the Kansas Power and Light power plant.

By the late 1880s, discerning Abilene shoppers could have purchases delivered to their door. This delivery wagon was from Harry Litts Clothier's.

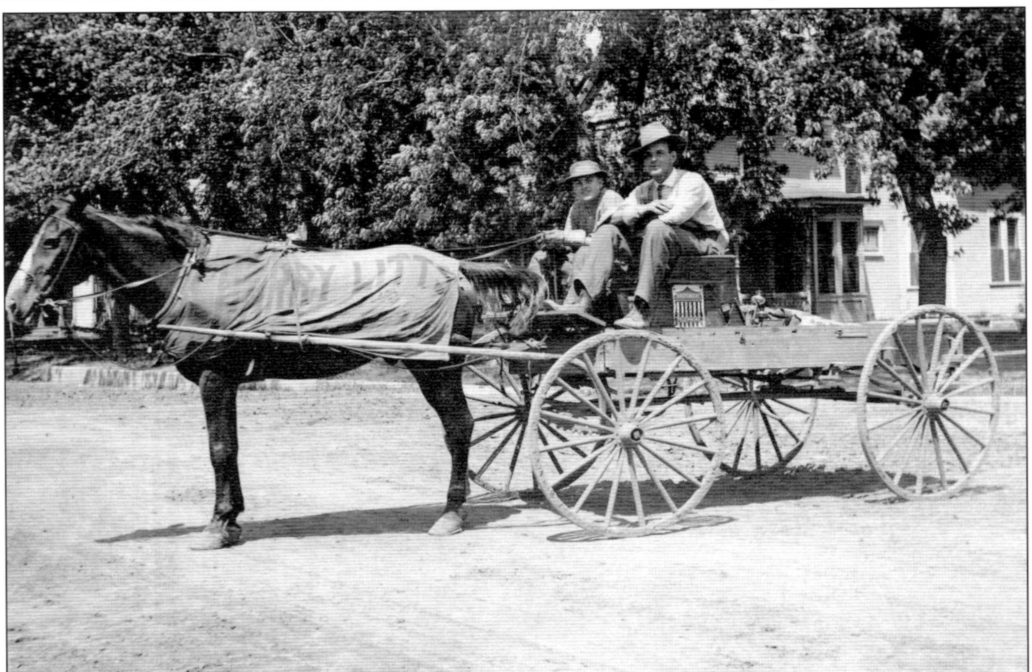

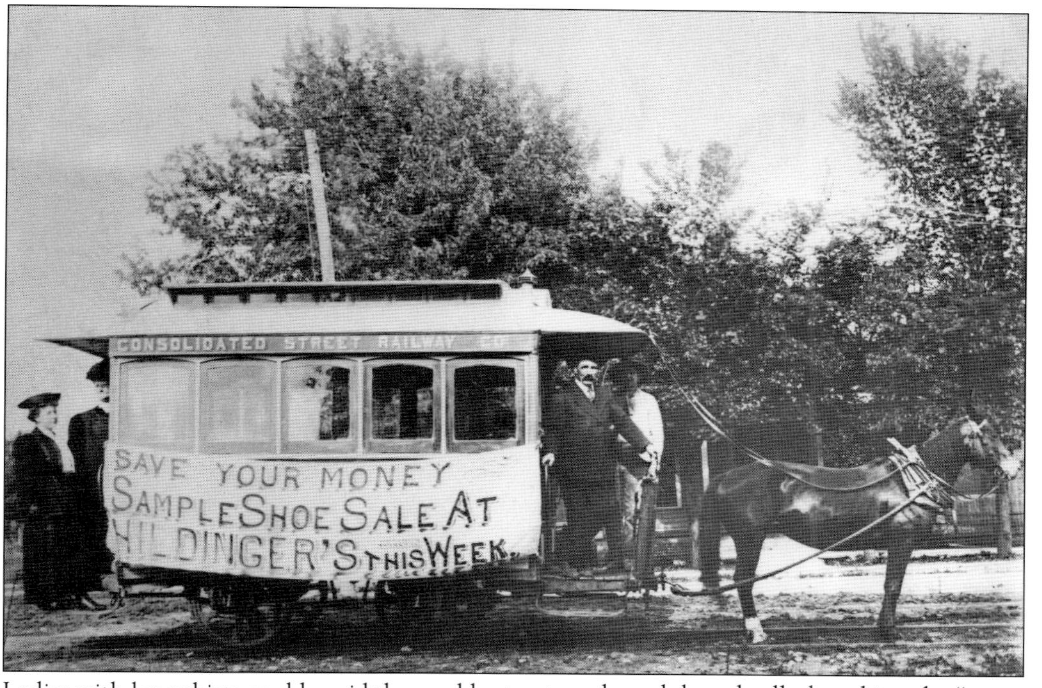

Ladies with long skirts could avoid the muddy streets and rough boardwalks by taking the "street railway" to Abilene stores. The horse-drawn trolleys ran on actual rails imbedded in the ground. Local merchants took full advantage of the advertising opportunity.

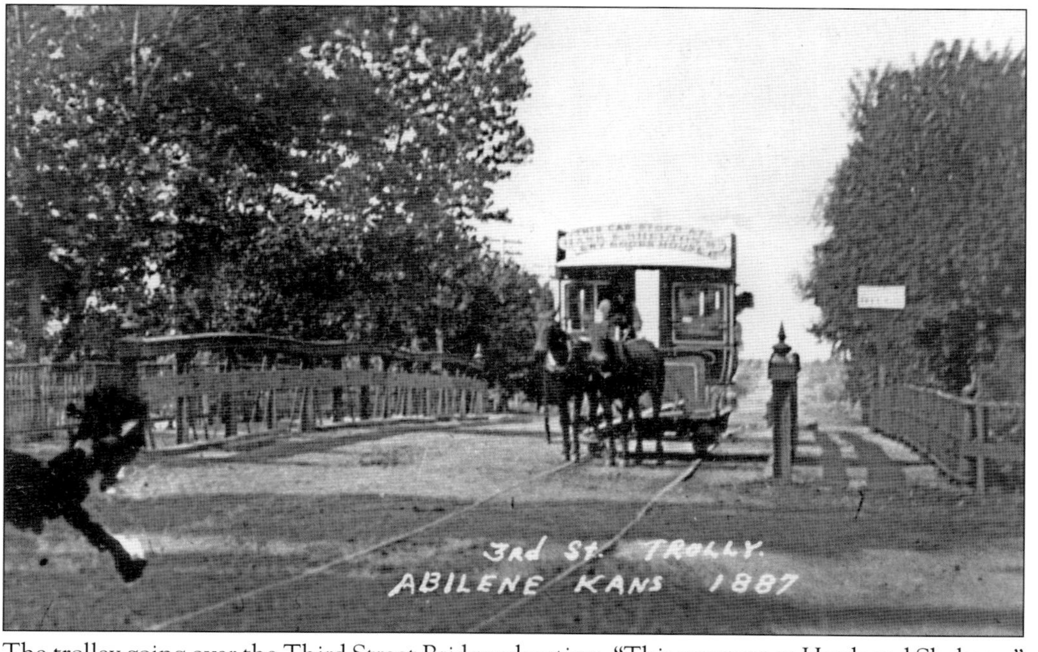

The trolley going over the Third Street Bridge advertises, "This car stops at Hawk and Sheltons."

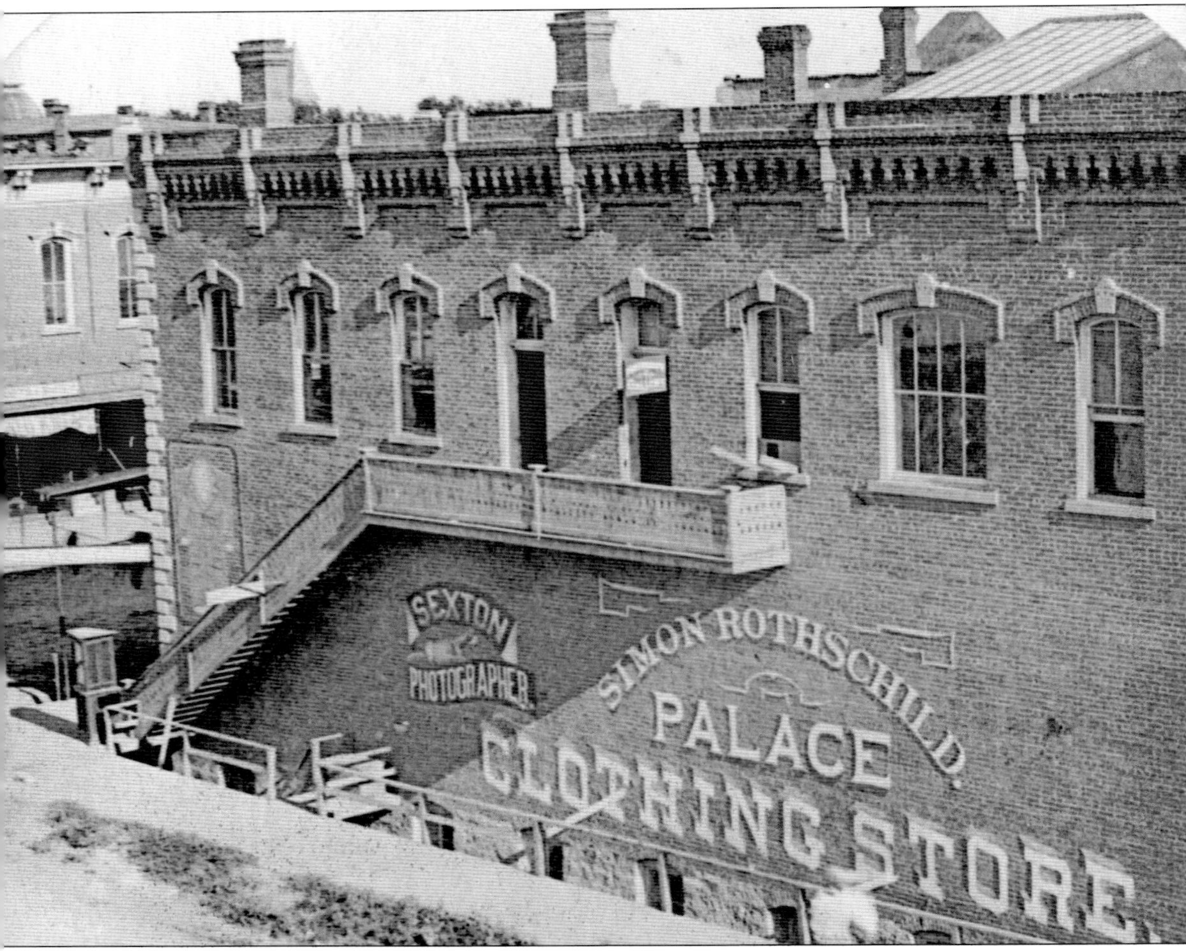

Shoppers from Abilene and the surrounding areas found a wealth of goods for sale. In less than 15 years, the town had grown from a few hastily built cabins to substantial stores and buildings like the Simon Rothchild Palace Clothing Store.

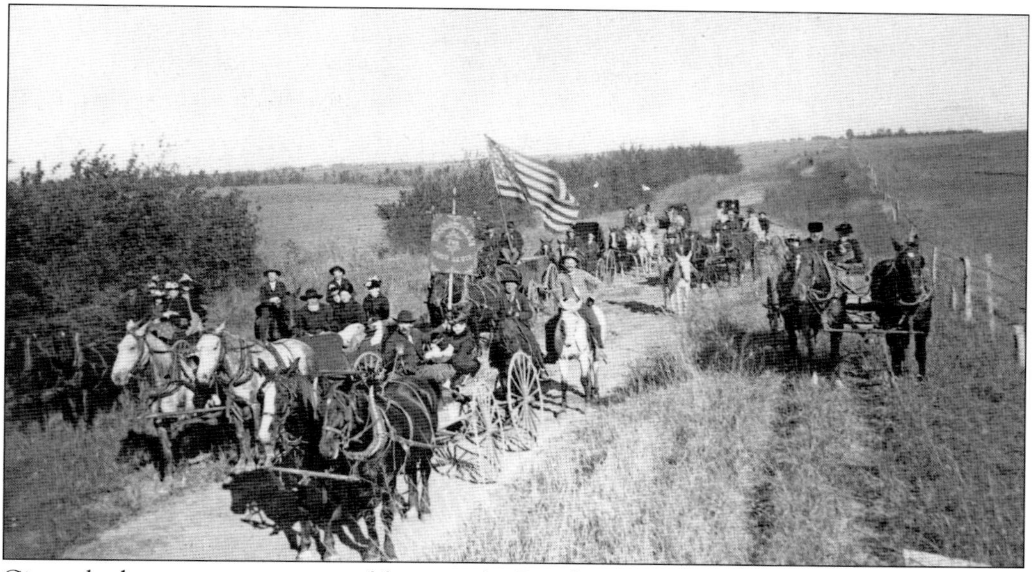

Given the heavy concentration of farmers, the Populist Party was heavily favored in Abilene's politics. This group of Abilene area farmers is riding to a Populist Party meeting. The party favored allowing senators to be elected by a vote of the people instead of by state legislatures. This became law with the 17th amendment.

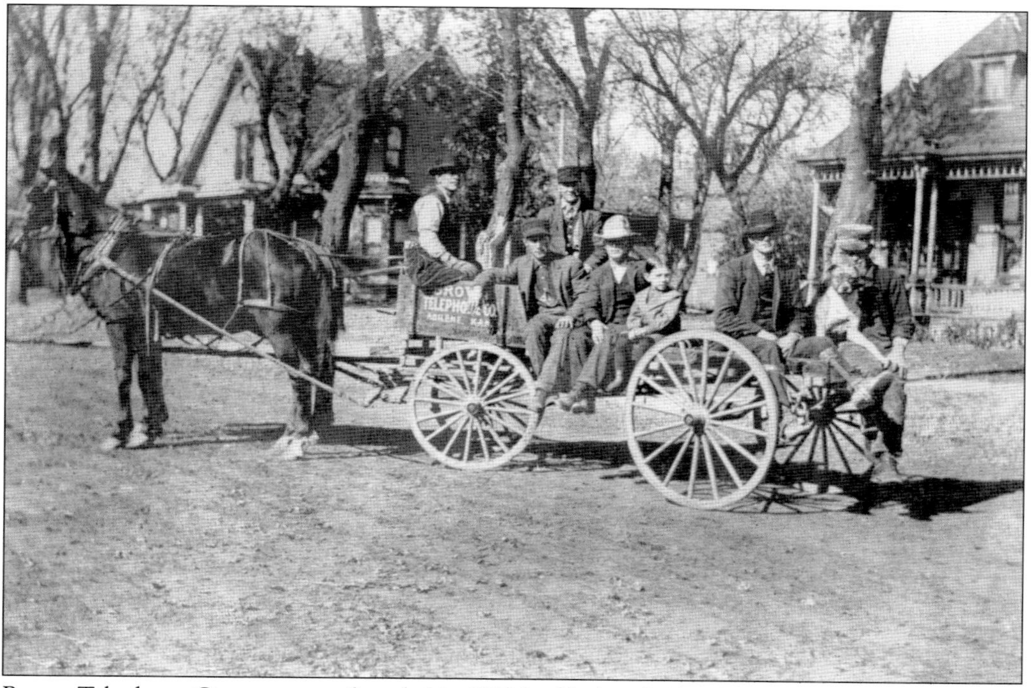

Brown Telephone Company was founded in 1899 by Chelson LeRoy Brown as a competitor to the Bell Telephone system. Today, the Brown Telephone Company is known as Sprint Nextel.

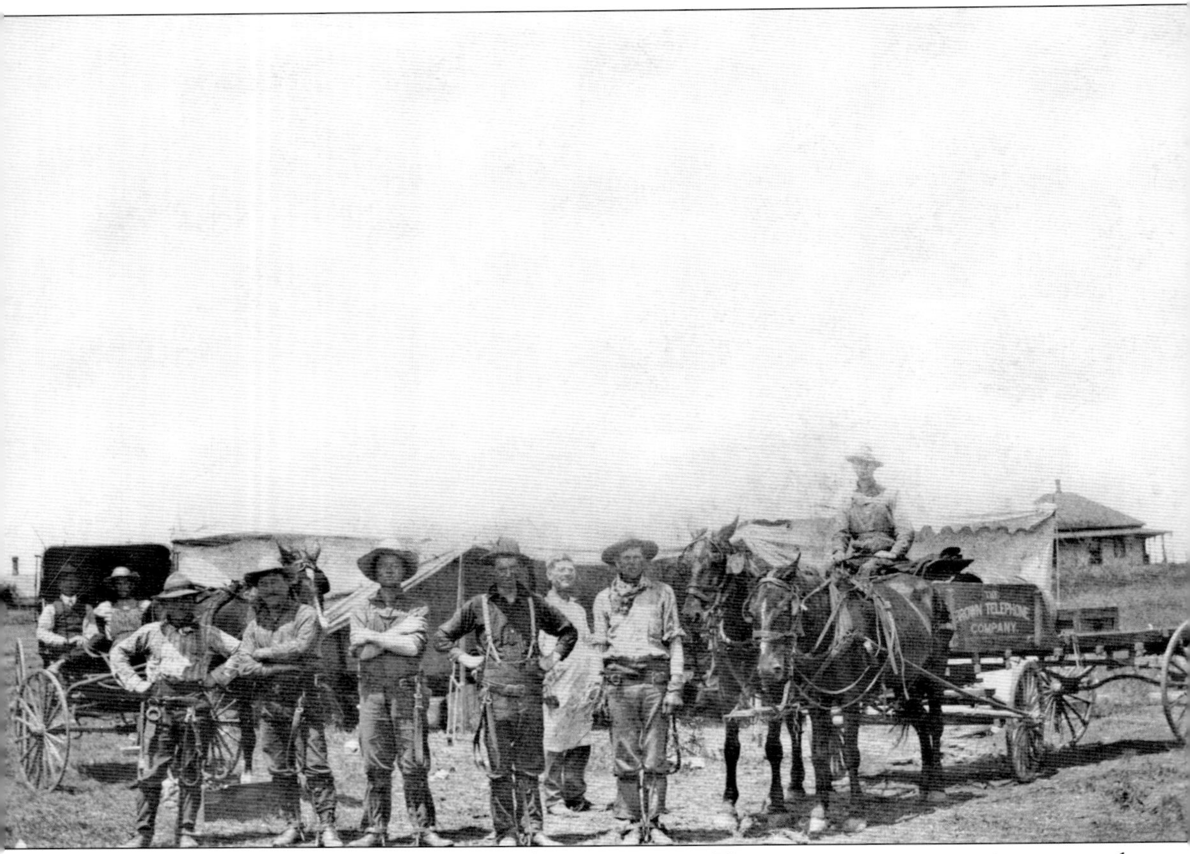

Pictured are workers from Brown Telephone Company. The men are wearing equipment used for stringing telephone lines.

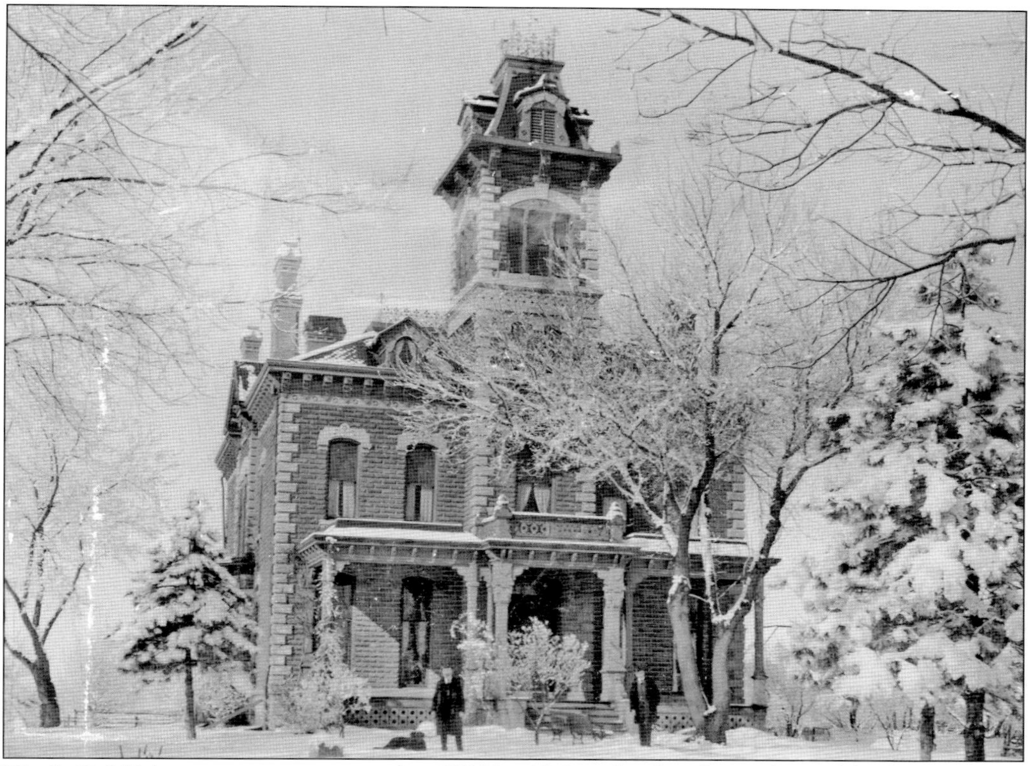

The LeBold Mansion was constructed in 1880 by Abilene banker Conrad LeBold. The mansion's tower was built over the site of the first home in Abilene. The dugout owned by Timothy and Eliza Hersey was preserved as a part of the LeBold tower foundation and is still there today.

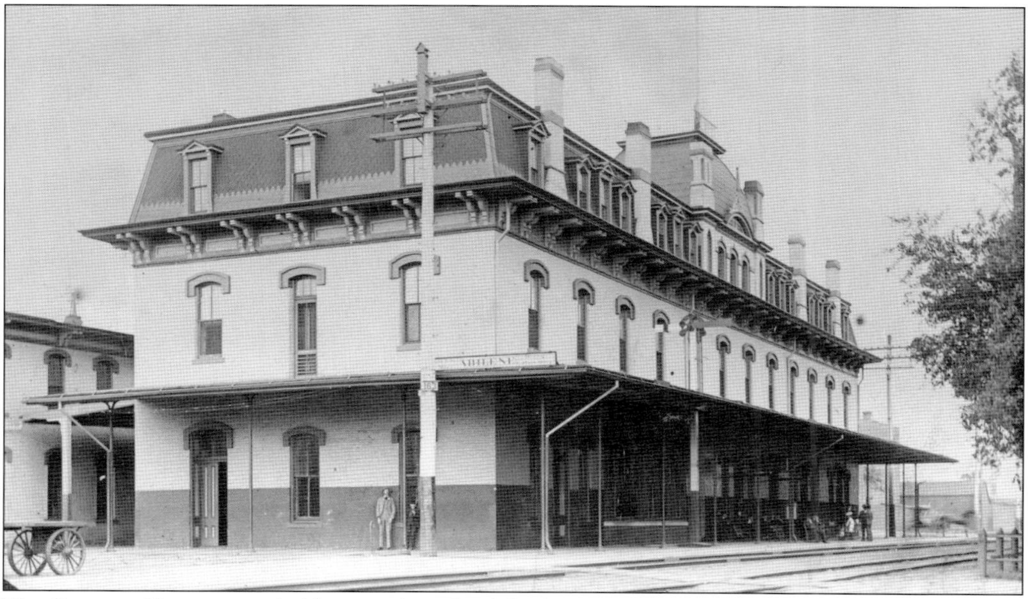

The Stanton House provided hot meals and soft beds to visitors. Originally built in 1875, the third story was added in 1881. It later became Pacific House and the Union Pacific Depot.

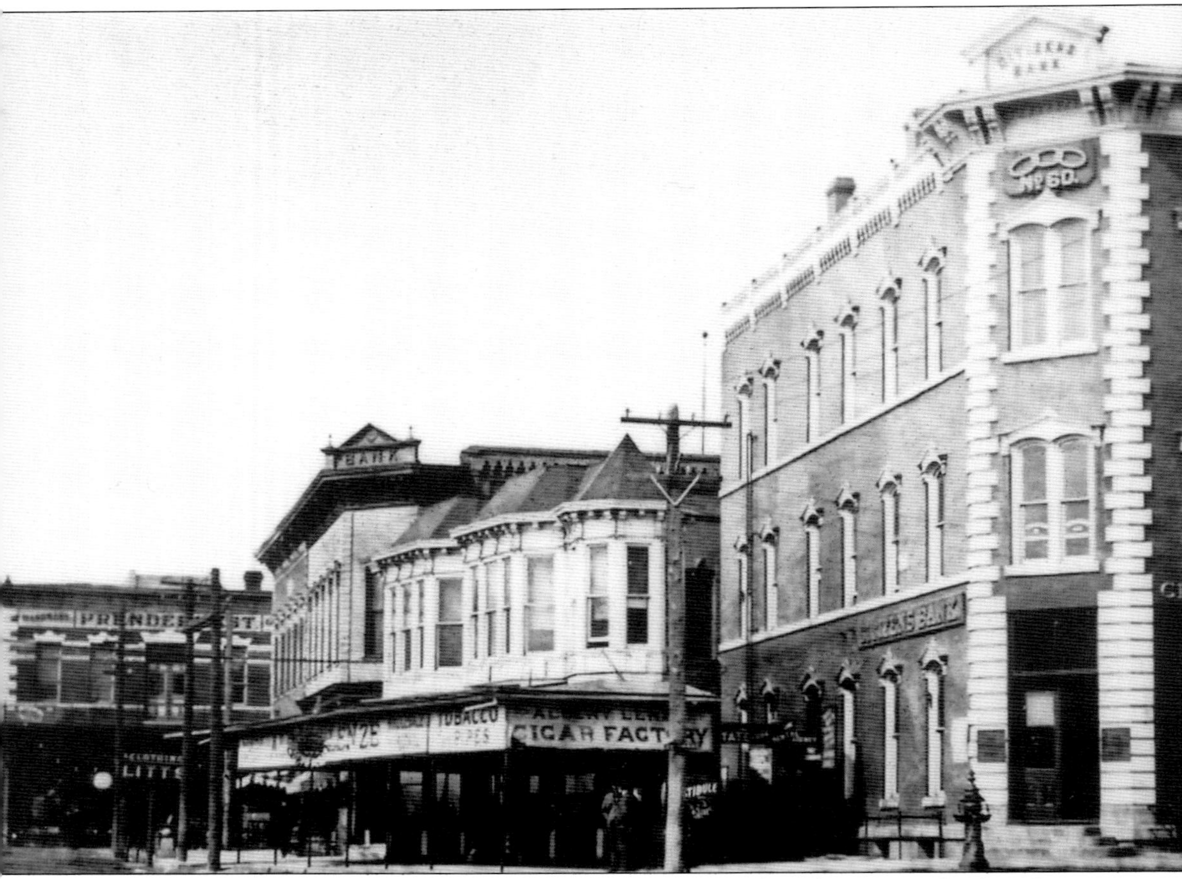

By the 1890s Abilene was a well-established town that offered residents even the finer luxuries of handmade cigars and a well-stocked smoke shop.

Three

Fairs, Festivals, and Fun

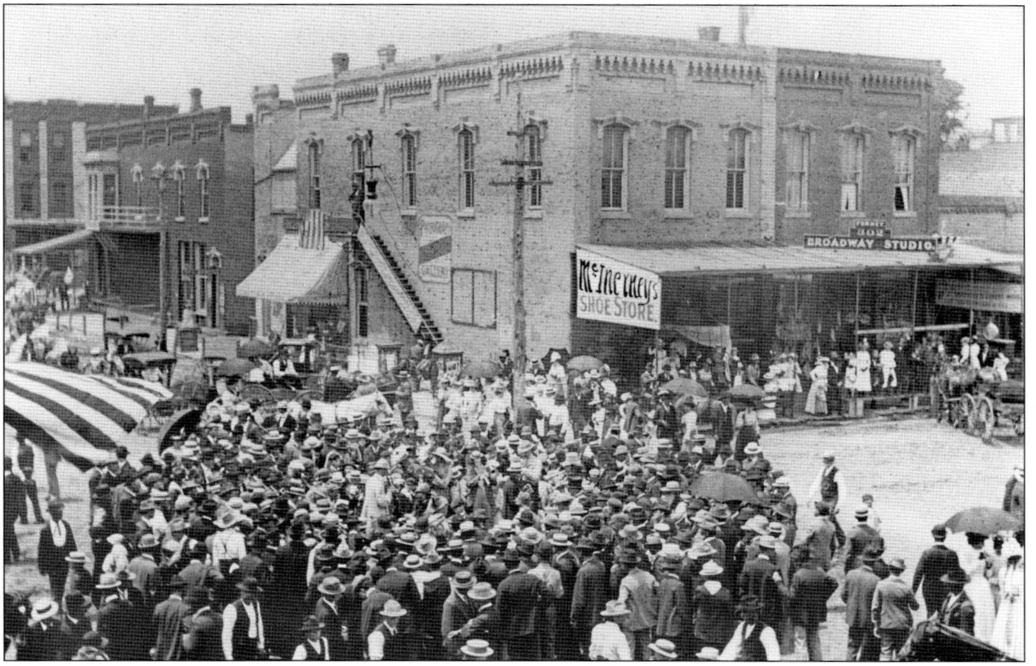

Life on the Kansas prairie was not easy. Farmers had to contend with too little rain, too much wind, and insects invading their crops. Abilene merchants worried just as much about the weather as the farmers, because their fortunes were tightly tied to agriculture. To relieve stress and bring enjoyment to life, the citizens of Abilene formed bands and civic organizations and held festivals and parades. People from throughout the county flocked to Abilene for special events like the annual Fourth of July celebrations.

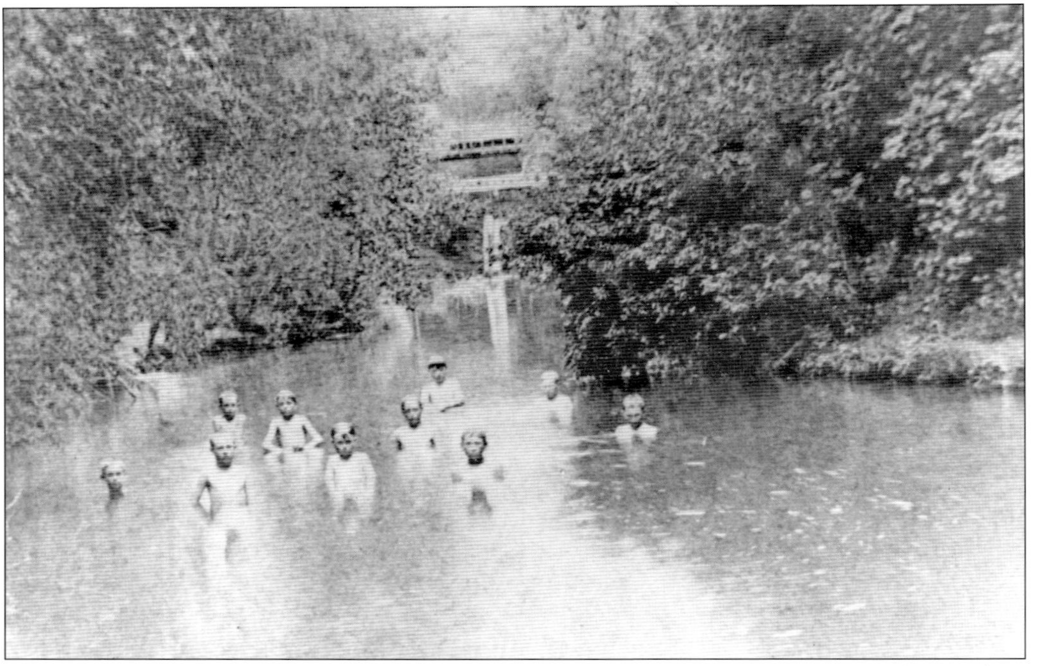

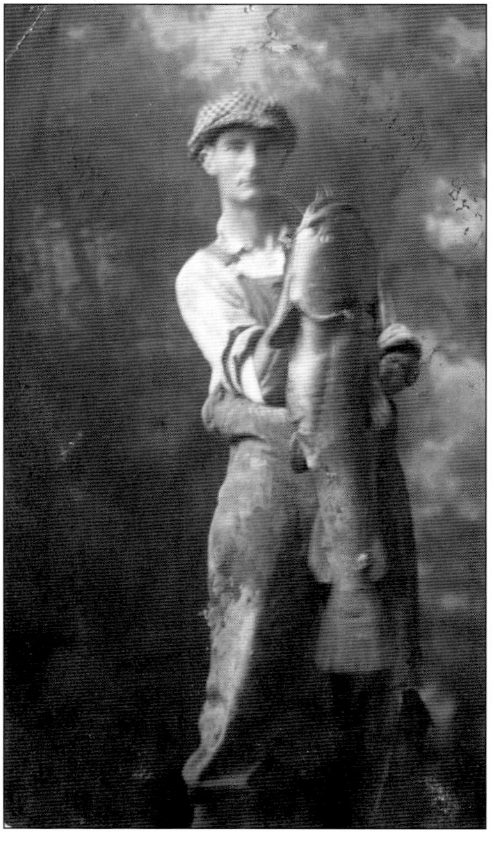

The best entertainment was often the simple pleasure offered by the natural landscape around Abilene. In the heat of the summer, the local swimming hole provided relief from the heat. This 1885 image shows a group of boys skinny-dipping in Mud Creek.

Fishing was popular hobby with men and women of all ages. Catfish grew big in the Smokey Hill River, and the hobby had the added bonus of providing a free supper.

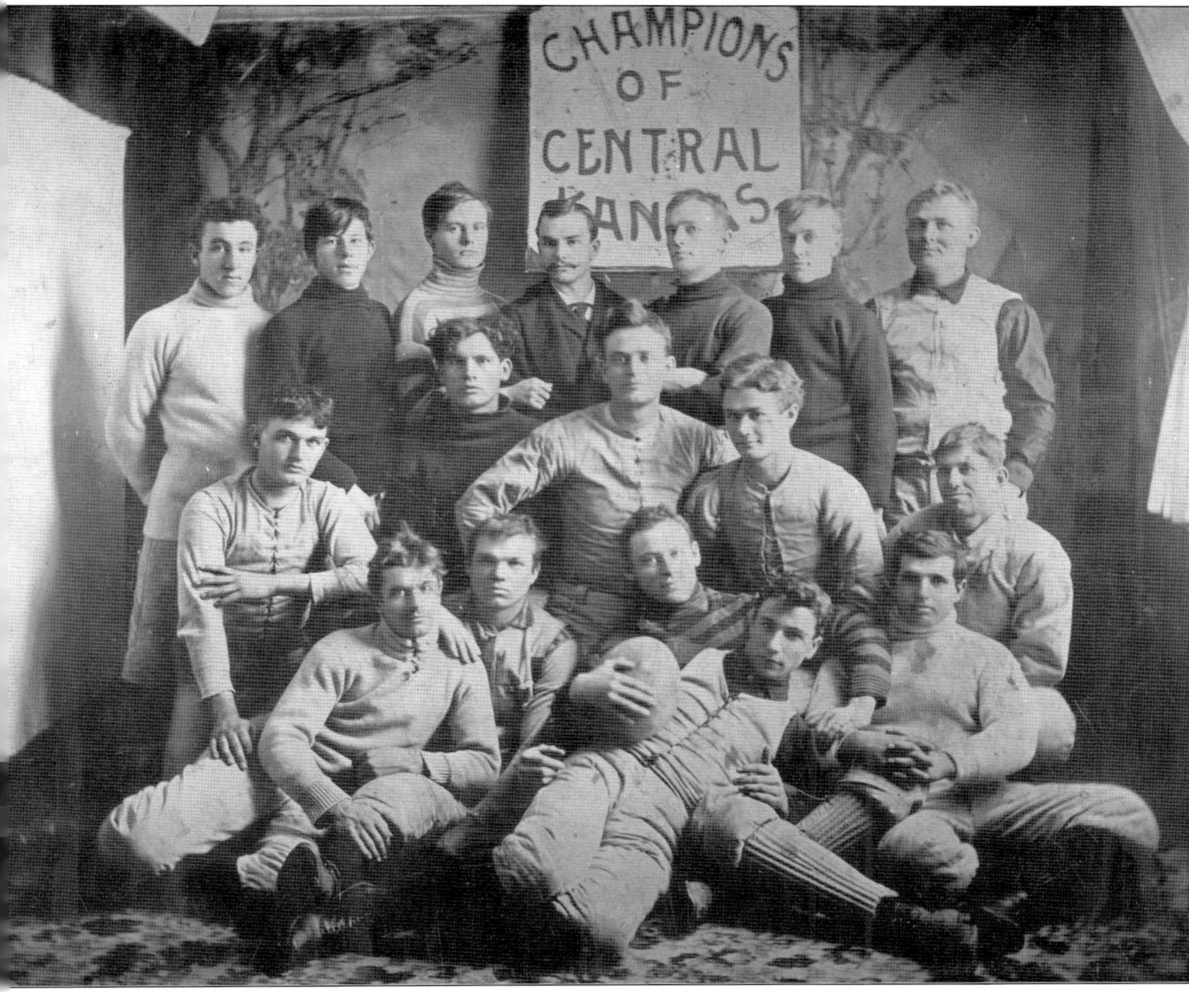

Sports were popular with both the players and spectators. Abilene and the surrounding townships organized football and baseball teams and traveled from town to town to compete against each other. Championships were highly prized and earned bragging rights for the whole year. The rough-and-tumble sport of football was quite popular among the young men of the area. In 1894, the football champions of central Kansas hailed from Abilene.

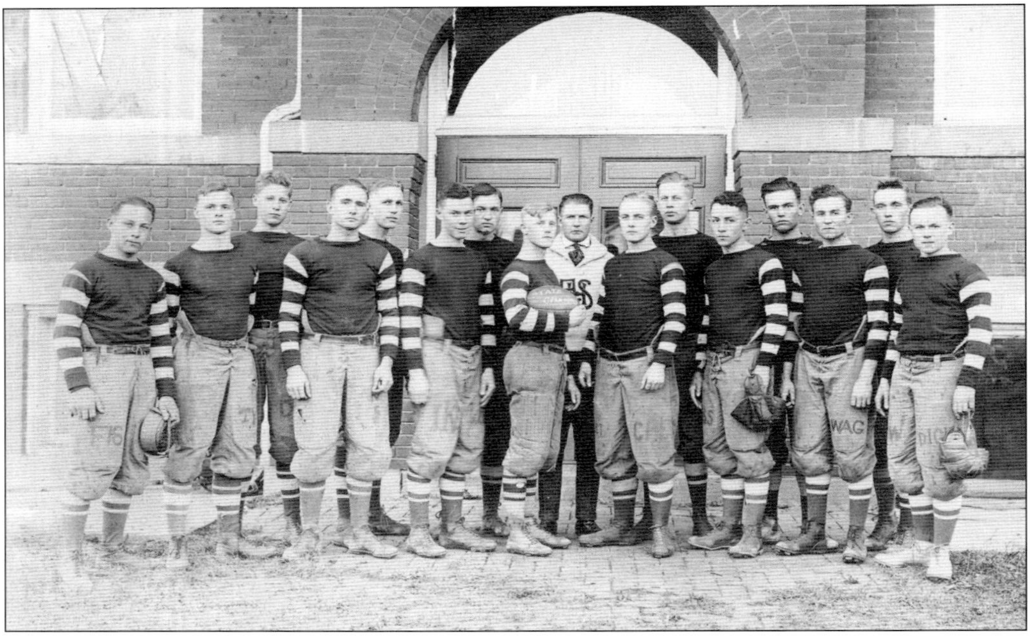

The football tradition continued, and Abilene High School brought home the state championship in 1916.

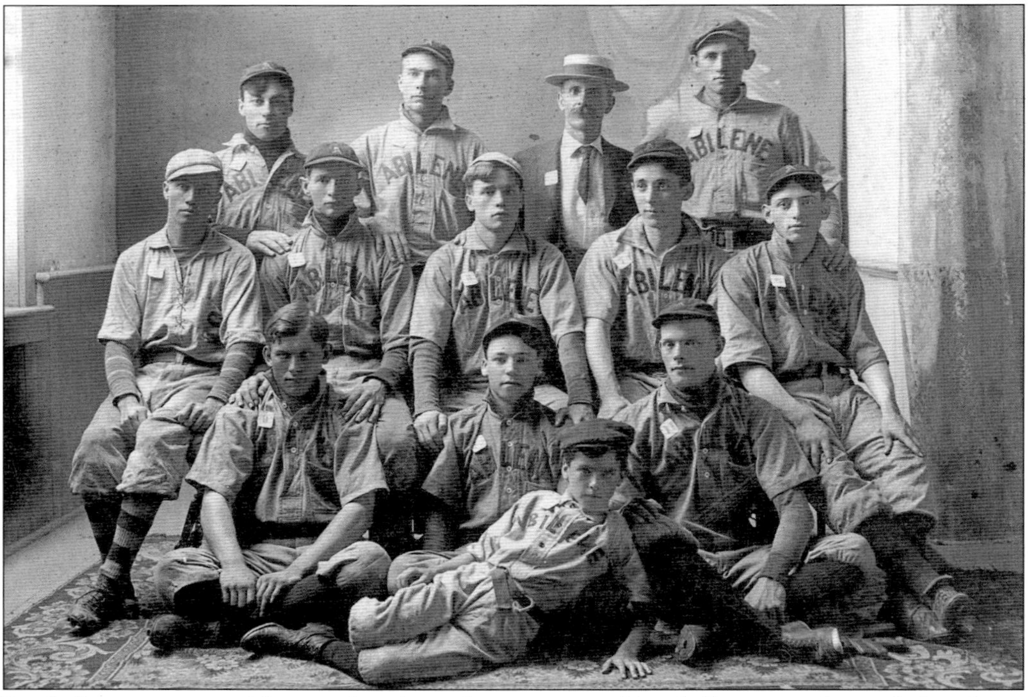

Baseball was a perennial favorite. Local merchants sponsored baseball teams and provided uniforms for the players. Civic pride demanded that everyone go to the ball field to cheer their boys on to victory. The ball games provided a sense of community solidarity and dose of good healthy fun. This is the 1906 Abilene baseball team, managed by John Eddy (man in the straw hat).

By the 1910s, Abilene and most of the surrounding communities had built simple baseball fields and stands for their avid fans. This is the 1910 Abilene baseball team.

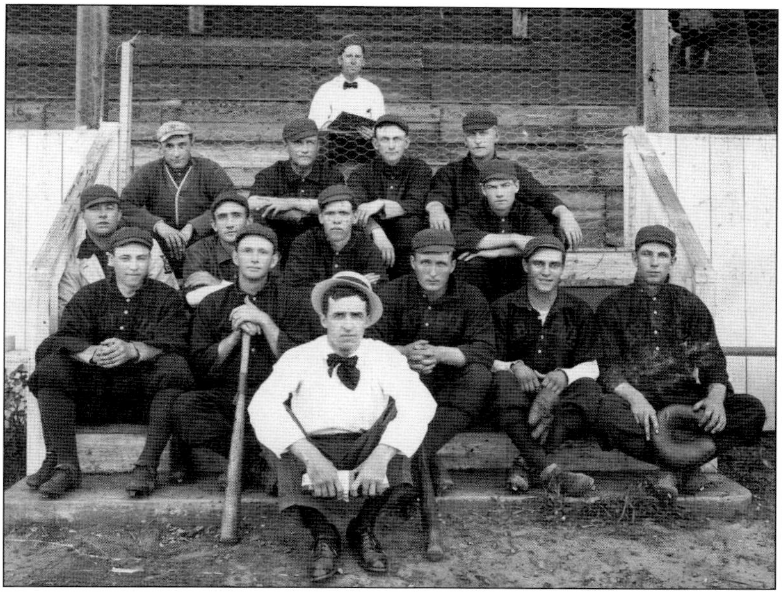

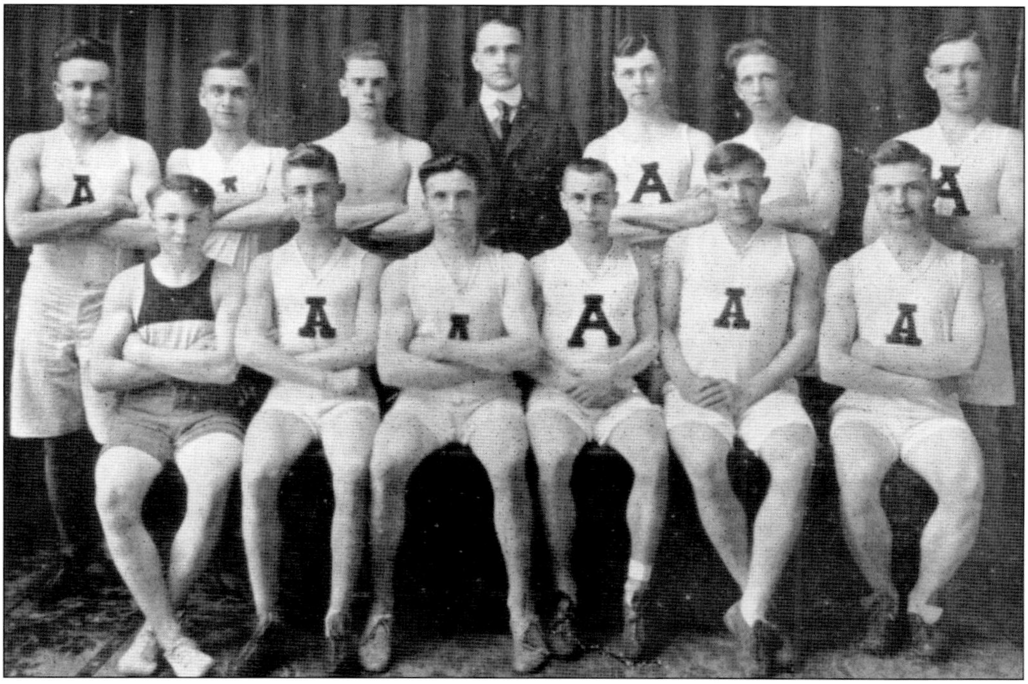

Track-and-field sports became popular with the introduction of high school sports teams. The 1918 Abilene boys' track team took the state championship.

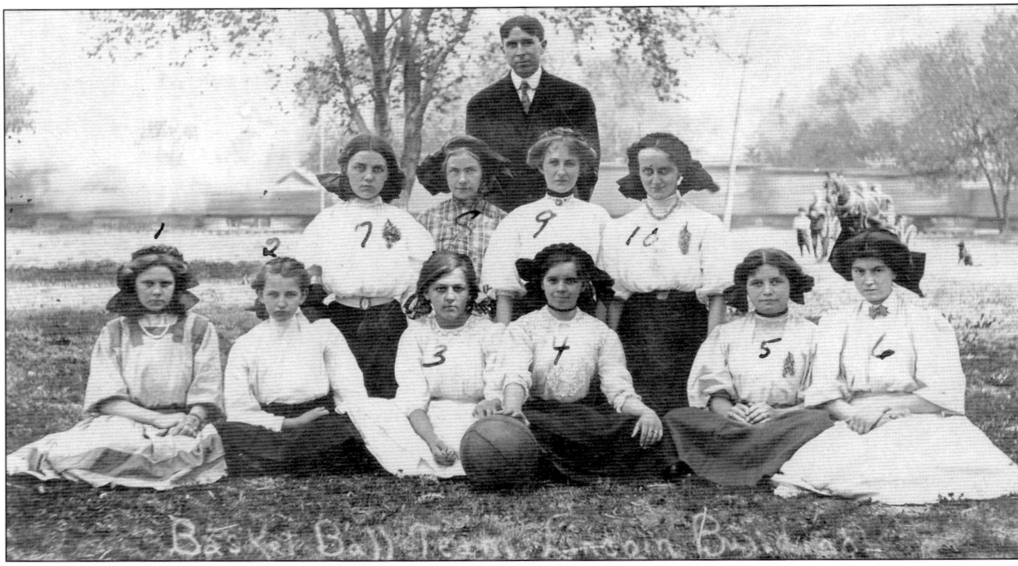

Not to be left out of sports, the girls of Lincoln School formed their own basketball team in 1910.

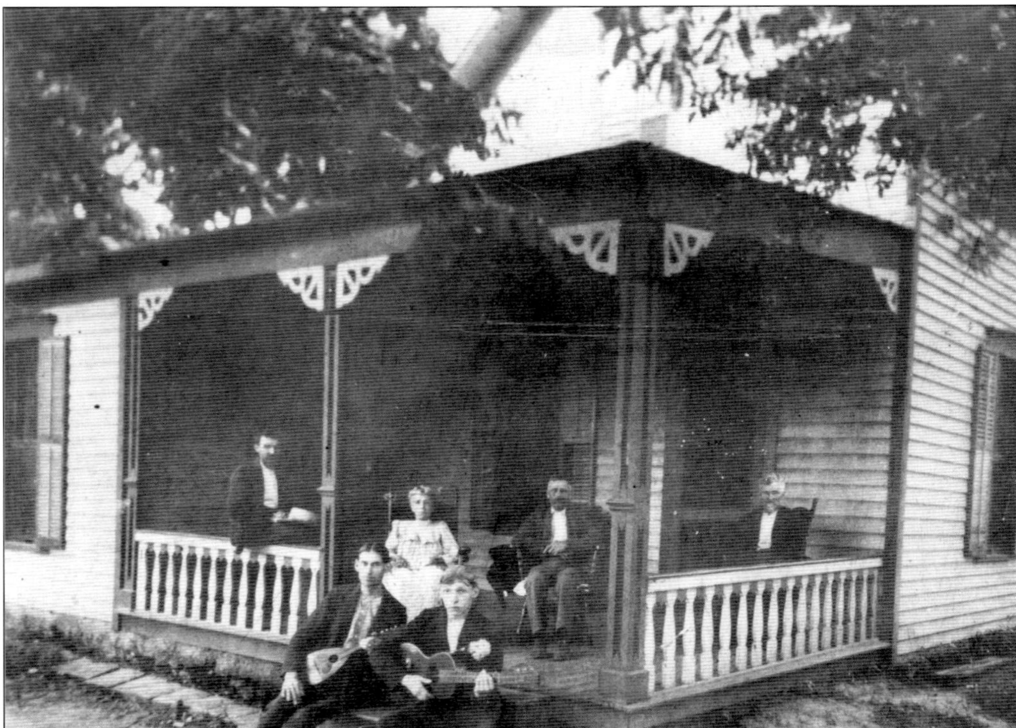

Music was a valued form of entertainment. Whole families learned instruments so they could play together. This 1900 image shows the family of Mrs. Joe Jeffcoat Rogers and their musical instruments. Sitting in the front is Danny Jeffcoat, holding his eight-string potbellied mandolin, and next to him is Clyde Jeffcoat with his guitar.

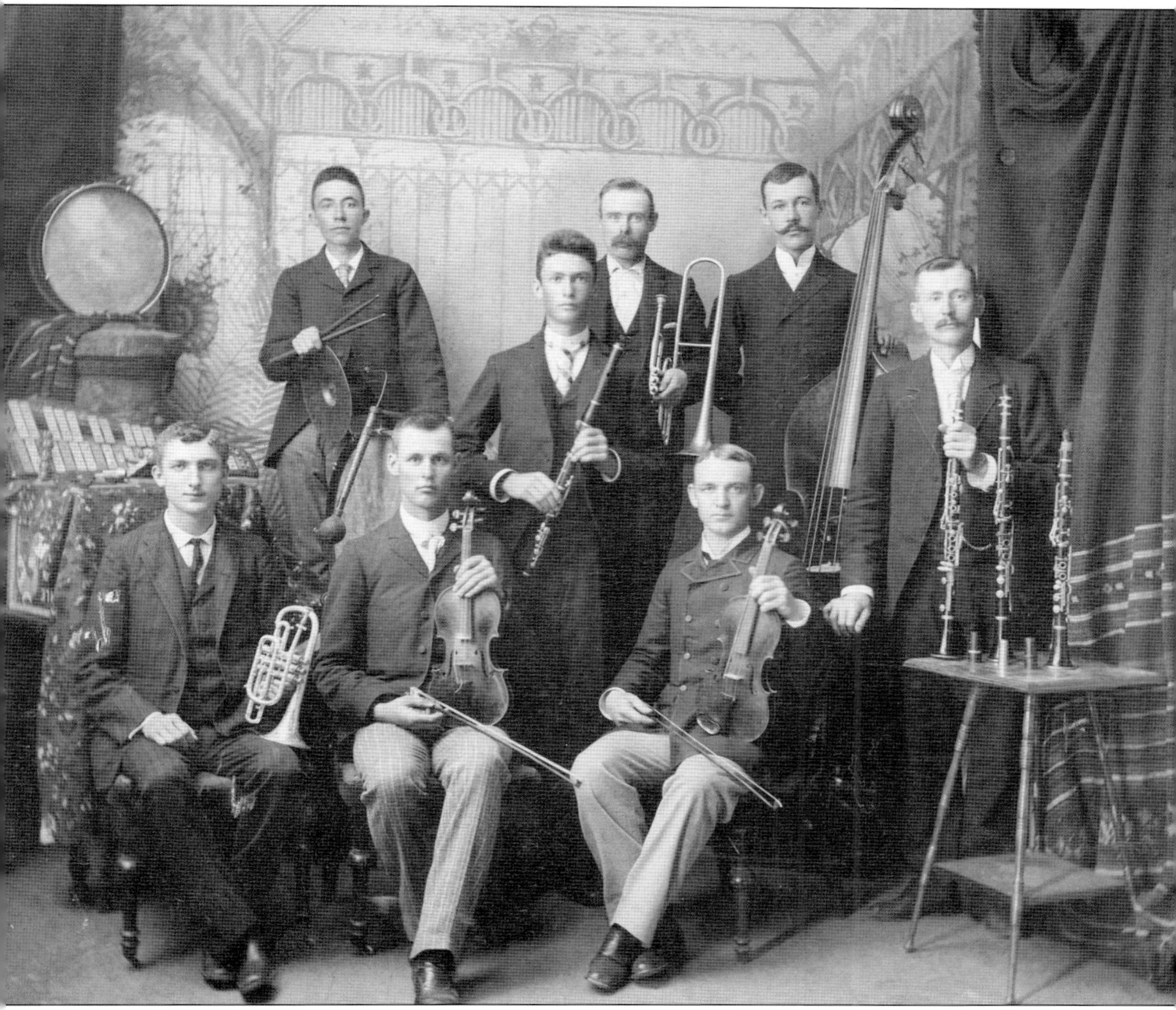

The men of Abilene formed their own city orchestra as early as 1894. Under the direction of Prof. Charles Harrison, the orchestra presented concerts at various venues around the county.

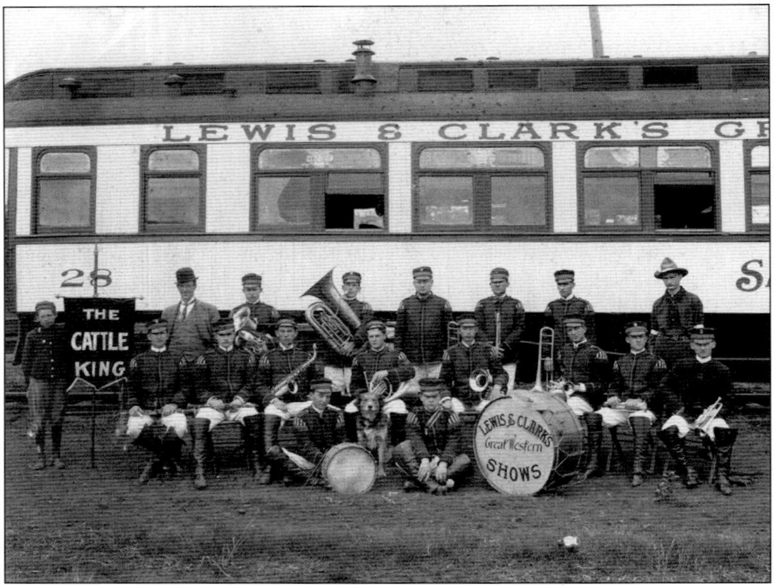

Traveling bands like Lewis and Clark's Great Western Show provided entertainment to the citizens of Abilene. Its shows played to sold-out audiences.

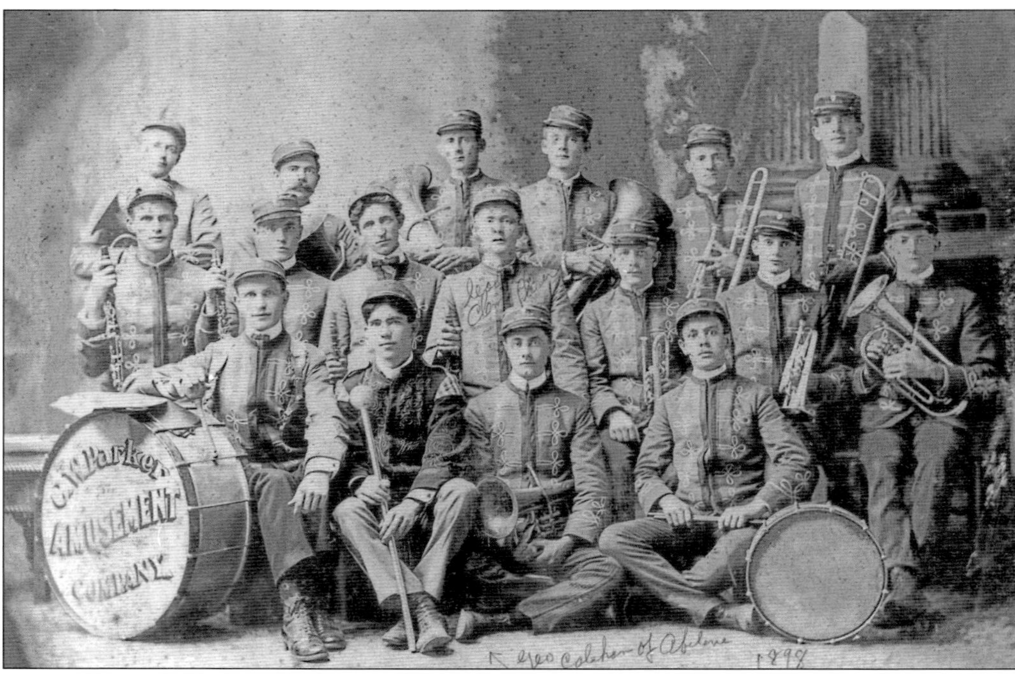

The C.W. Parker Amusement Company was located in Abilene and manufactured amusement rides and carousels. The company also had its own band that traveled to different towns and communities.

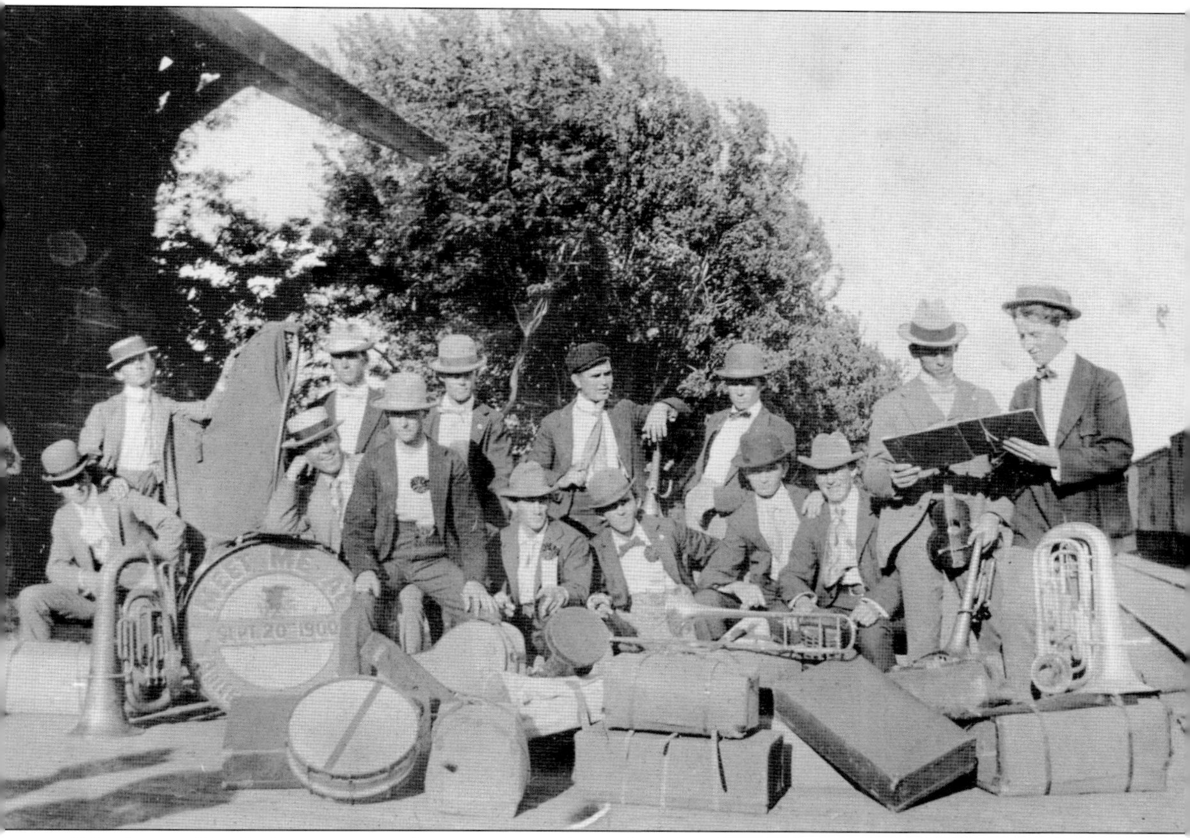

The best of both the sports and musical world was had by the Abilene Baseball Band. Each of the ballplayers also played an instrument. They could slug with the baseball bat and swing with the music. Instruments included in the band were cornets, trombones, drums, violin, and an Italian harp.

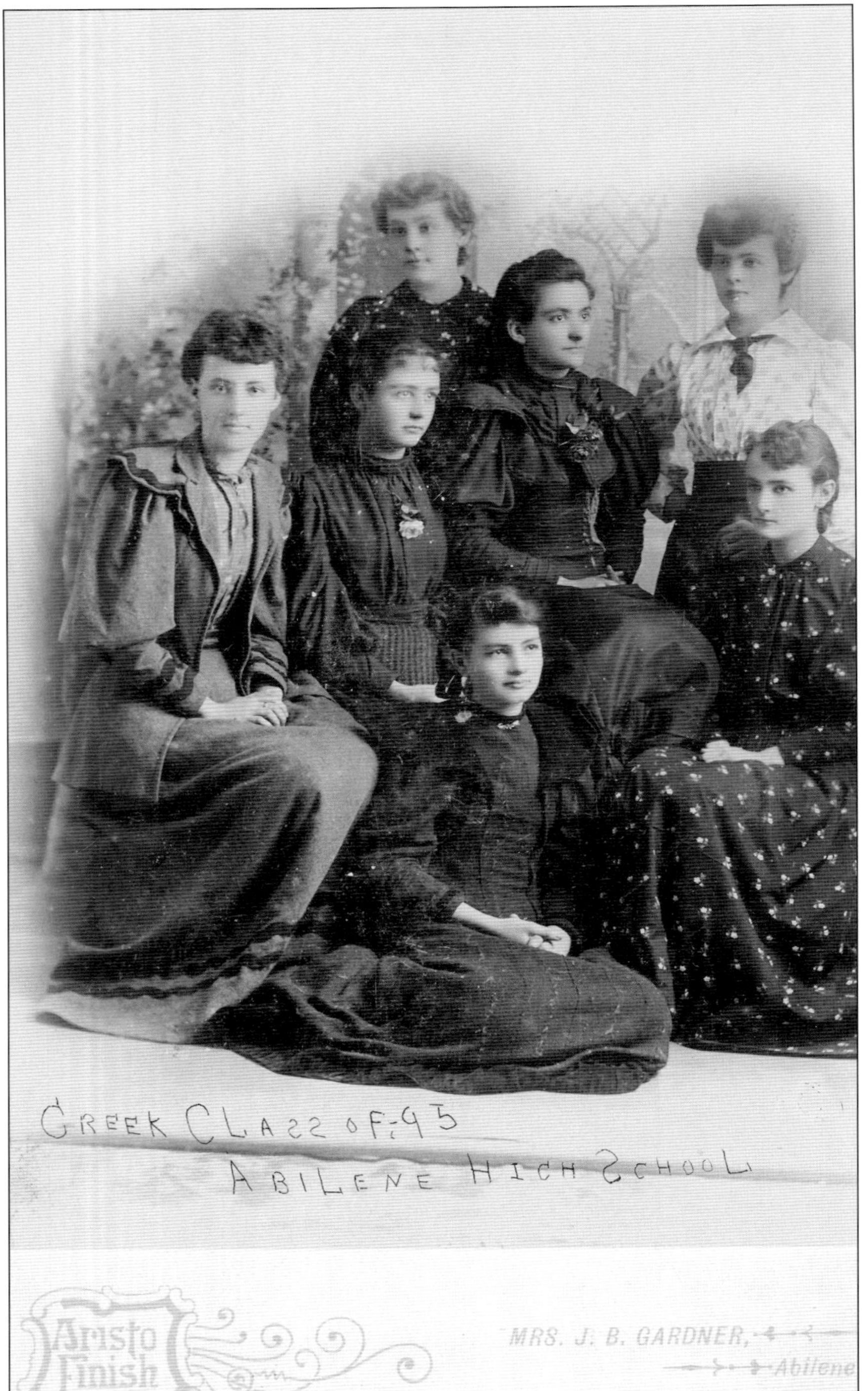

The young ladies of Abilene pursued cultural activities through clubs and classes like the Greek class of Abilene High School. Identified in this 1895 photograph are Beatrice Waring, Daisy Hunton, Lilly Jackson, and Bertha Parring (at the top).

Fashion became increasingly more important to the ladies of Abilene. With the advent of photography studios, young people and families could have their picture made. This 1897 photograph shows four young ladies of Abilene in the most up-to-date fashions. Pictured from left to right are Dollie Davis, Clara Call, Fladd Hawk, and Alice M. Sterl.

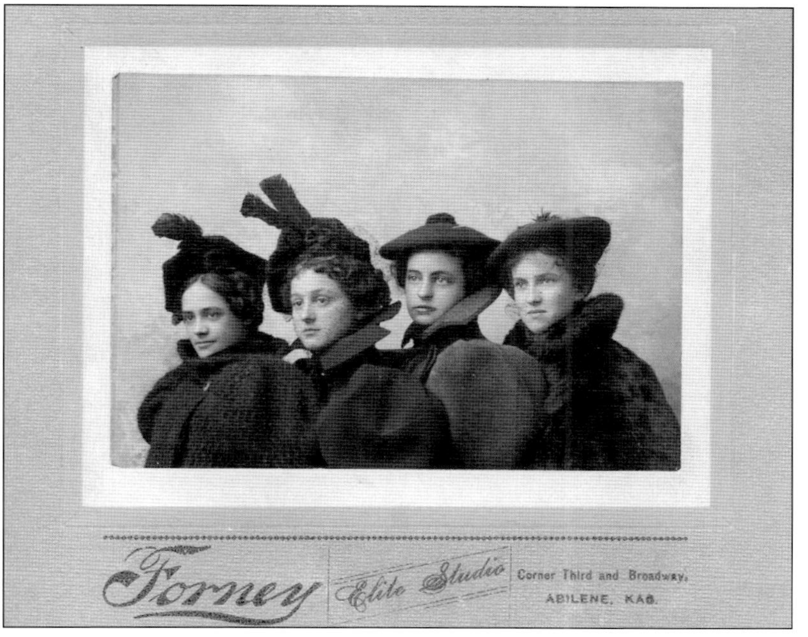

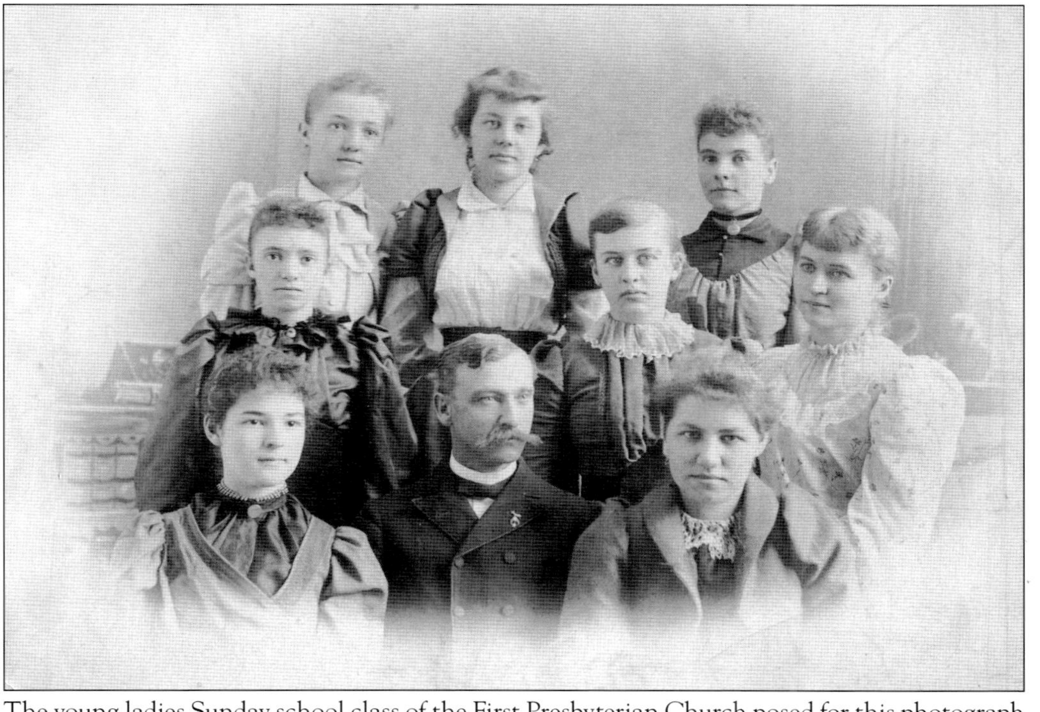

The young ladies Sunday school class of the First Presbyterian Church posed for this photograph in 1891. The girls not only studied the Bible but also enjoyed social activities and organizing charity drives.

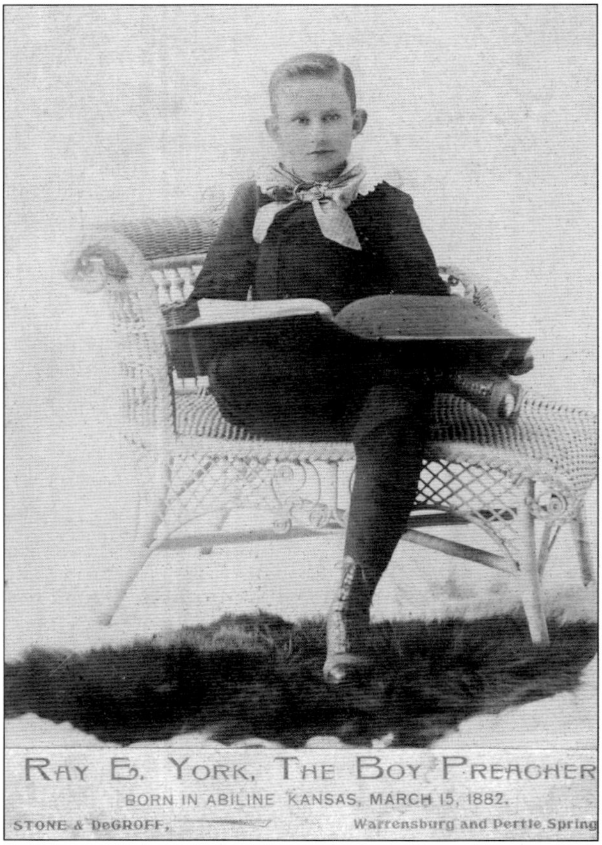

Traveling speakers like Ray York, the boy preacher, drew large crowds of interested people.

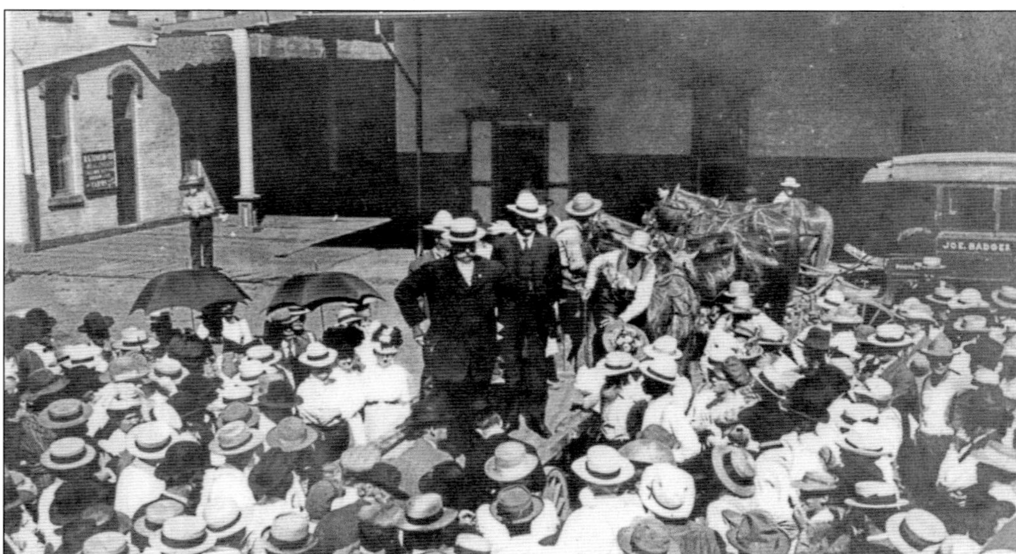

A visit by presidential candidate William Howard Taft drew large crowds to Abilene in 1905. Without radios or television, the only way to hear a candidate speak was in a face-to-face speech. But just as important as the campaign was the opportunity for a social gathering.

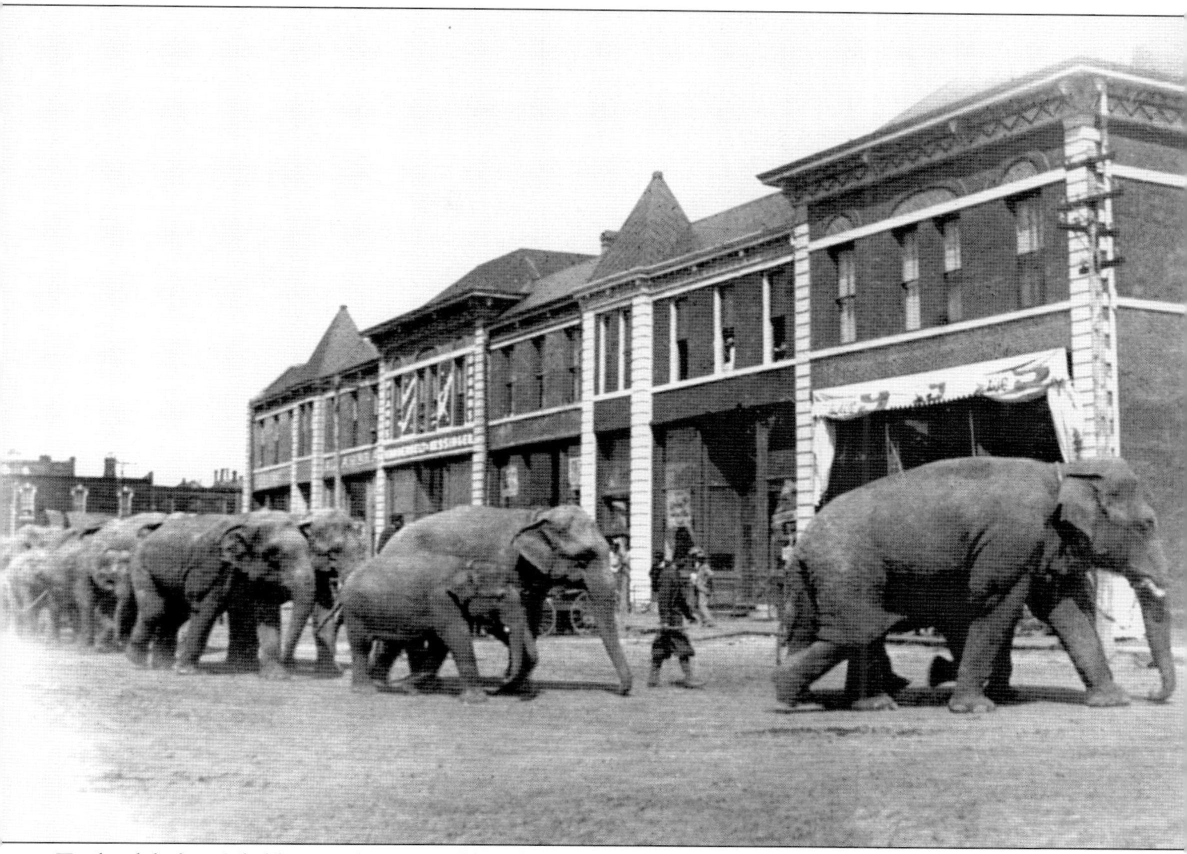

To the delight of children and parents alike, the Ringling Brothers Circus visited Abilene in the late 1800s. Instead of cattle moving through the streets, there was a herd of elephants on parade.

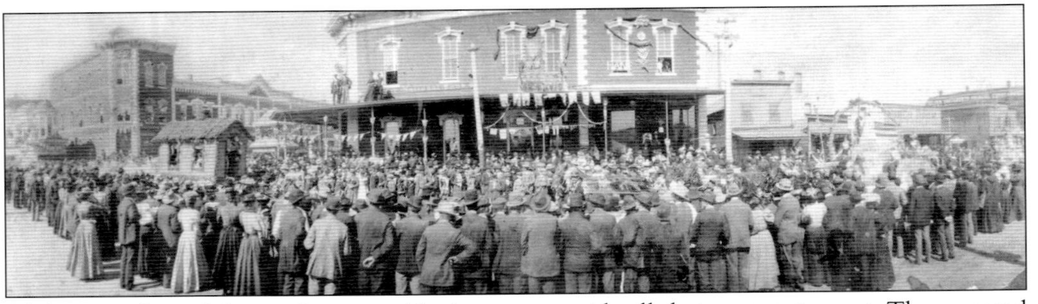

Abilene residents did not rely on outside shows to provide all their entertainment. They created their own parades, festivals, and celebrations. The Kaffir Corn Carnival was first held in 1899 and drew large crowds from throughout the county. Kaffir corn was sorghum grown as feed for animals. Harvest was in the fall, and that was a perfect time for a community gathering.

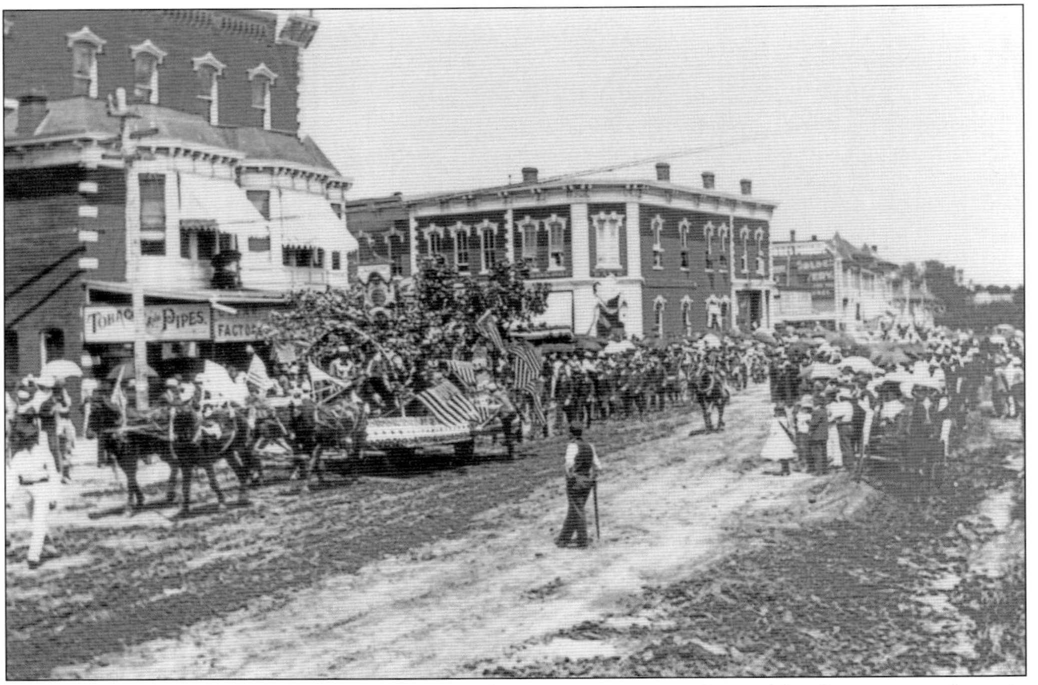

The Kaffir corn was used to decorate floats and to create costumes. It was like the rose parade, only a bit pricklier. Corn was a plentiful resource and an inexpensive way to decorate for a festival. This float has an Americana theme and sports American flags along with the Kaffir corn heads.

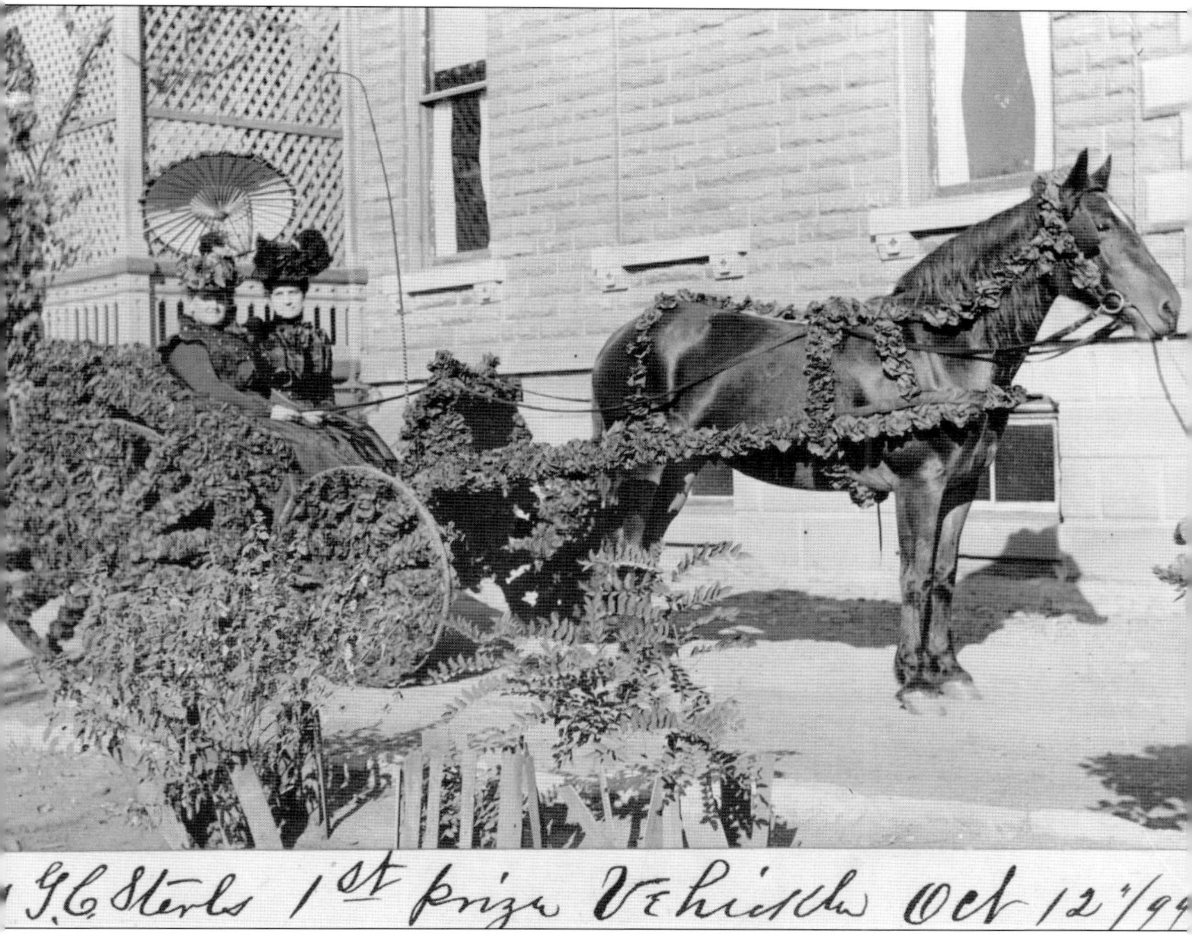

The first-place vehicle sports Kaffir corn heads laced through the buggy wheels and attached to the horse's harness.

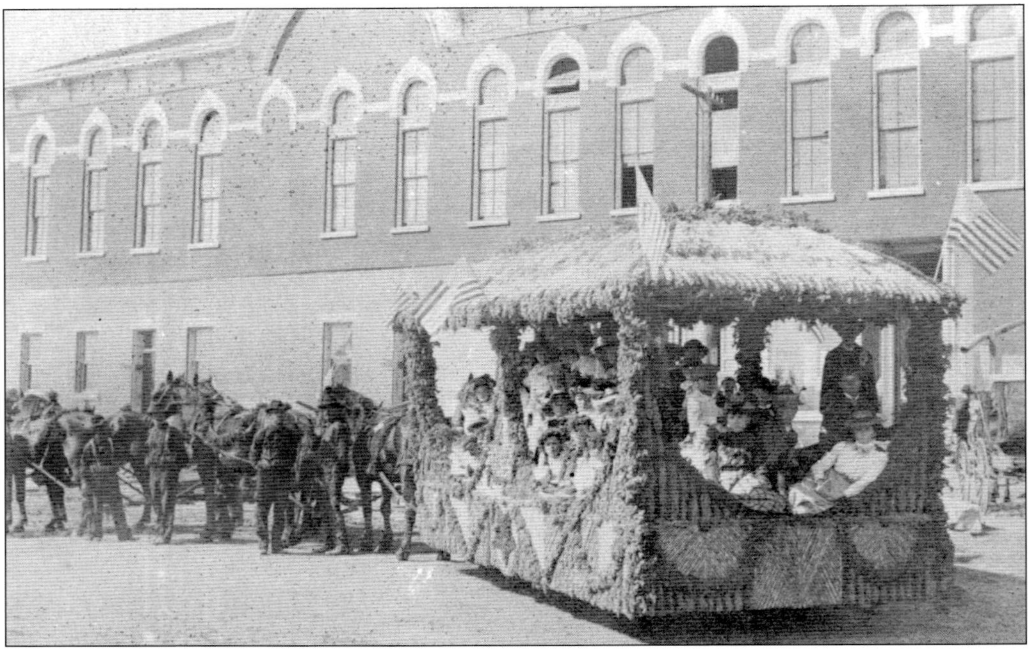

This float has elaborate sides and roof made from corn stalks and husks. It was built on a wagon bed and pulled by a full team of horses.

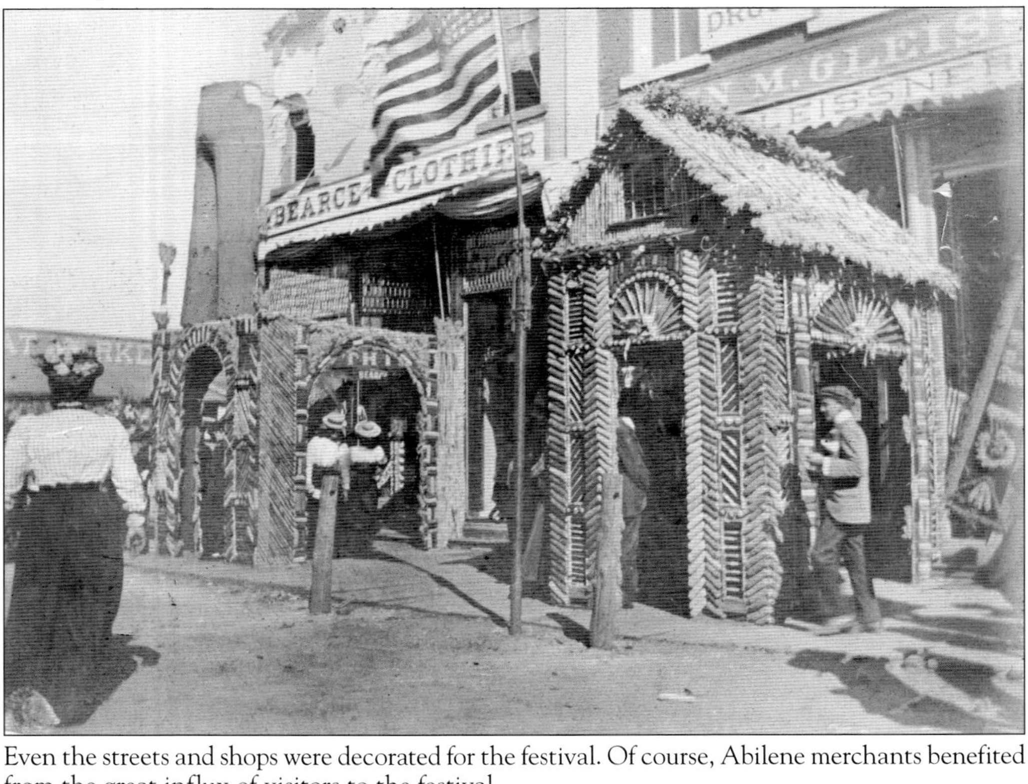

Even the streets and shops were decorated for the festival. Of course, Abilene merchants benefited from the great influx of visitors to the festival.

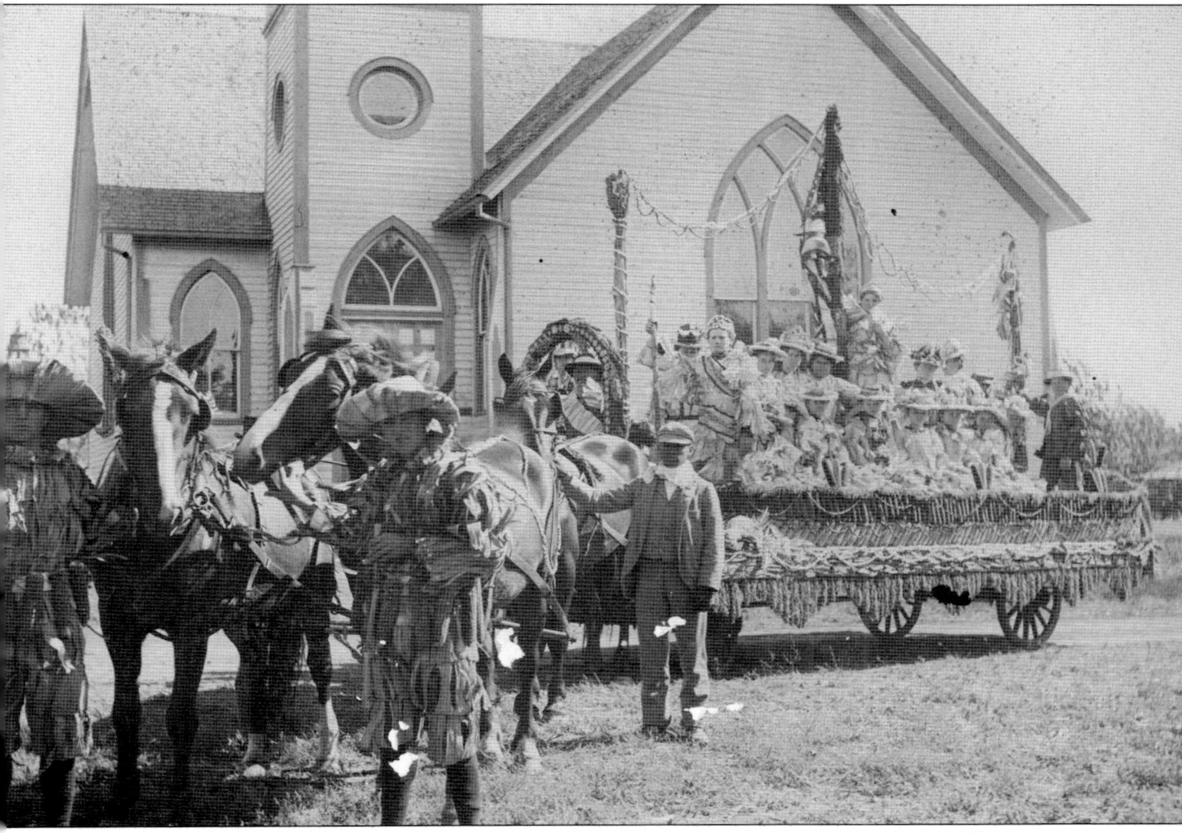

The first-place float at the 1899 Abilene Corn Carnival was created by the students of Harmony Hall School. They wore costumes and hats created out of corn husks.

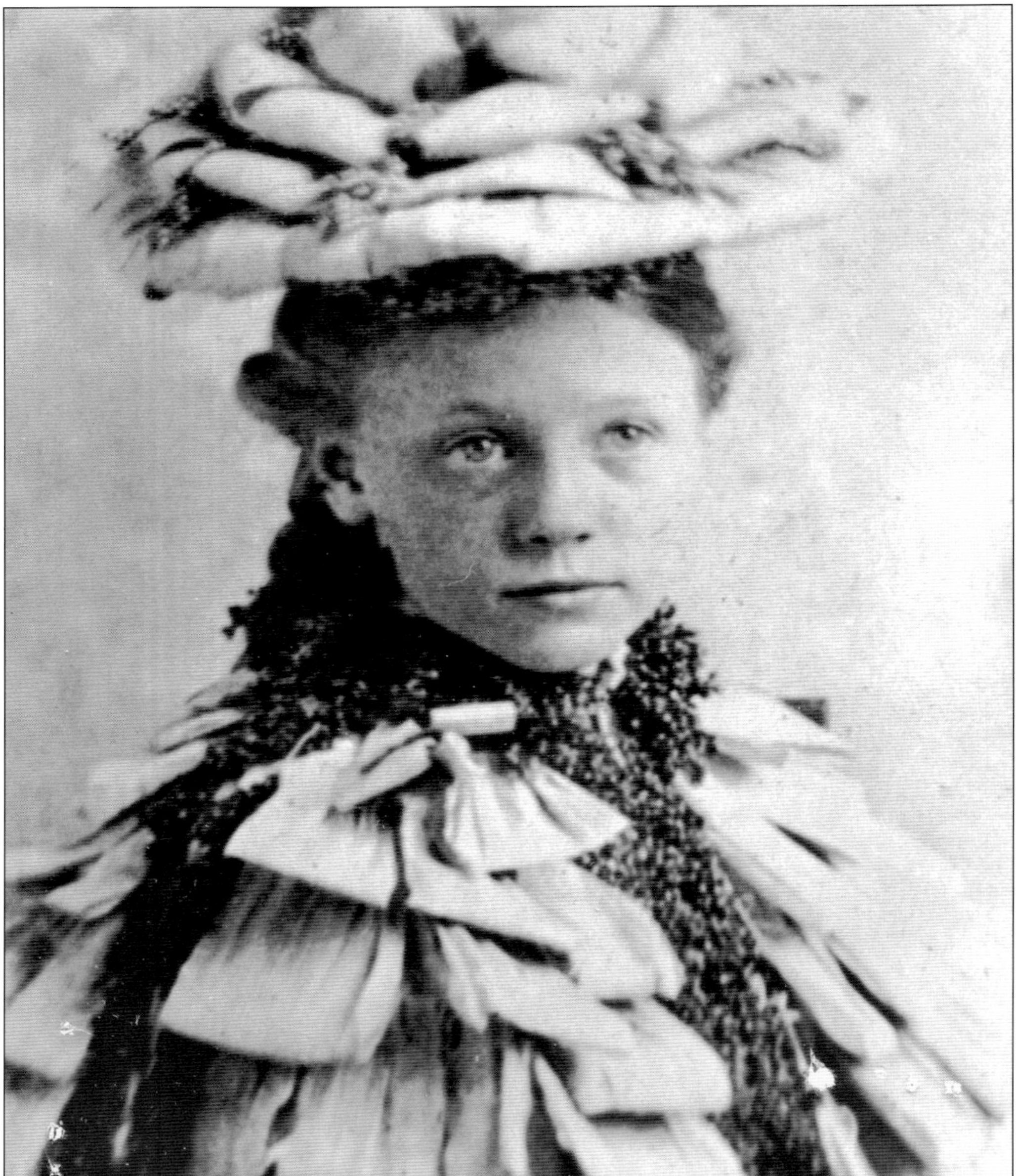

This girl shows off an elaborate costume made from husks of Kaffir corn and a necklace from Kaffir corn heads.

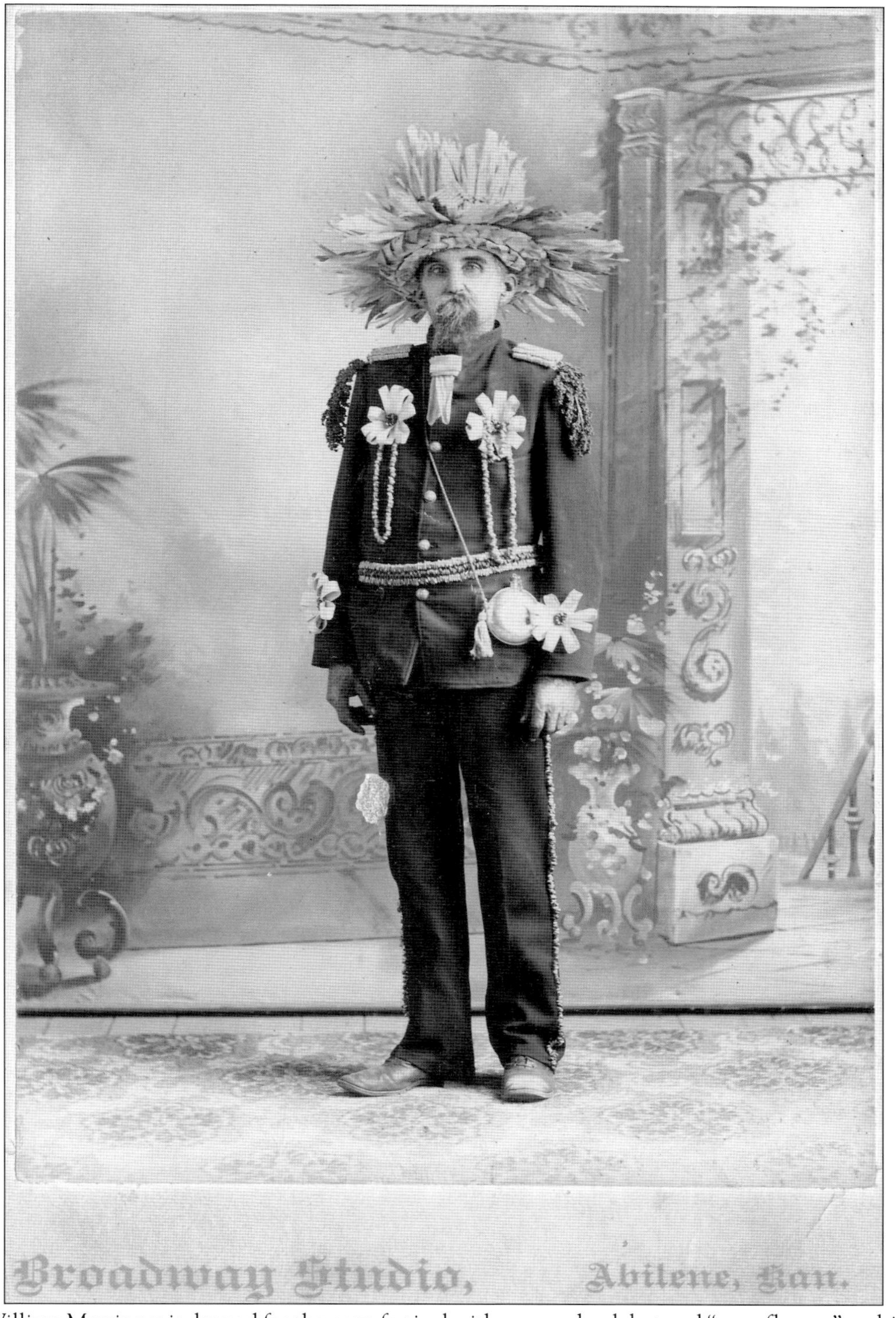

William Messinger is dressed for the corn festival with a corn-shuck hat and "corn flowers" on his suit. Messinger served as city commissioner and was by trade a well-known stone mason.

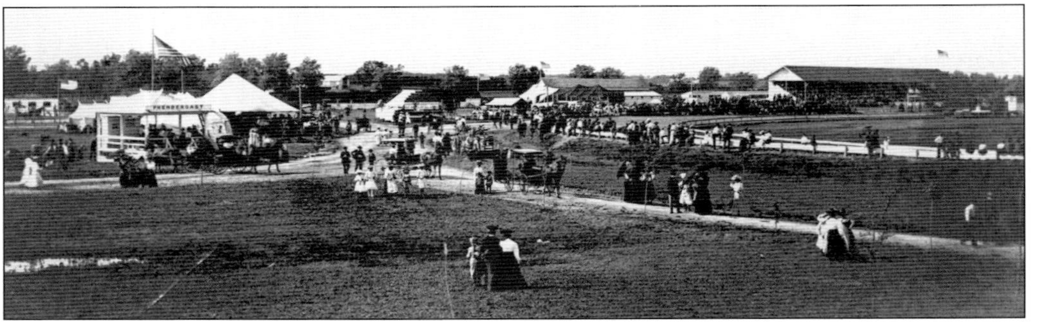

To accommodate fairs and festivals, the community built a fairgrounds. It was completed in the early 1900s and was used for county fairs, horse racing, and eventually automobile races.

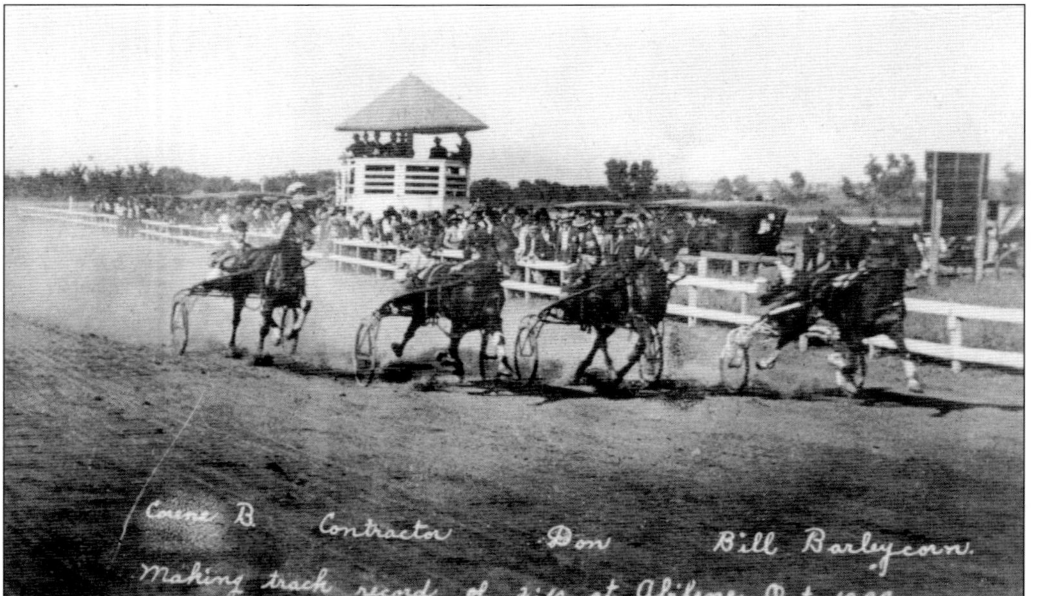

Horse races were a popular attraction at the fairgrounds. The races were a proving ground for horse breeders. The more ribbons a horses won, the more valuable it became. Crowds gathered in dust and mud to cheer on their favorite teams.

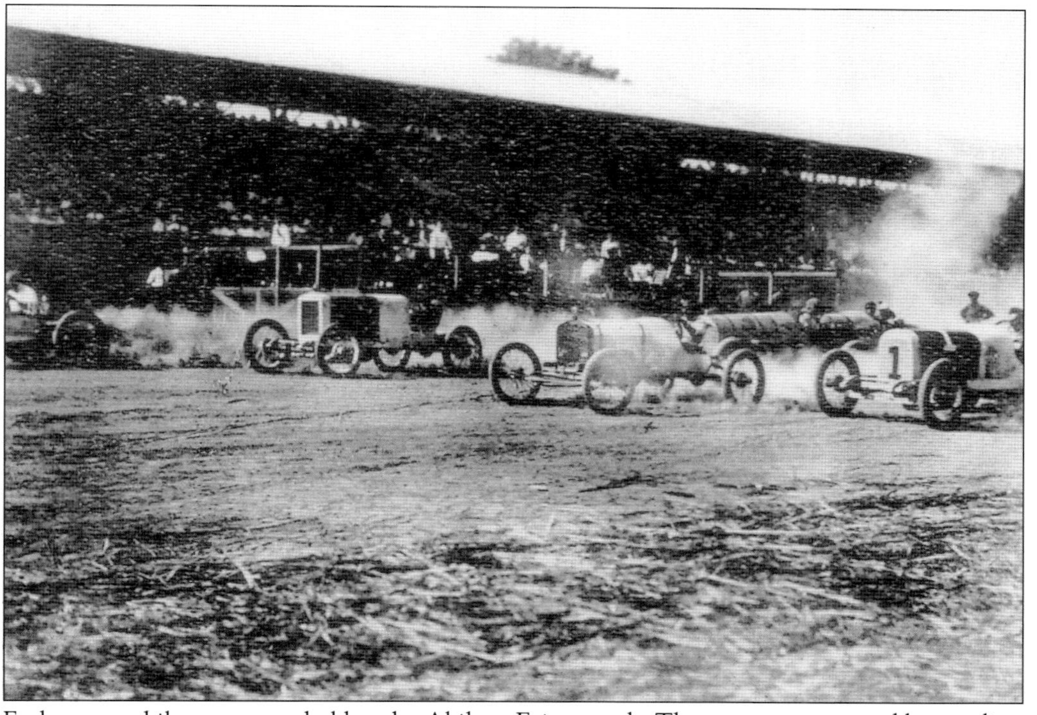

Early automobile races were held at the Abilene Fairgrounds. The cars were powered by gasoline and were little more than tin cans on buggy wheels, but the stands were full to see the newfangled machines race.

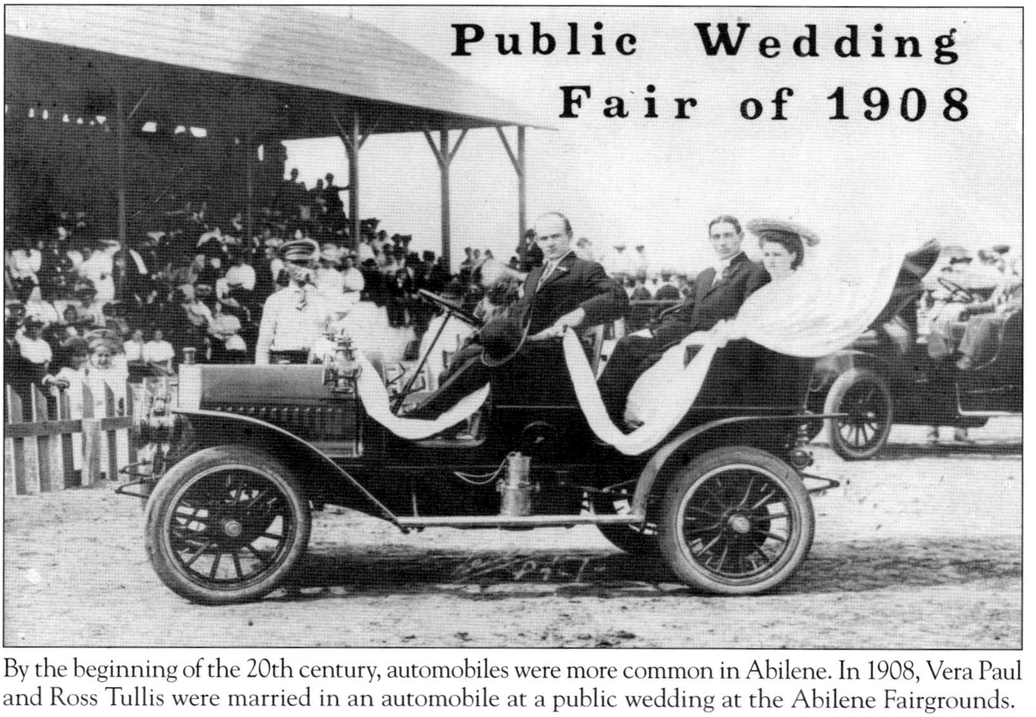

By the beginning of the 20th century, automobiles were more common in Abilene. In 1908, Vera Paul and Ross Tullis were married in an automobile at a public wedding at the Abilene Fairgrounds.

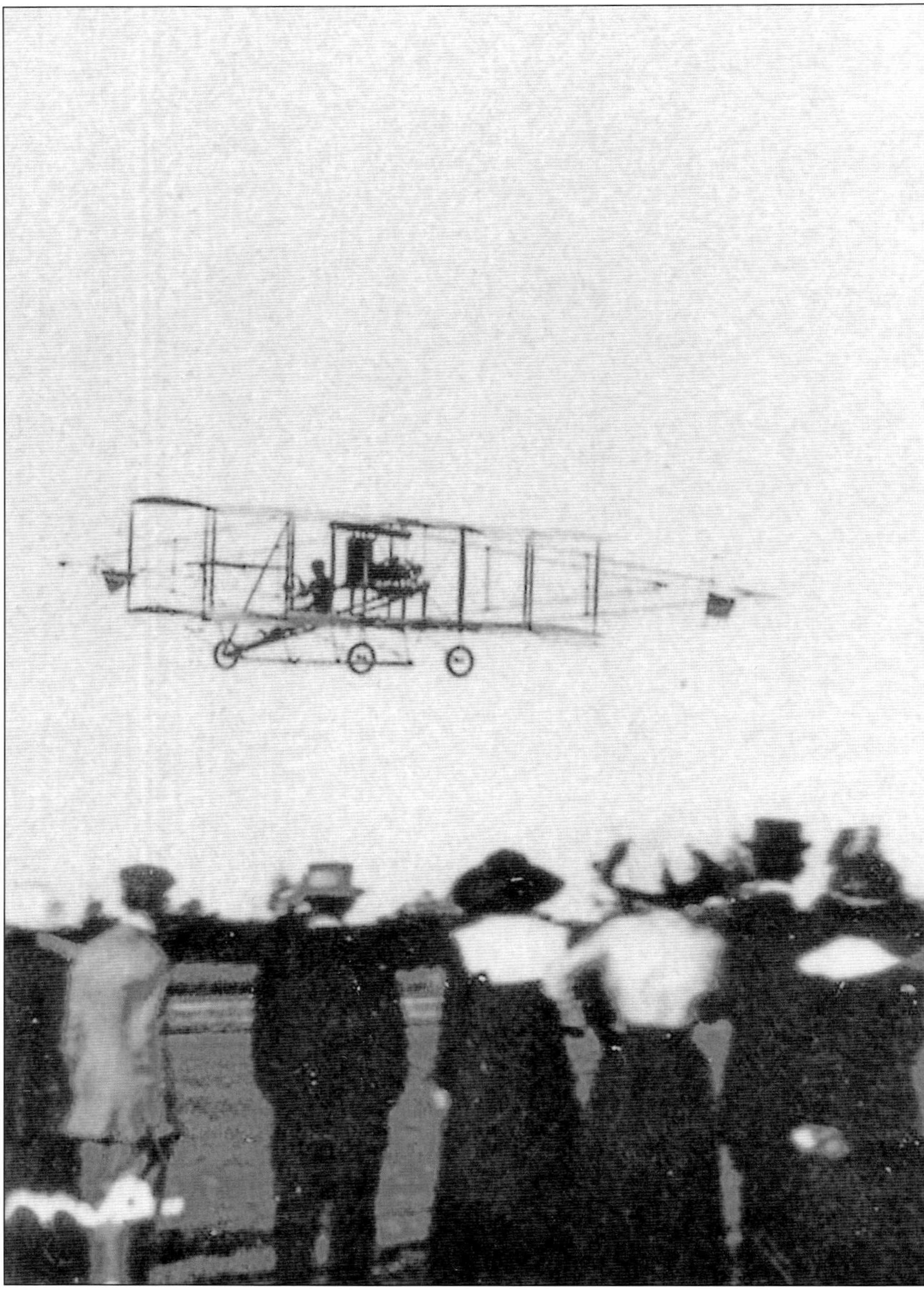

The turn of the century brought amazing new inventions to the world and to Abilene. In 1904, the Wright brothers took to the air for the first manned flight. And, in 1912, a flying machine took wing at the Abilene fairgrounds. It was the start of a whole new era.

Four

The Boom Years

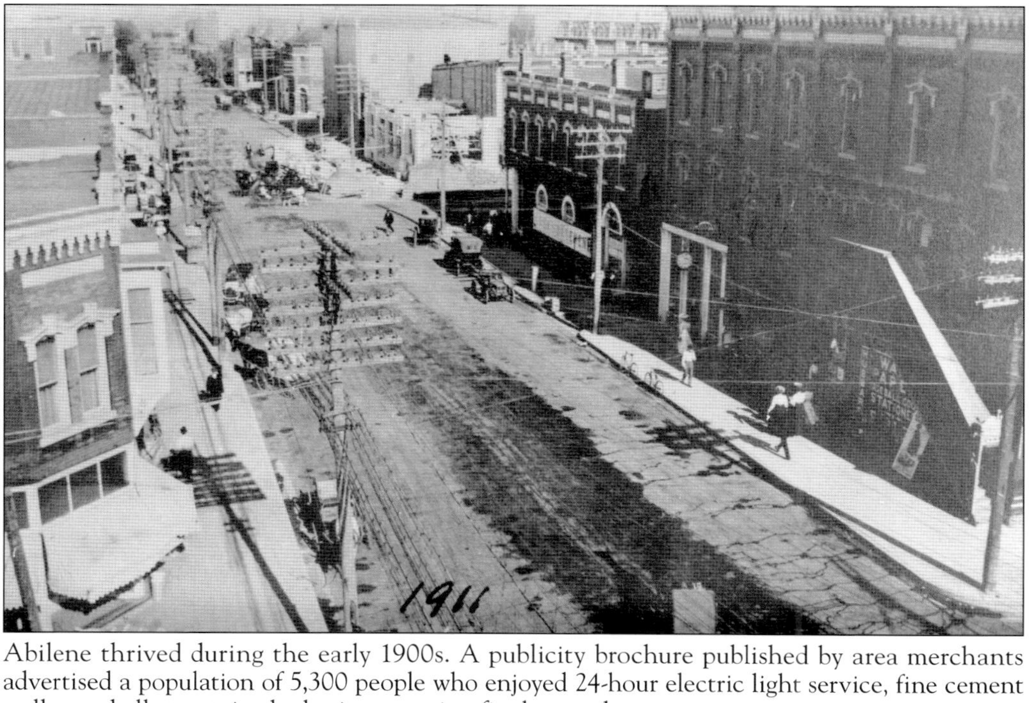

Abilene thrived during the early 1900s. A publicity brochure published by area merchants advertised a population of 5,300 people who enjoyed 24-hour electric light service, fine cement walks, and all streets in the business section finely paved.

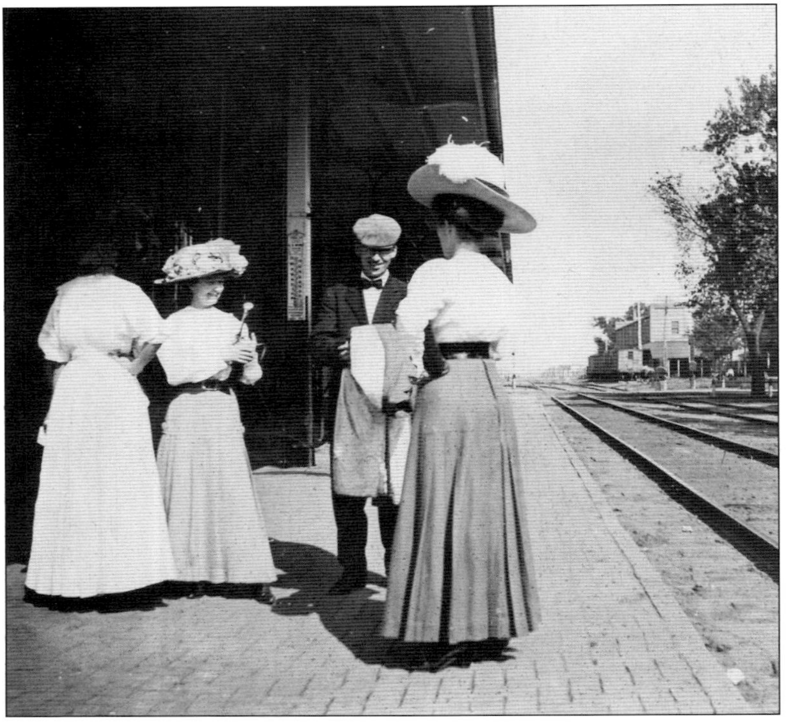

Trains continued to play a central role in the vitality of Abilene. Three rail systems had routes through town. The Union Pacific, Sante Fe, and Rock Island Railroads provided transportation to market for crops and livestock. Travelers could board the train in Abilene and move easily across the country.

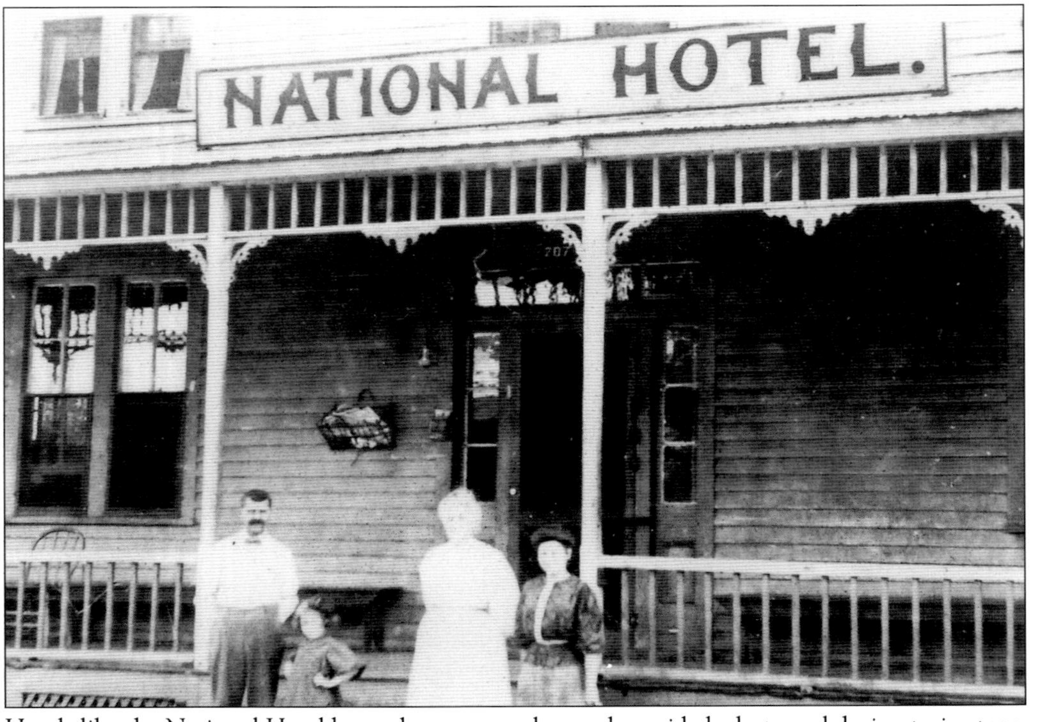

Hotels like the National Hotel housed weary travelers and provided a hot meal during train stops.

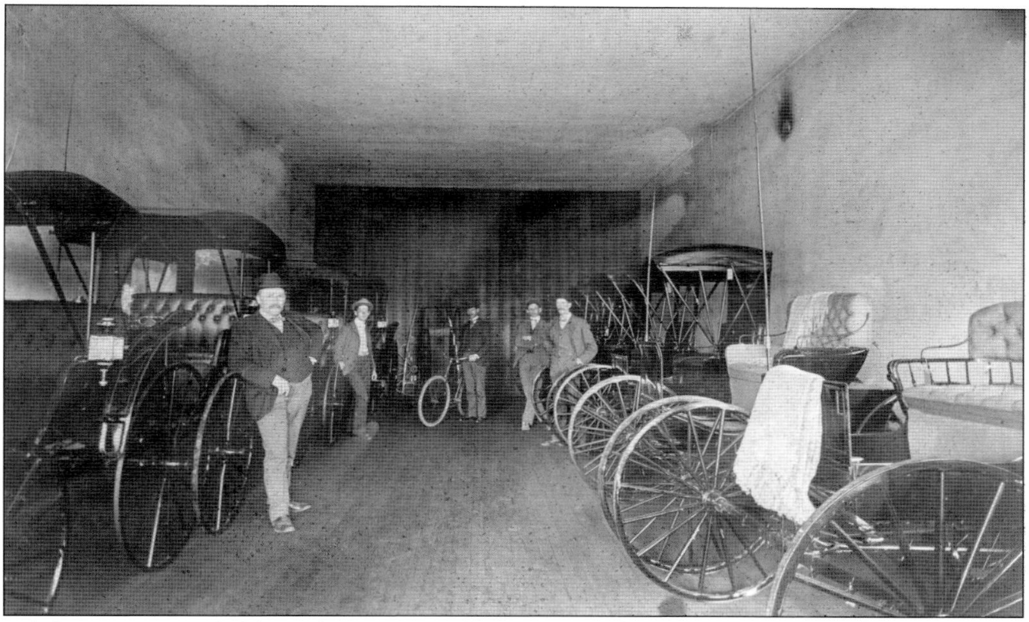

While trains provided long-distance travel, a horse and buggy were still the standard form of transportation in 1900 Abilene. The Shockey & Landes buggy show room offered customers the opportunity to check out the merchandise before they bought their wheels.

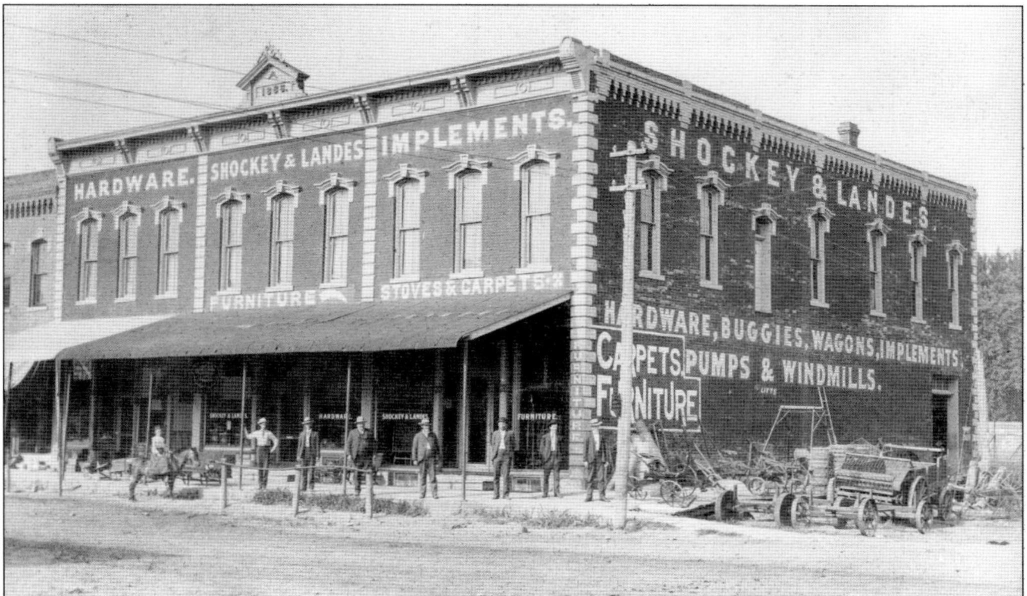

Shockey & Landes, at the corner of Fourth Street and Broadway, was one of the largest retail companies in Abilene. It offered hardware, farm machinery, vehicles, furniture, and carpets. The original partnership was between Isaac Shockey and J.G. Landes. Their sons continued to run the business well into the 20th century. Some of the people who can be identified in this c. 1900 image include Bessie Shockey (on the horse), Jacob Landes, Isaac Shockey, E.M. Shockey, and O.B. Landes.

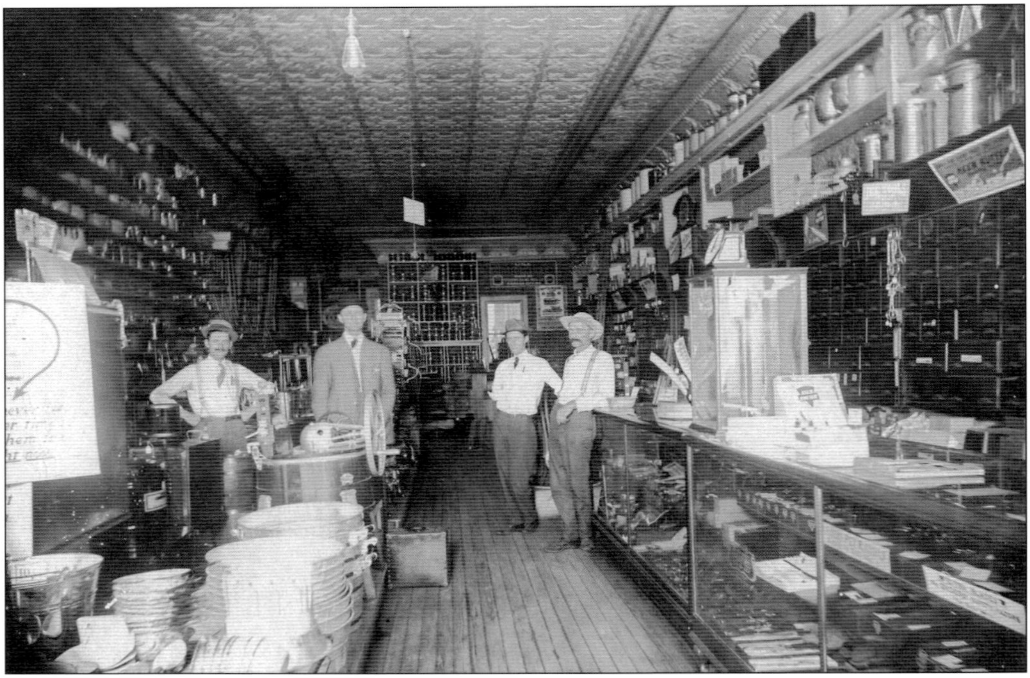

Shockey & Landes sold everything from galvanized washtubs to penny nails. The men in this c. 1900 image are, from left to right, J.G. Landes, Isaac Shockey, Simon Shockey, and O.B. Landes.

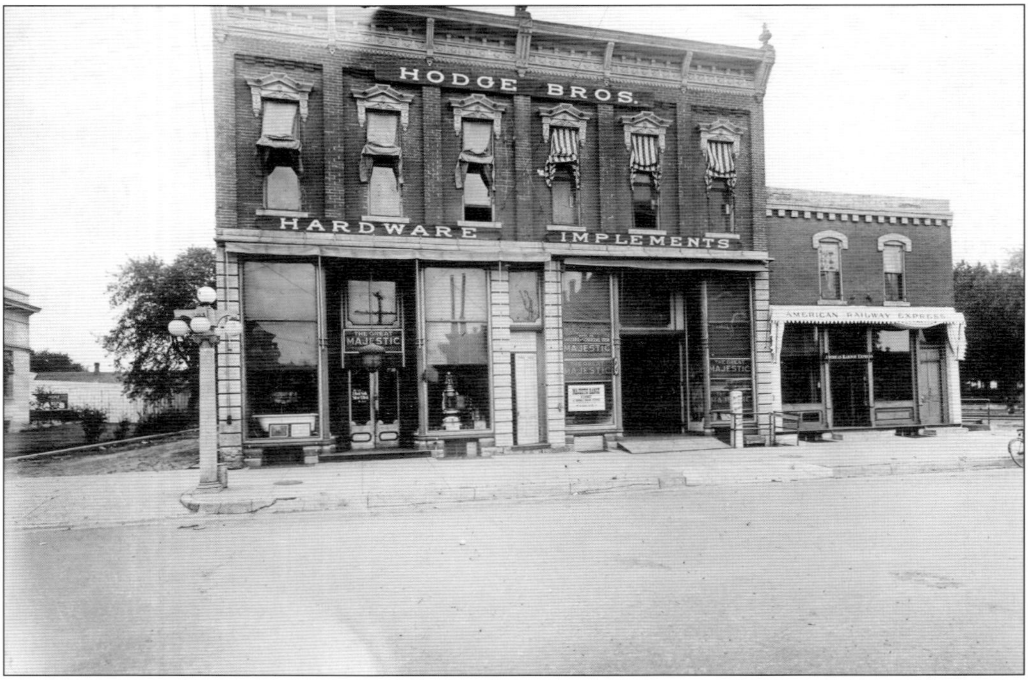

Shockey & Landes was not the only hardware in town. Stiff competition was offered by the Hodge Brothers' line of tools and farm equipment.

Abilene became the regional hub for shopping, with people from the smaller towns of Enterprise, Chapman, and Detroit coming to Abilene for a variety of shopping needs. The Armitage Novelty Store provided children's rocking toys, doll buggies, and household items.

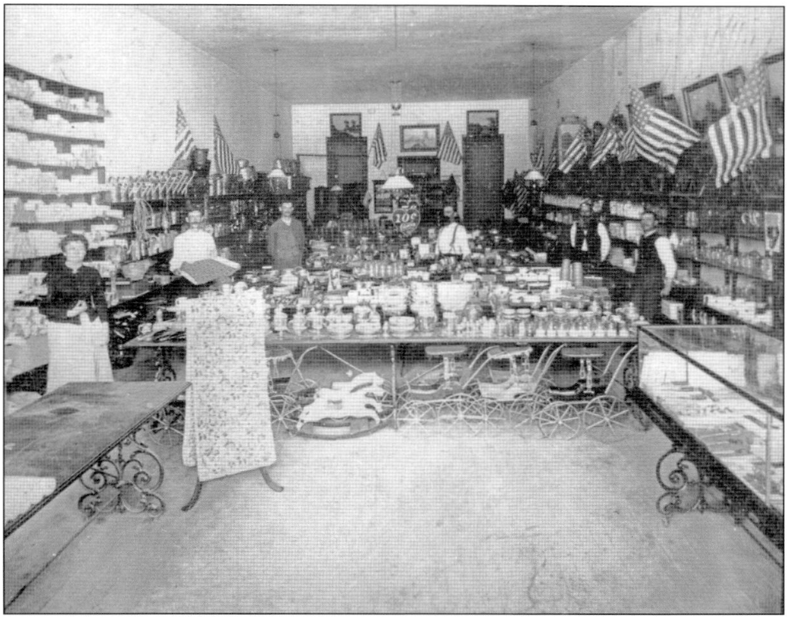

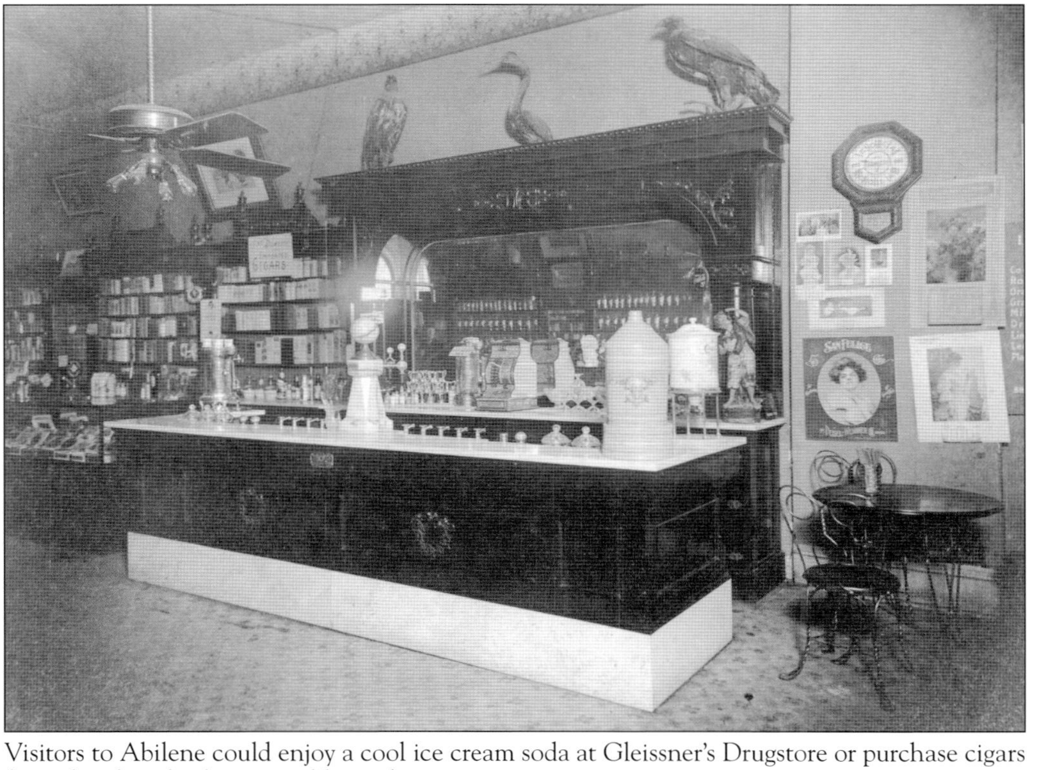

Visitors to Abilene could enjoy a cool ice cream soda at Gleissner's Drugstore or purchase cigars from the glass display case of fine tobaccos.

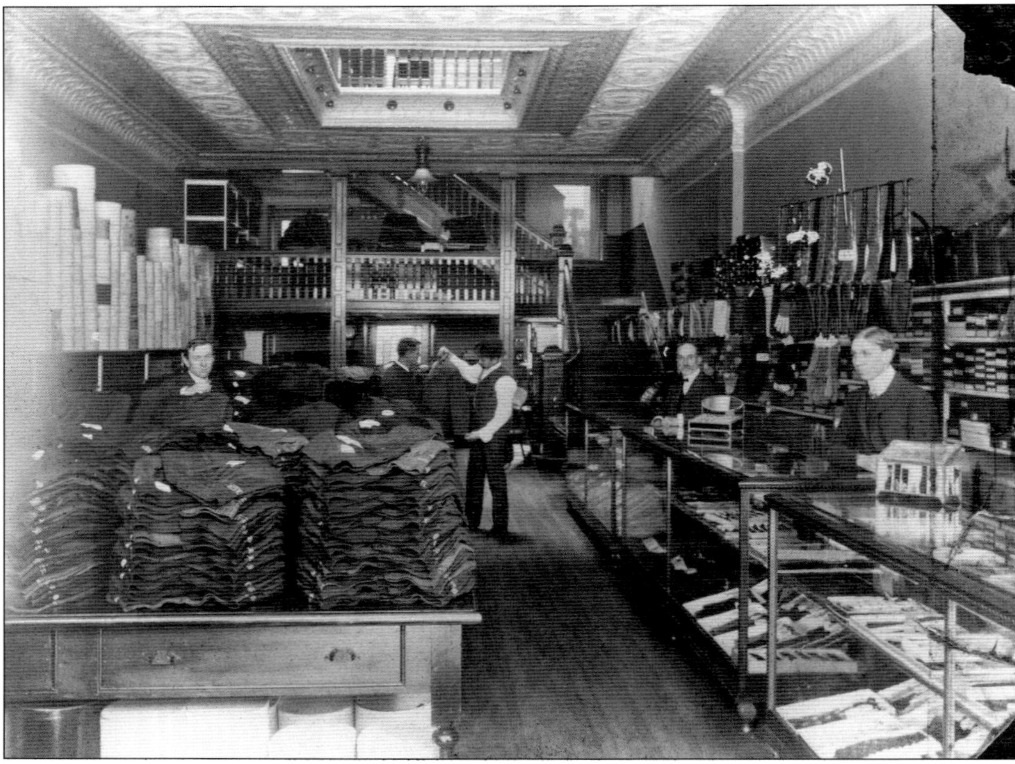

Clothing stores offered a wide selection of pants, vests, jackets, bowler hats, and neckwear. Stiff white collars were detachable from shirts to allow the shirts to be laundered more frequently.

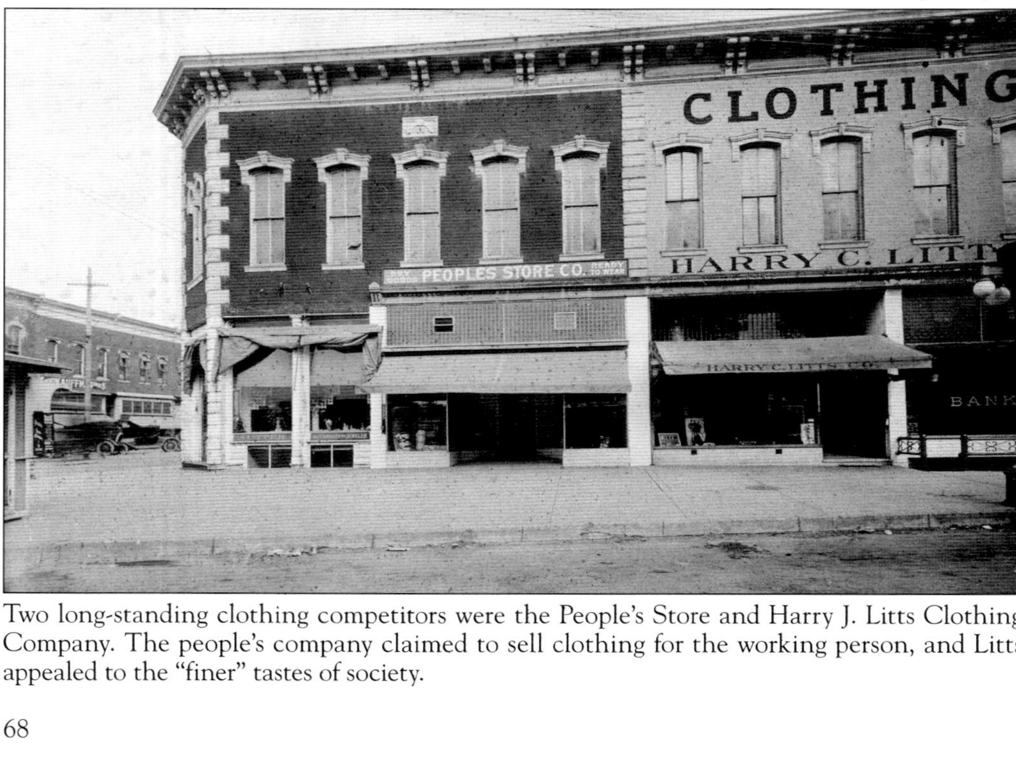

Two long-standing clothing competitors were the People's Store and Harry J. Litts Clothing Company. The people's company claimed to sell clothing for the working person, and Litts appealed to the "finer" tastes of society.

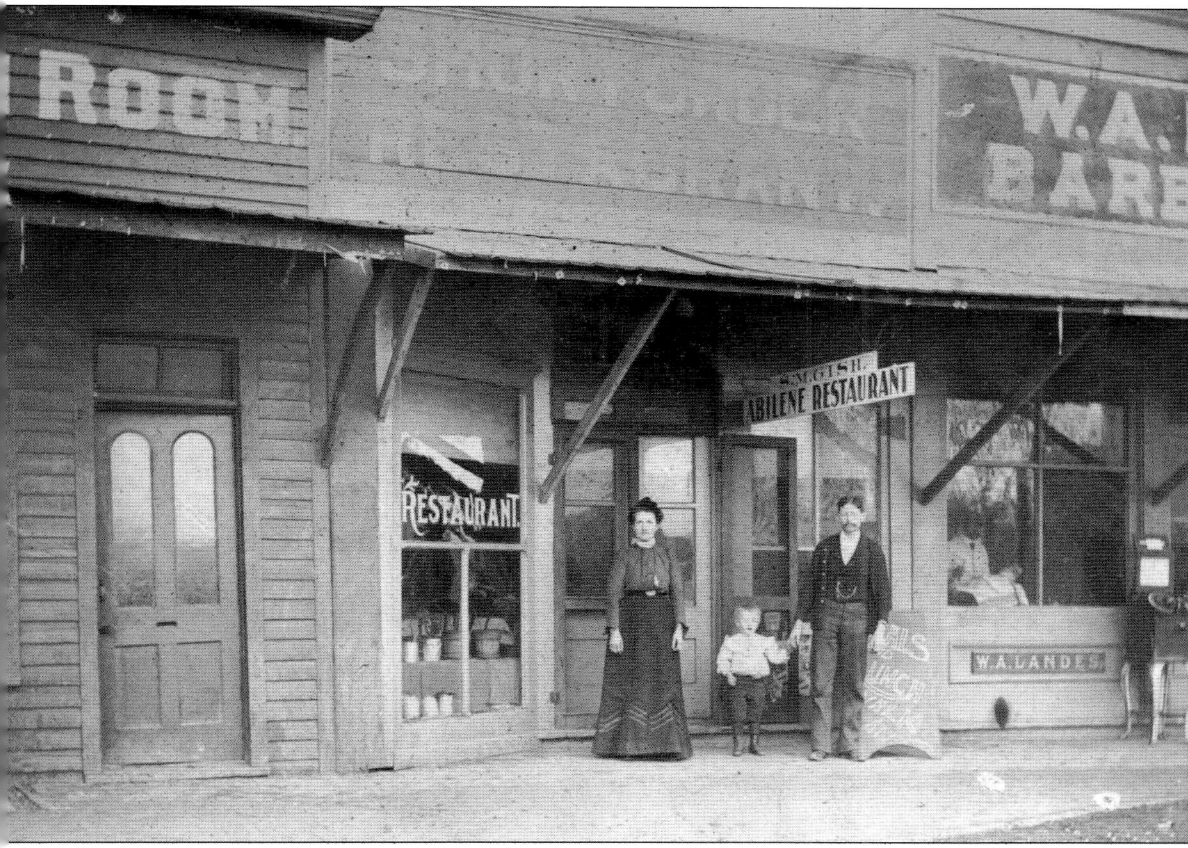

The S.M. Gish Restaurant offered shoppers, travelers, and locals home-cooked meals and daily lunch specials. Pictured in front of their business are Sam Gish, his wife, and his son.

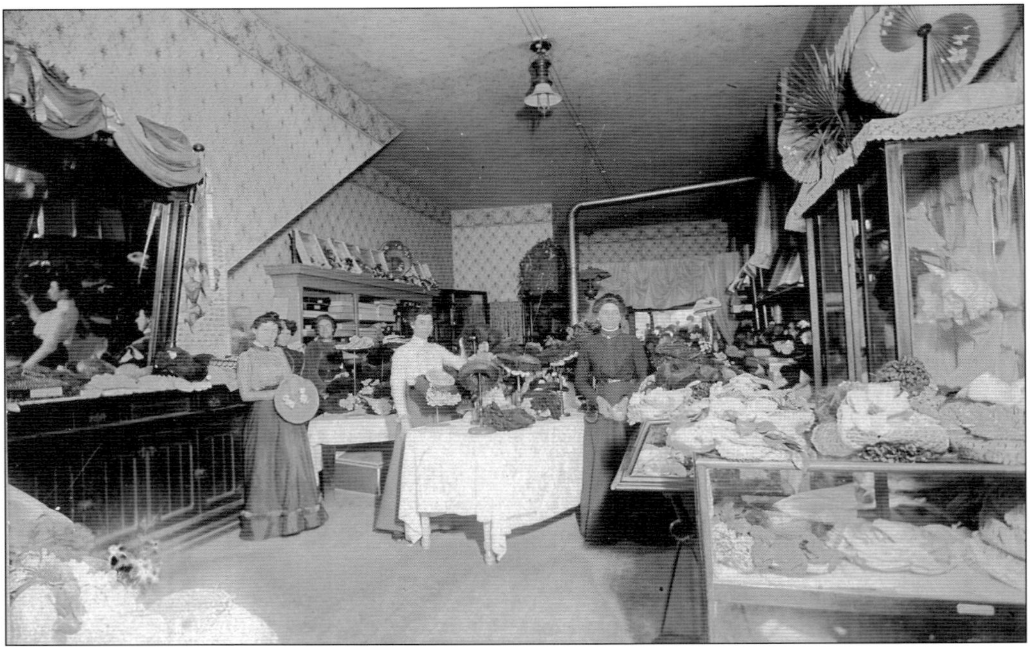

Mrs. Jolley's Millinery store offered discerning shoppers the finest in ladies' fashion. Custom-made hats, fine handbags, gloves, and undergarments were all available for purchase.

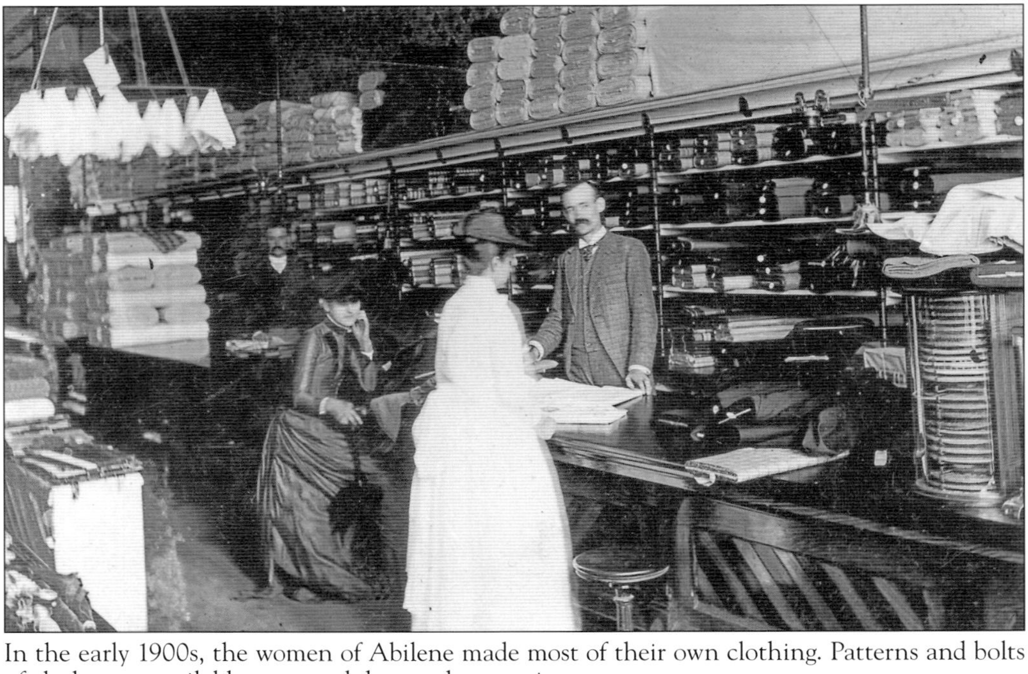

In the early 1900s, the women of Abilene made most of their own clothing. Patterns and bolts of cloth were available at several dry goods stores in town.

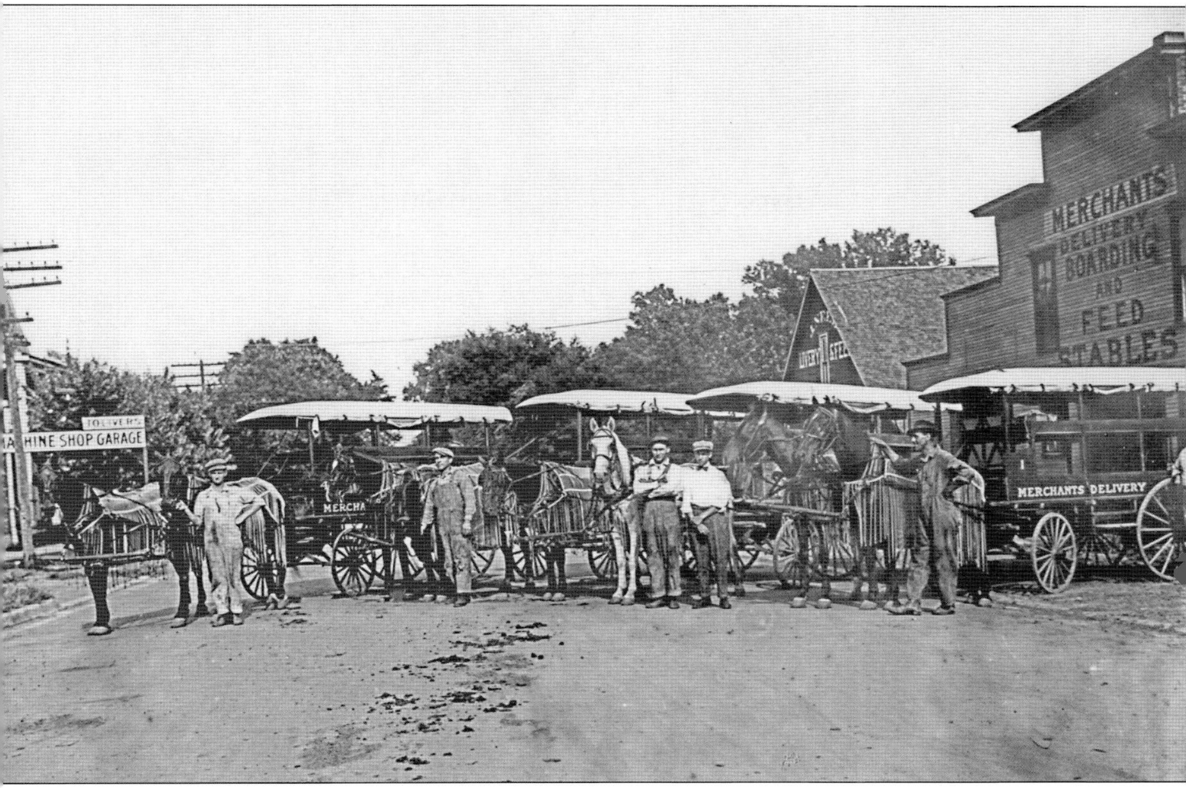

Abilene shoppers had the added luxury of using Merchants Delivery. Organized by Henry Matteson, the horse-drawn delivery wagons would deliver all shoppers' purchases directly to their doorstep.

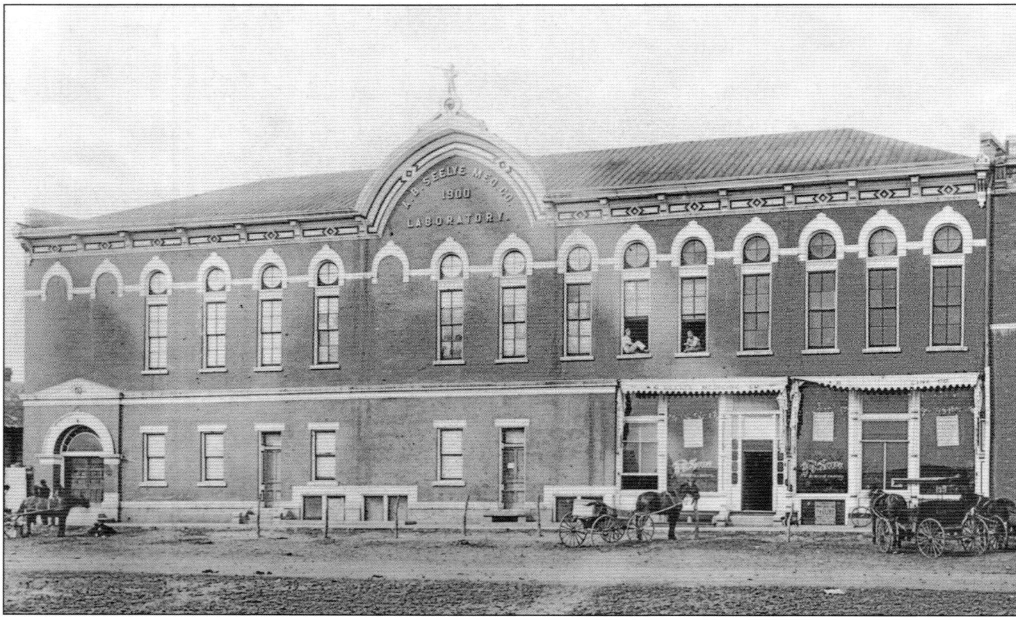

In addition to being the host to a wide variety of merchants and shops, Abilene also offered the citizens an upscale entertainment venue. The Seeley Opera House brought in music and theatrical performers from around the country. Formerly the Bonebrake Opera house, Dr. Seeley purchased and refurbished the building for use as his laboratory as well as the theater.

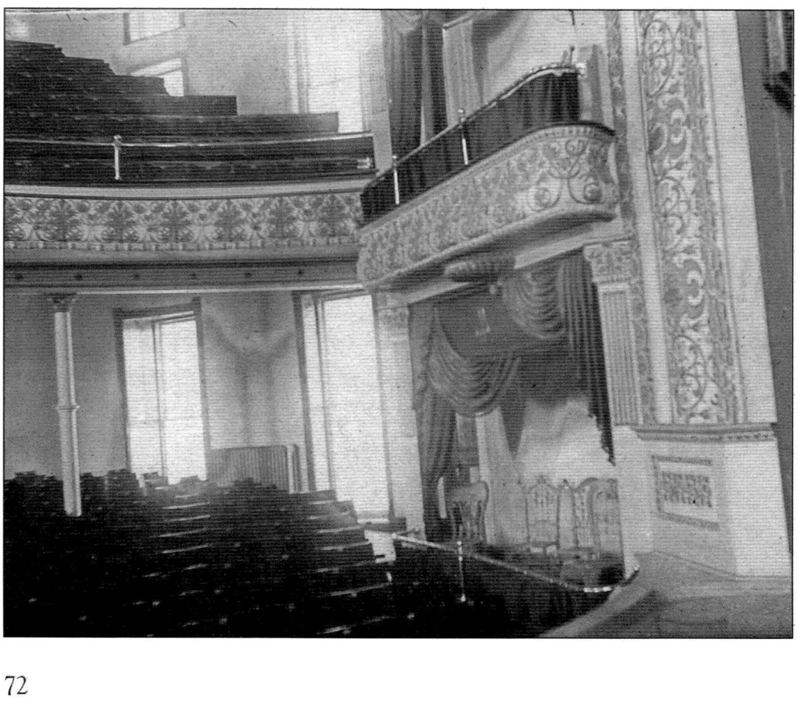

Abilene citizens boasted that the Seeley Opera House was the finest theater west of Kansas City. Citizens enjoyed plays, bands, and shows like the "Lewis and Clark Western Show."

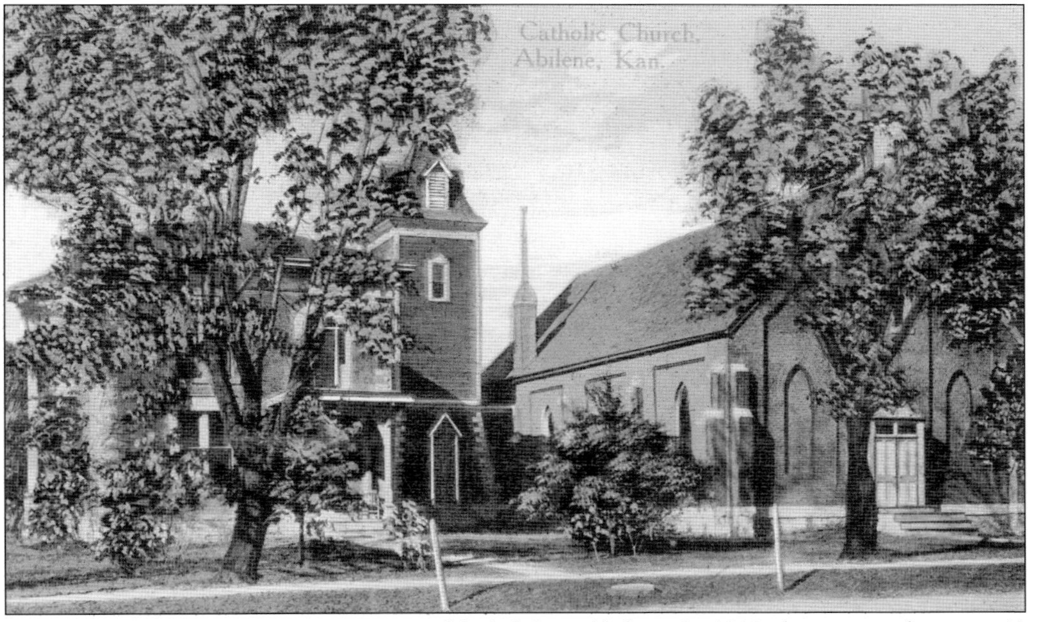

Local churches were an important part of daily life in Abilene. In 1910, the city was home to 14 churches and a variety of religious denominations. Church organizations included the Ladies Aid Society, bible study groups, and men's clubs.

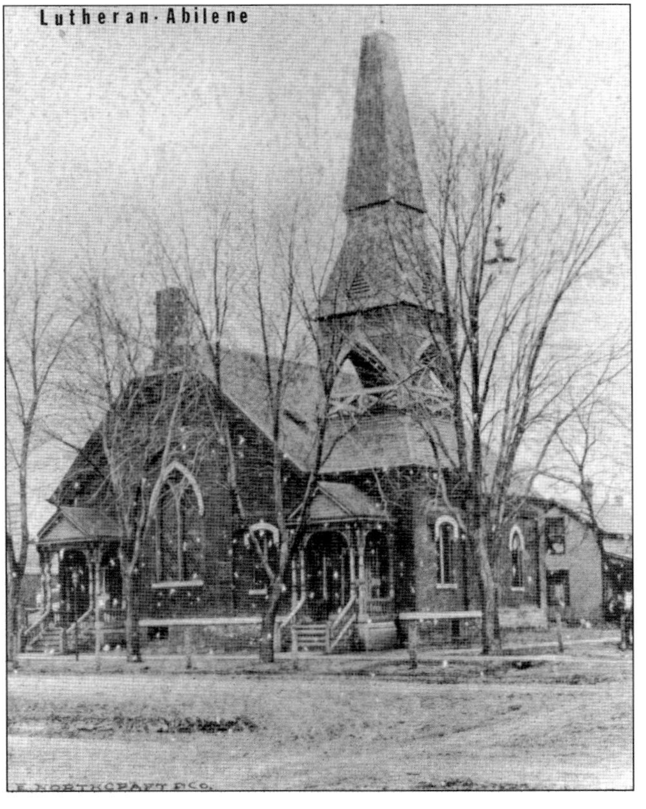

The Lutheran church was one of the first churches in Abilene, dedicated on August 18, 1878. The stately brick building cost the congregation an astonishing $5,500. In order to help pay off the debt, the congregation sold their parsonage.

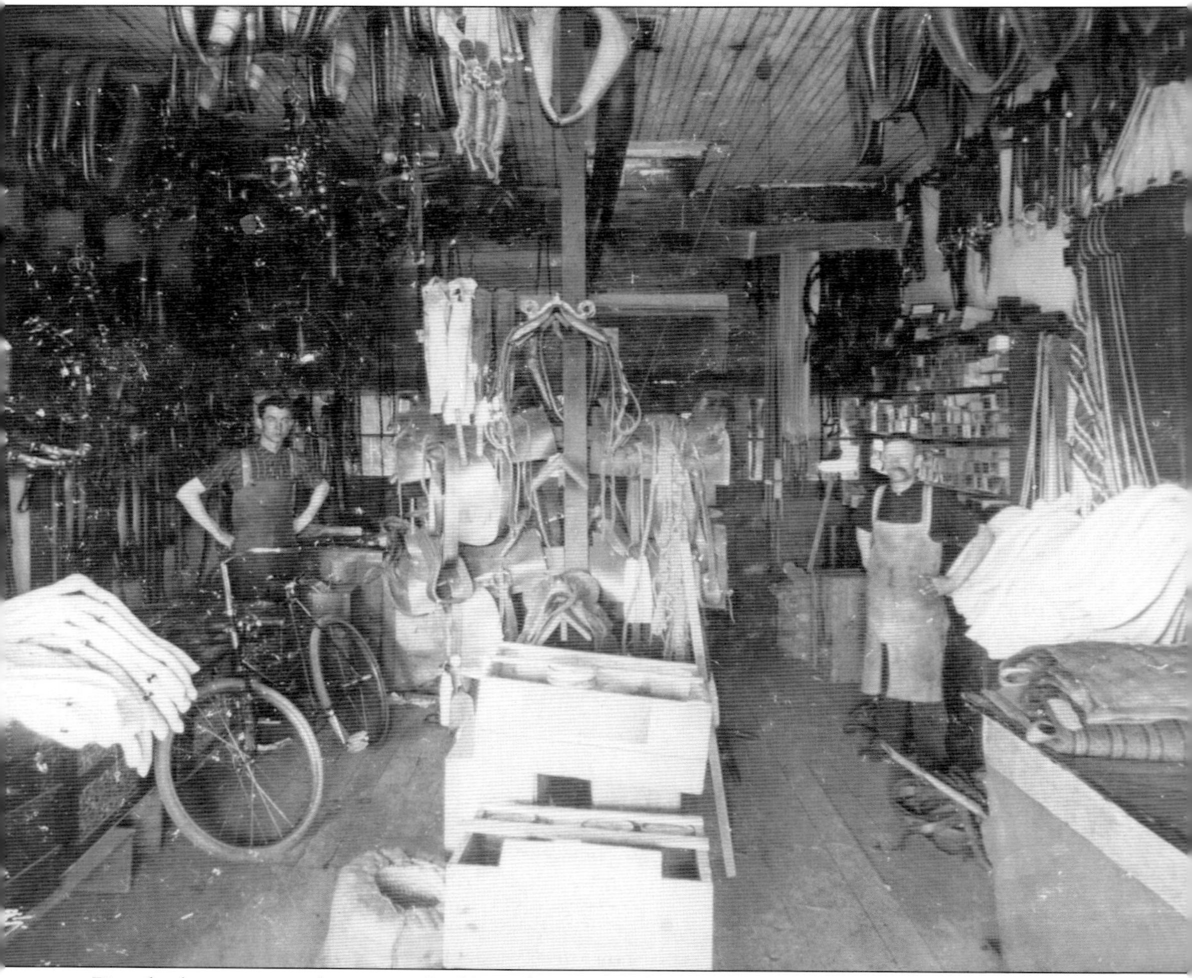

Bicycles became popular across the United States in the early 1900s. Abilene's citizens also enjoyed the fun of traveling on two wheels instead of riding on horseback. The local harness shop started catering to bicycle enthusiasts and offered both bicycles and horse tack.

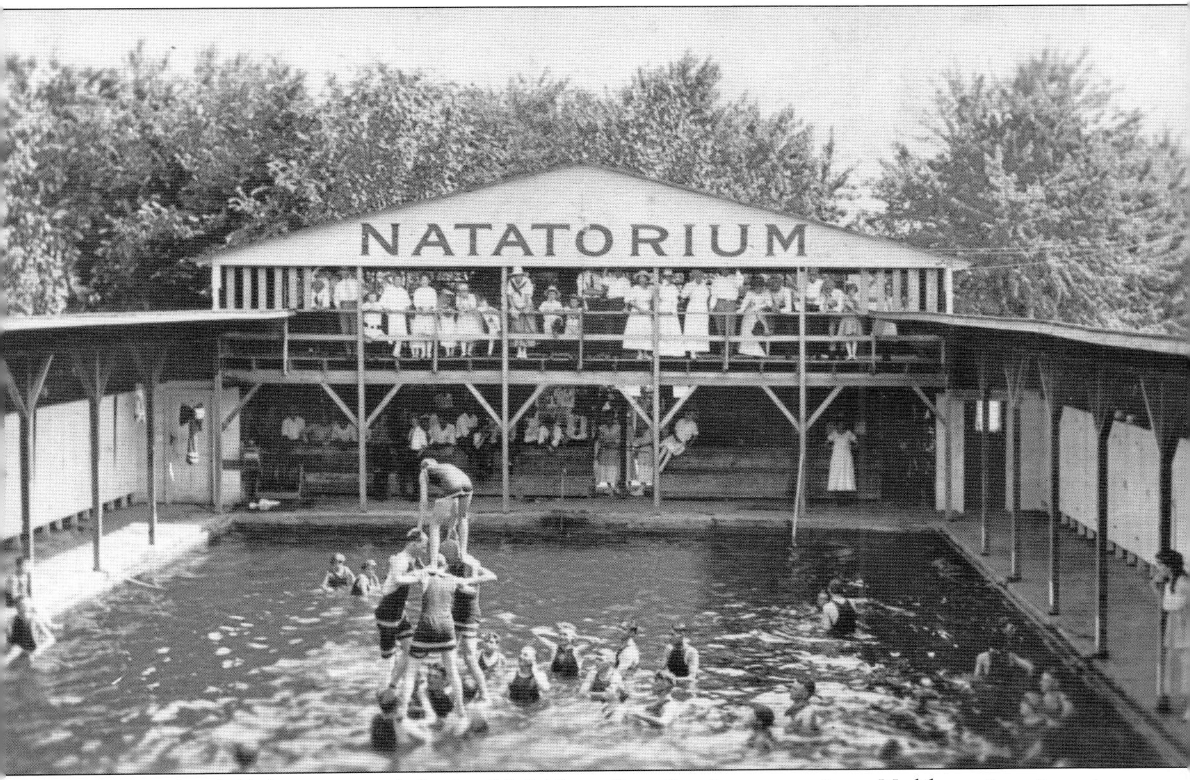

The youth of Abilene enjoyed the healthful benefits of a city natatorium. Unlike swimming at Mud Creek, swimsuits were required for all males and swim dresses for females. Onlookers who preferred to stay dry could watch the hijinks from the safety of viewing stands. Located on East Cottage Avenue, this shot of the Abilene Swimming Pool was taken in the early 1900s.

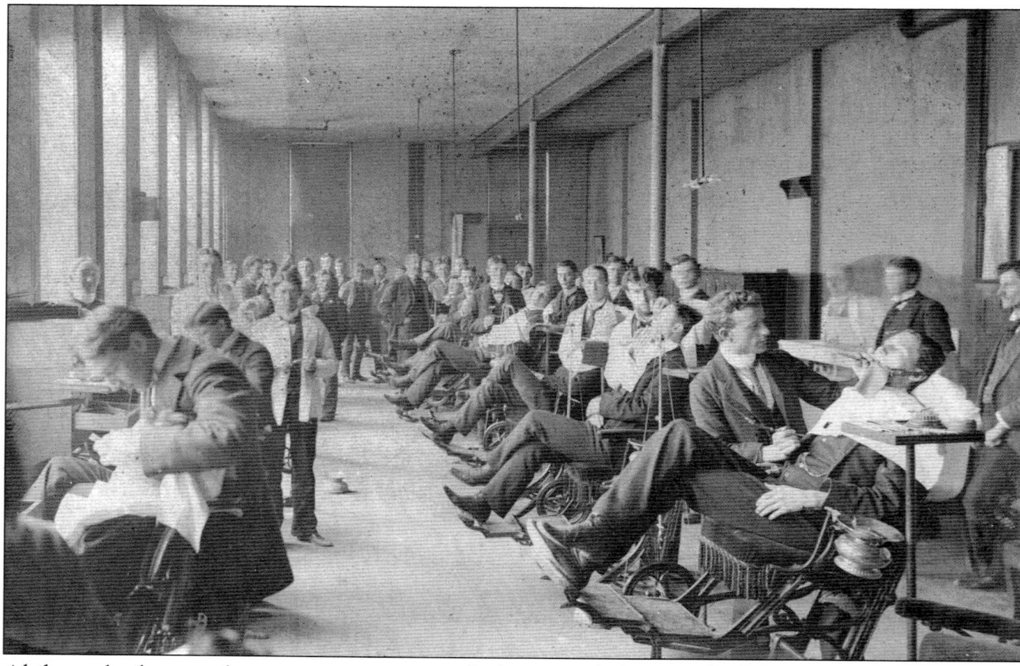

Abilene also became host to conventions and educational classes. The barber school taught classes in shaving as well as some basic dental techniques.

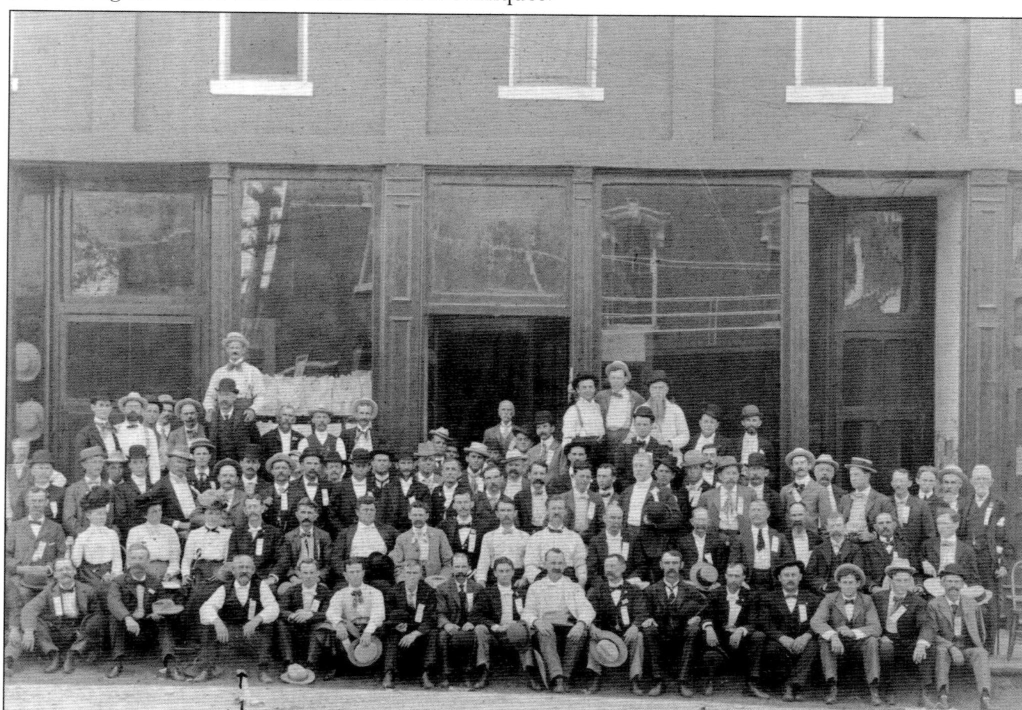

A regional undertakers convention was held in Abilene. Attendees discussed modern methods of embalming and burial practices, as well as tactful advertising.

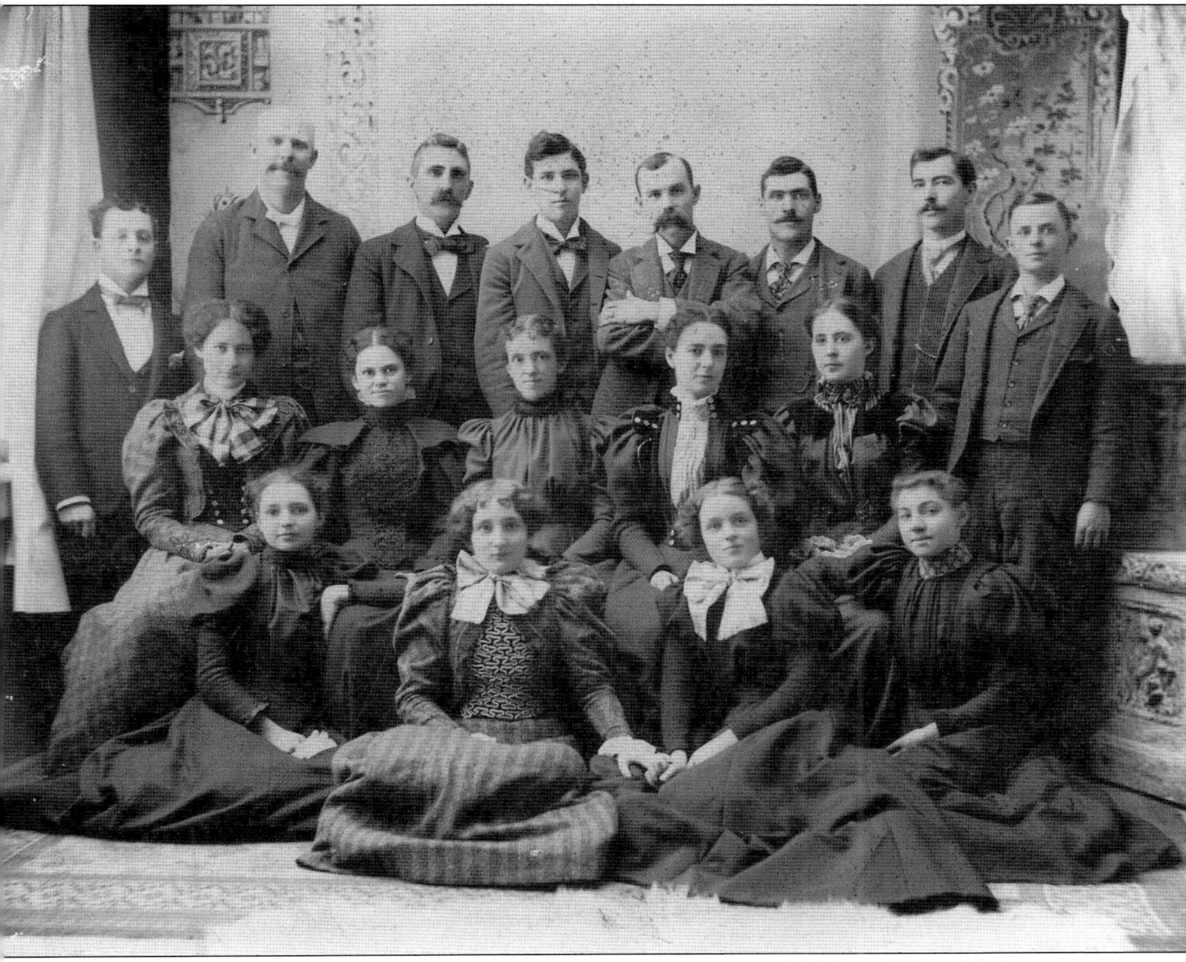

Civic responsibility was taught and practiced by the young people of Abilene. The 20th Century Club was a service organization open to both young men and young women.

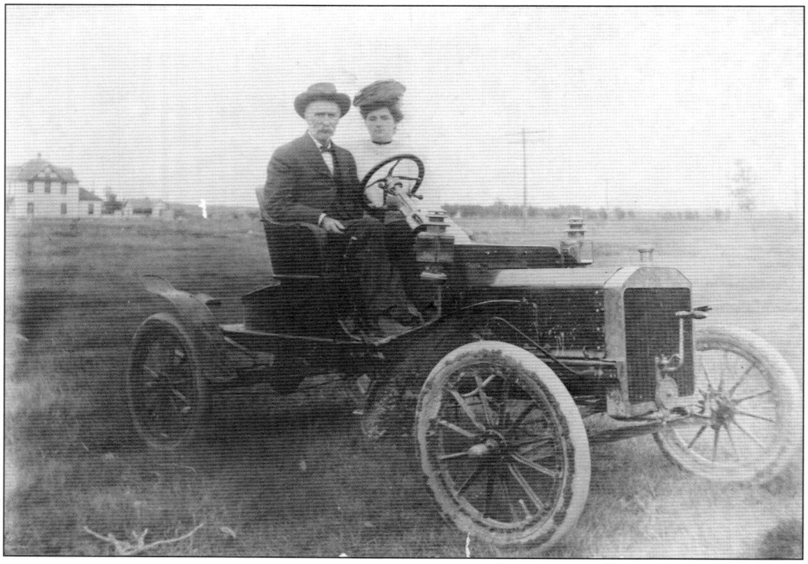

The citizens of Abilene embraced the age of the motorcar. Mr. Pinkham of Abilene owned the town's first automobile. He is pictured here giving a ride to his daughter.

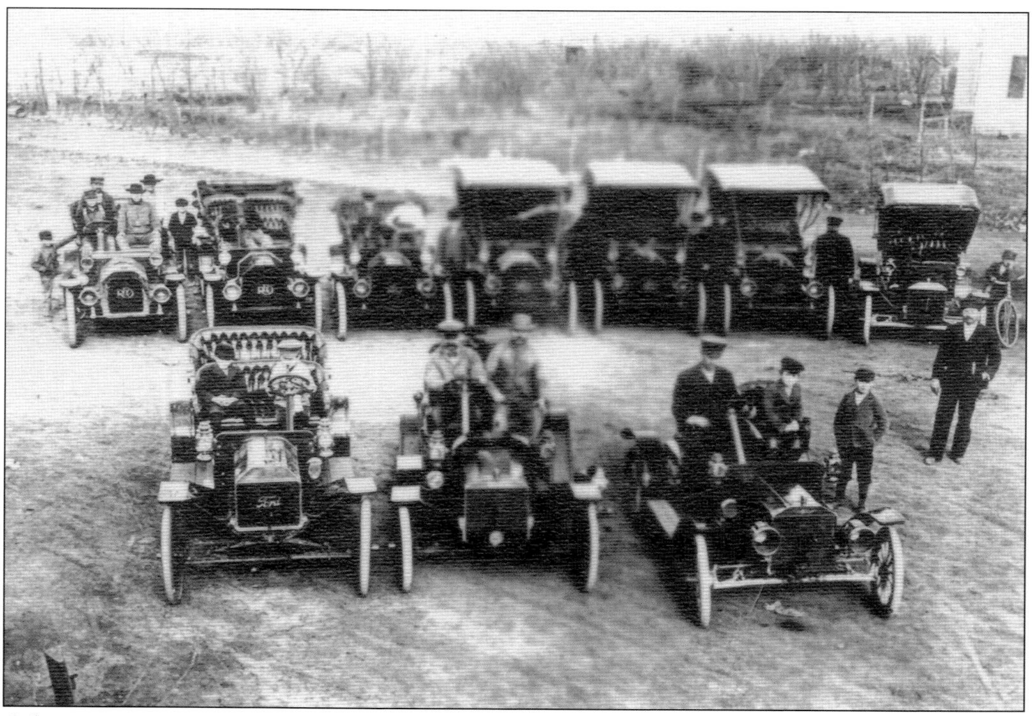

Other progressive citizens soon joined the prestigious club of motorcar owners. For a time, the streets of Abilene were shared by both horses and automobiles.

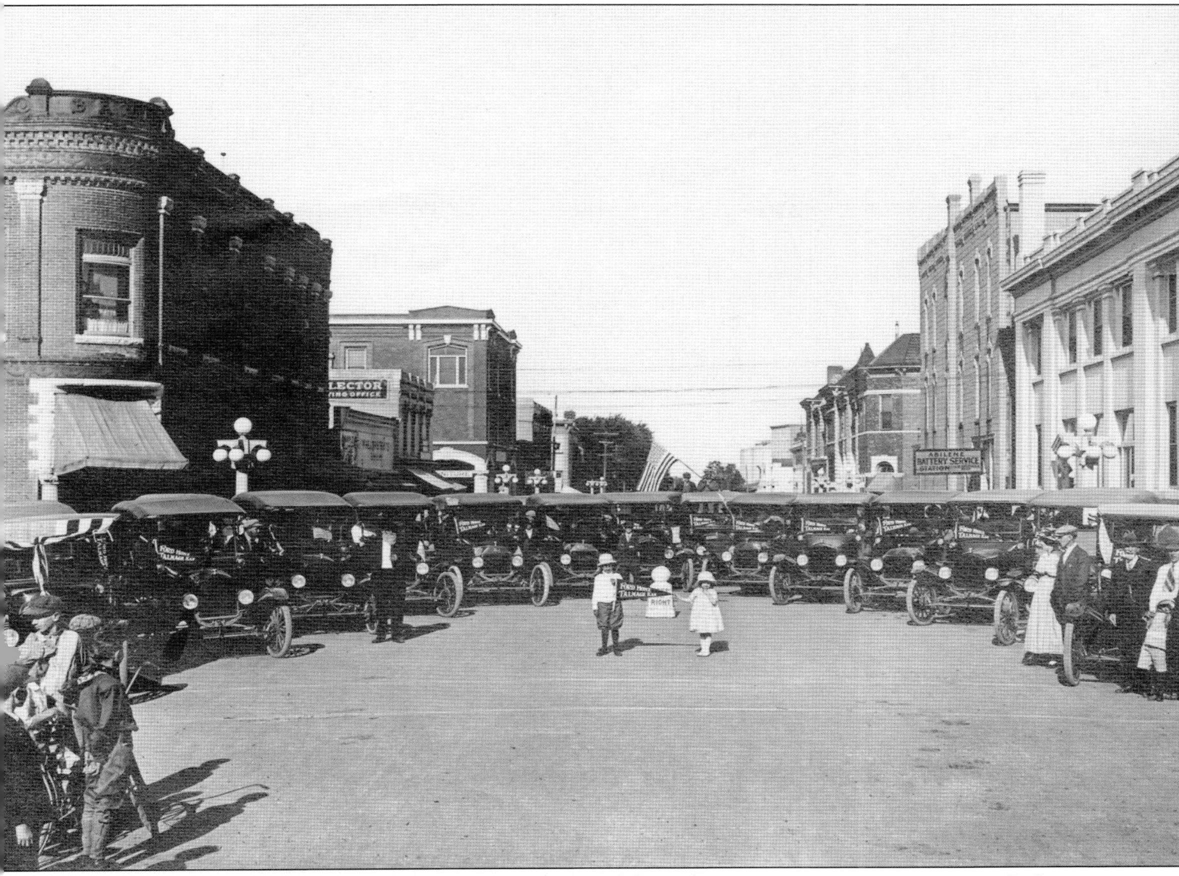

With the 1908 introduction of Henry Ford's Model T, the entire county was excited about automobiles. The motorcar was now affordable for many people, and the citizens of Dickinson County went on a buying spree.

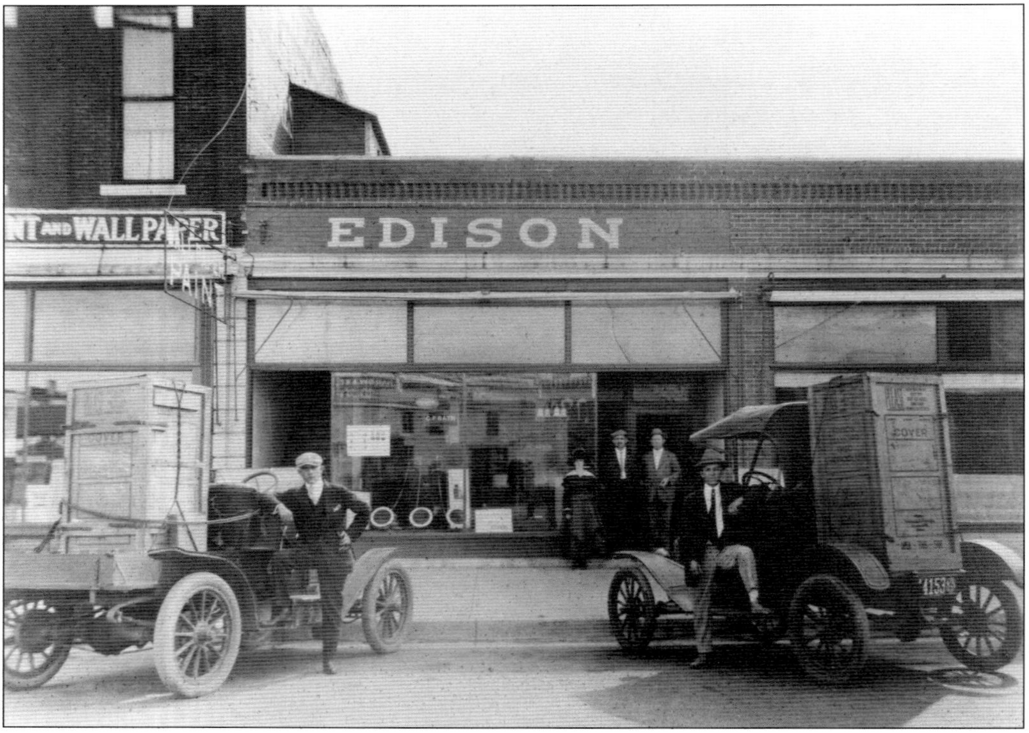

Despite poor road conditions, salesmen began using automobiles on their routes. Roads were still mainly dirt, and often cars became mired in the mud, but the prestige of a driving a motorcar added to the salesman's mystique.

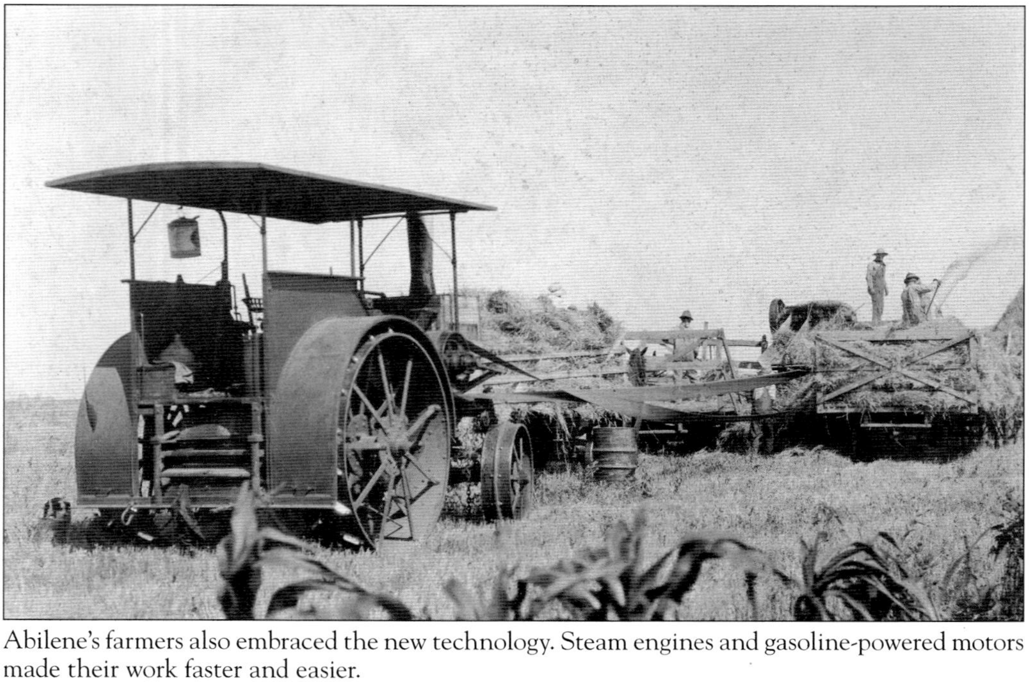

Abilene's farmers also embraced the new technology. Steam engines and gasoline-powered motors made their work faster and easier.

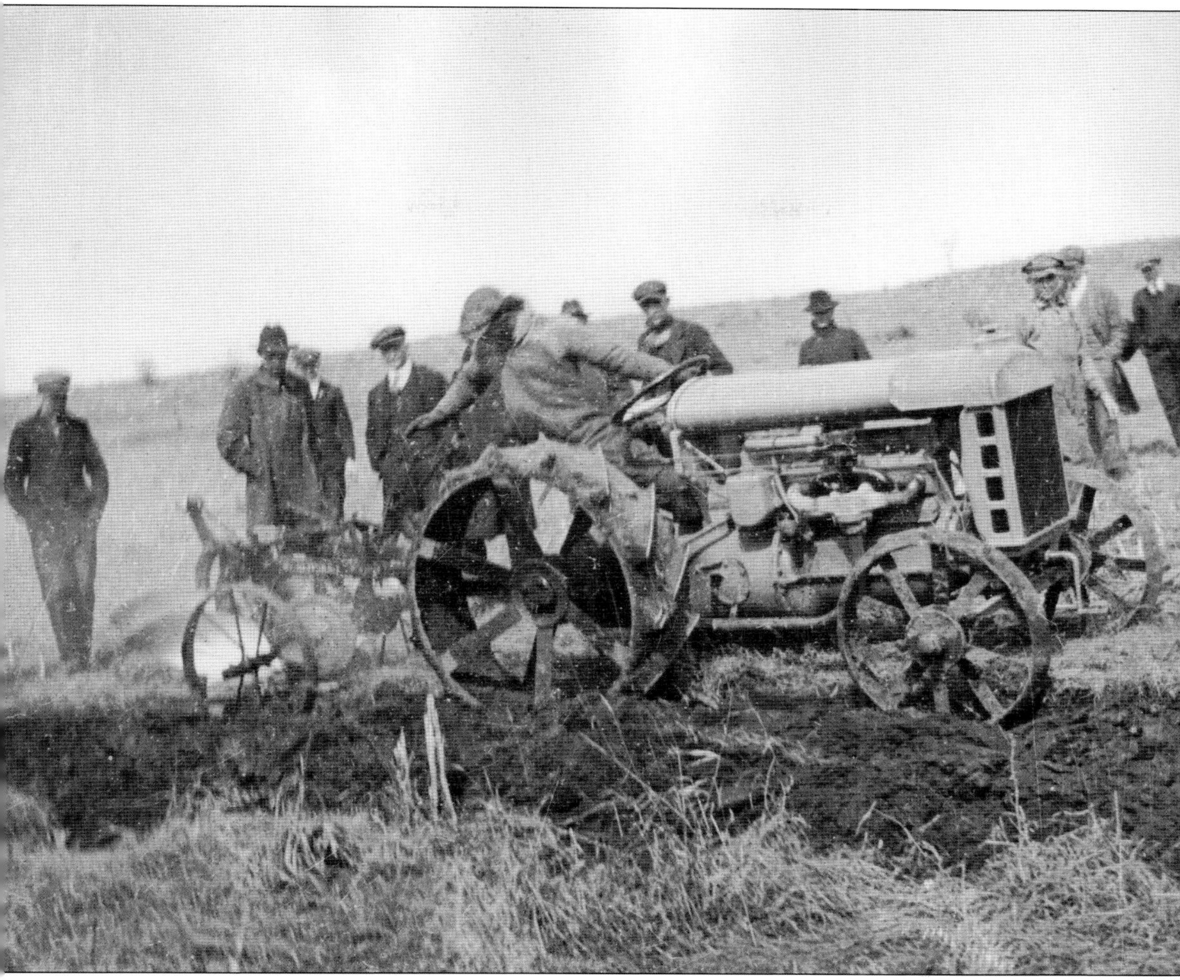

Tractor dealers took their merchandise directly to the fields and demonstrated their value to the farmers. Here, a dealer shows how easily the tractor and a plow can break the prairie sod.

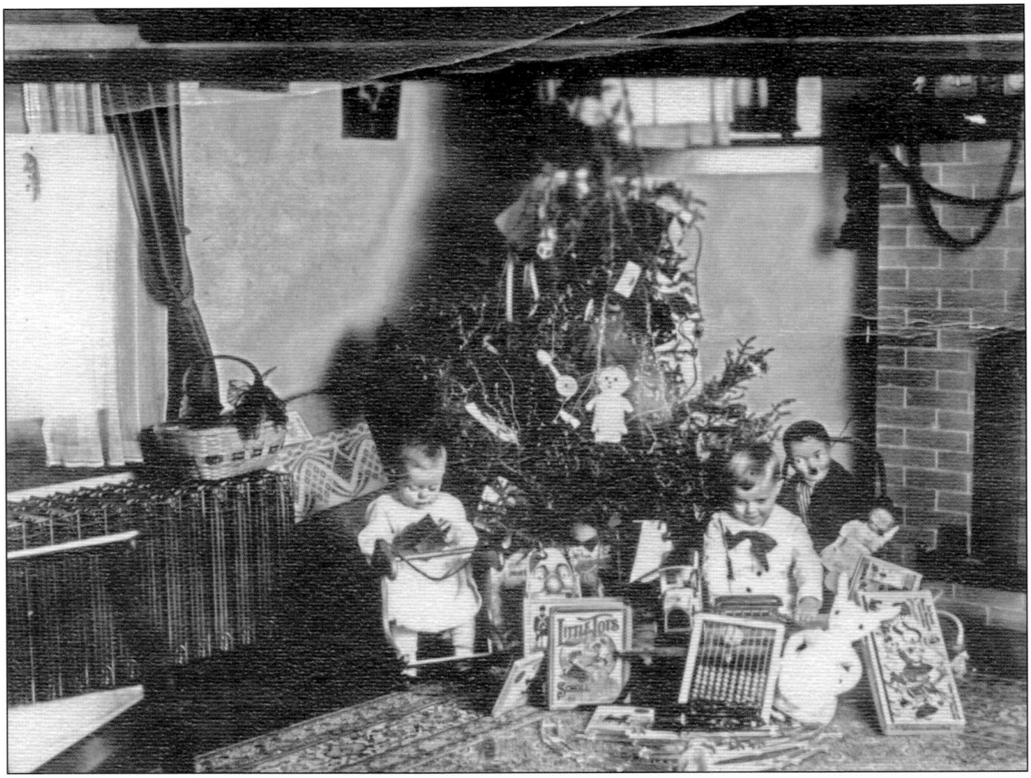

Goods from markets provided relative prosperity for the citizens of Abilene, as evidenced by this Christmas photograph. Gifts included books, games, an abacus, and a Charlie Chaplin doll.

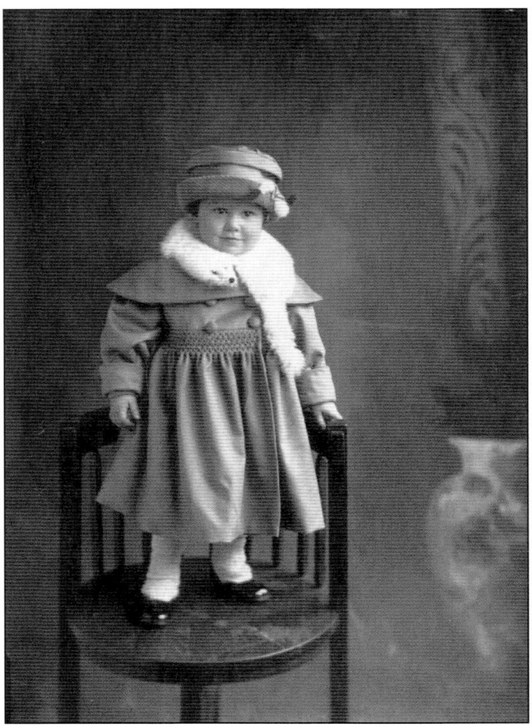

Parents also had enough disposable income to have photographs taken of their families and children. This image is of three-year-old Alice Hess. She is dressed in her Sunday best, including a stylish hat.

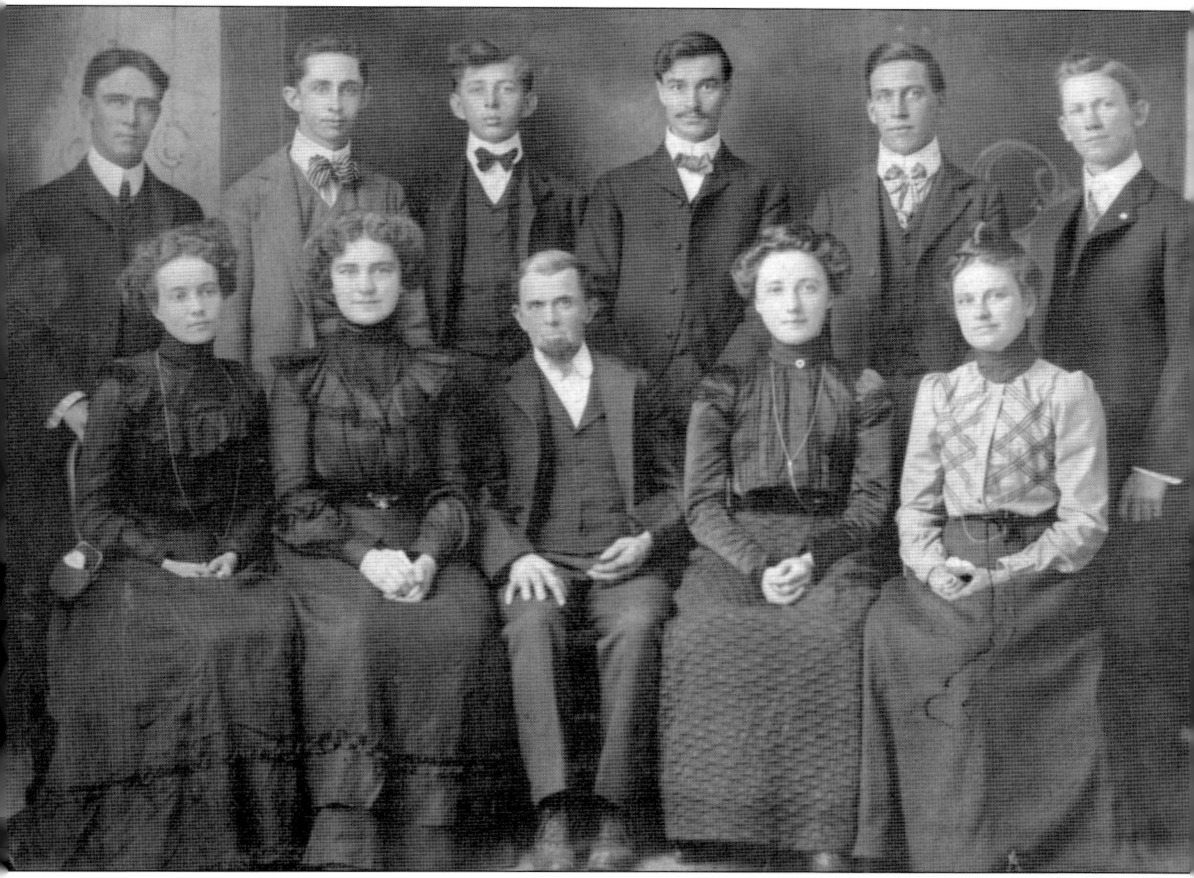

Jobs were plentiful, and women were welcome in the workforce. These men and women were employees of the Brown Telephone Company.

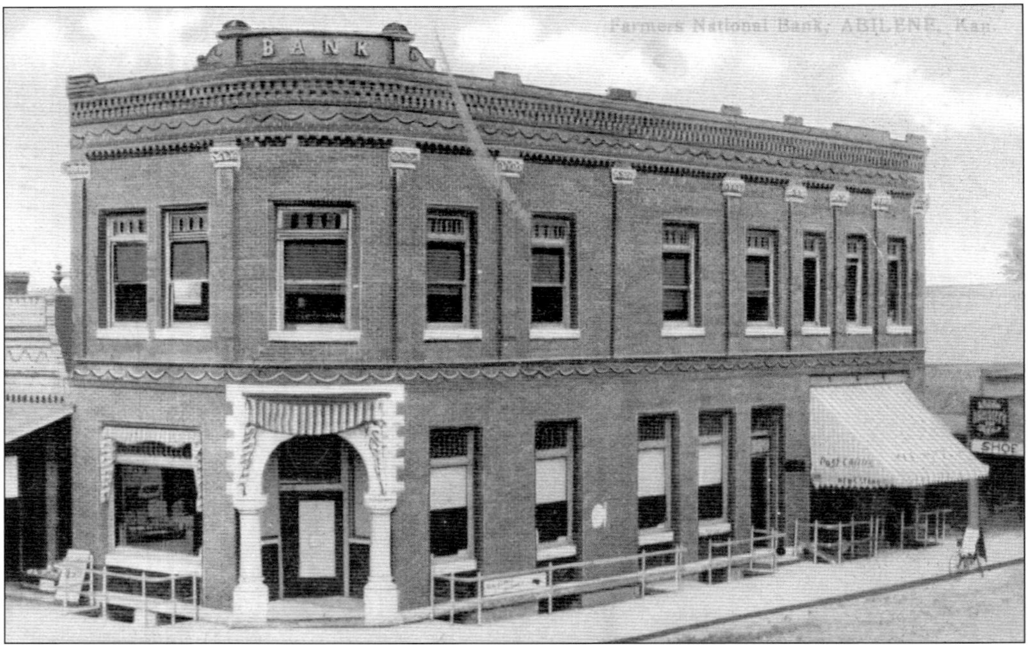

In 1910, Abilene boasted four banks in town. Their cumulative deposits totaled an amazing $1 million. A total of 18 banks resided in all of Dickinson County.

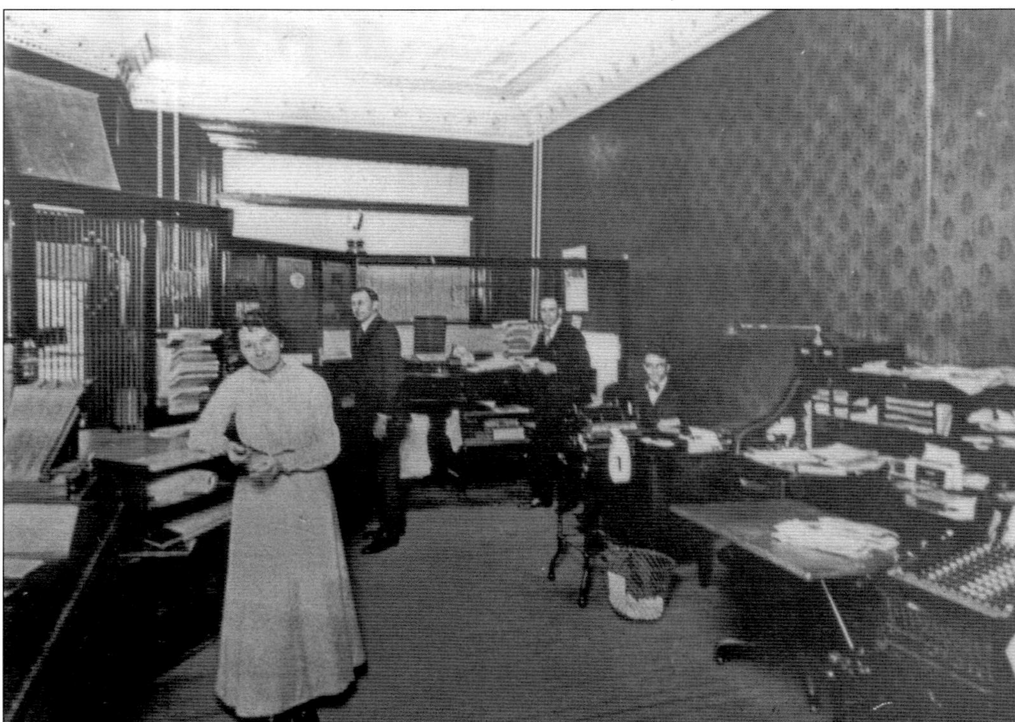
A bank job was considered prestigious employment. Employees had to have a smart head for figures and be able to deal well with the public.

ABILENE'S NEW POSTOFFICE BUILDING

OPENED NOVEMBER 23, 1914

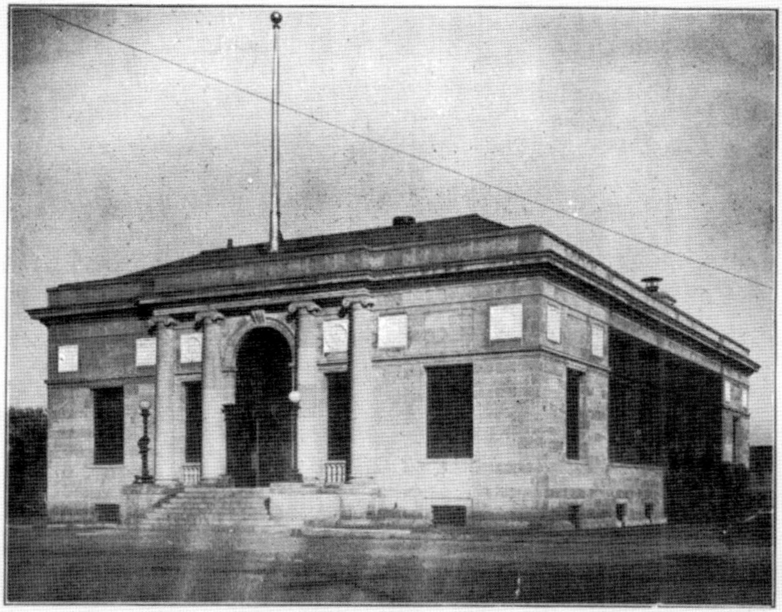

Clerks

. D. Focht
. G. Shearer
. E. Cavender
C. Hutchison, Jr.
L. Goodell

City Carriers

H. Johntz
. L. Young
L. Waring
. W. Loyd

Rural Carriers

W. L. Stowits
H. Mohler
J. A. VanDuyne
M. H. Gardner
R. E. Huston
J. M. Stewart
F. Sullivan

Janitors

H. M. Turley
H. Bell

W. A. MATTESON, Postmaster
T. M. JONES, Assistant Postmaster

The post office was the central hub of the city. Telephone service was expensive, so all long-distance communication was done by letter. A 1910 promotional brochure bragged that the City of Abilene provided free postal delivery to all city residents. This image depicts Abilene's post office building that opened in 1914.

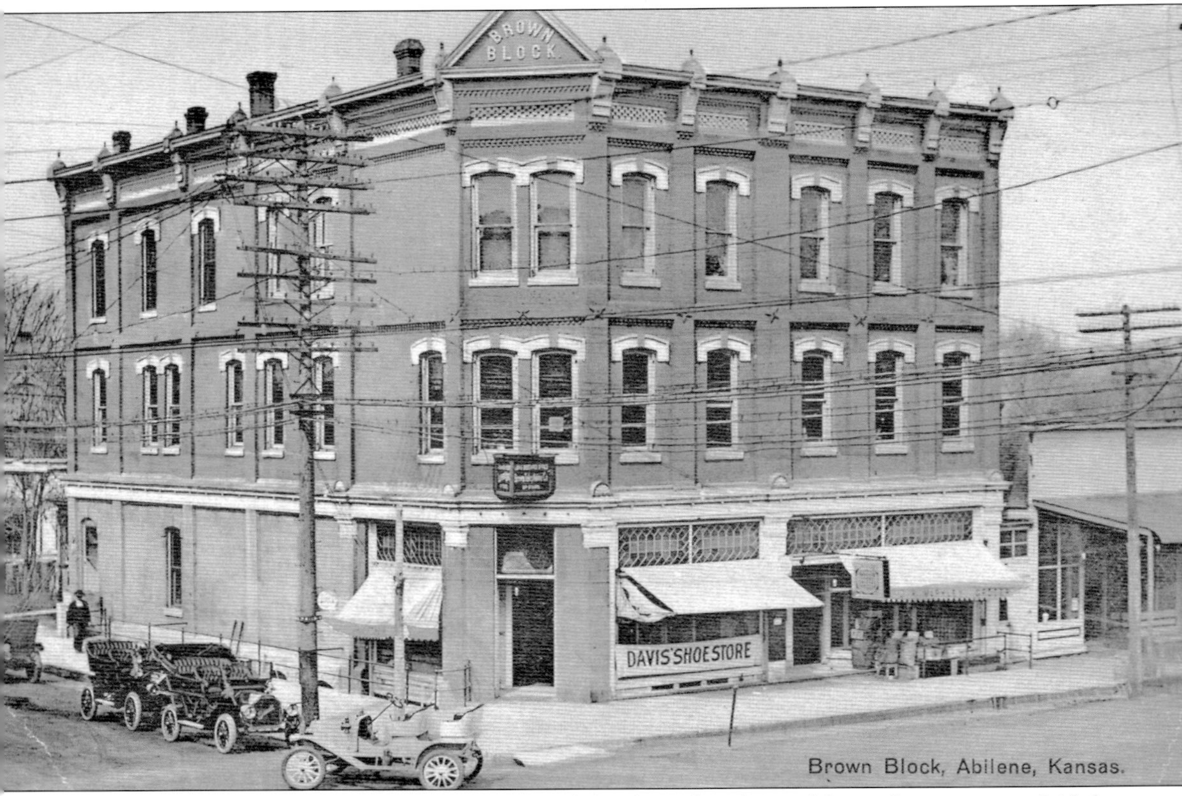

Telephone poles, electric lights, and automobiles show that the world was changing—and Abilene was changing with it. The next decades would bring the unprecedented challenges of war and economic depression.

Five

Parker's Carousels

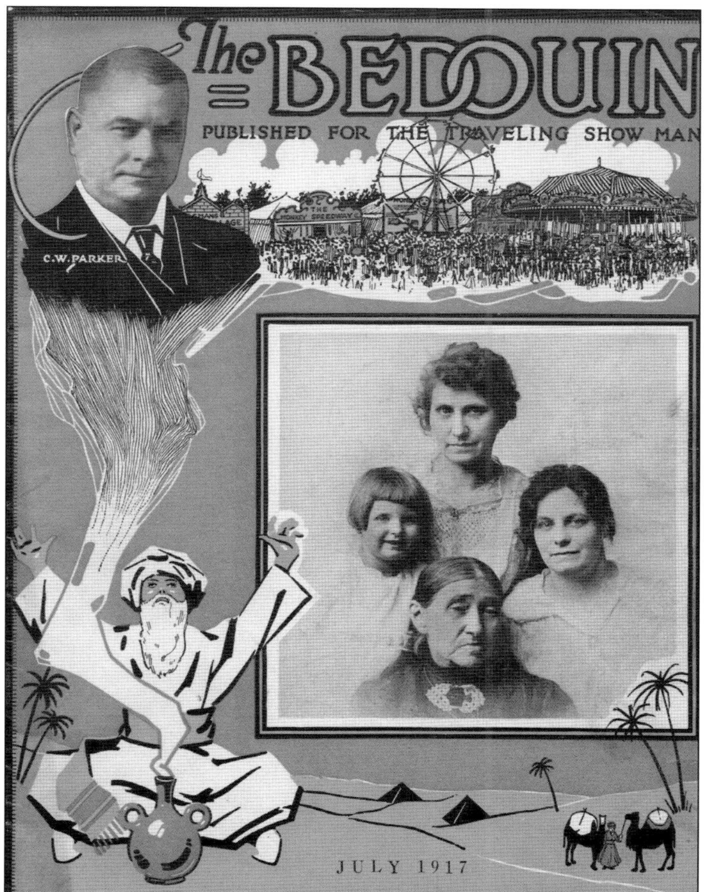

Out of the land of cattle and corn came an unexpected enterprise. The C.W. Parker Amusement Company had its birth in Abilene, Kansas. Charles Wallace Parker always had an interest in mechanics, especially mechanical amusements. He owned a shooting gallery and was fascinated by carnival equipment. When his young daughter became captivated by a carousel, Parker purchased one and took it apart to learn how it worked.

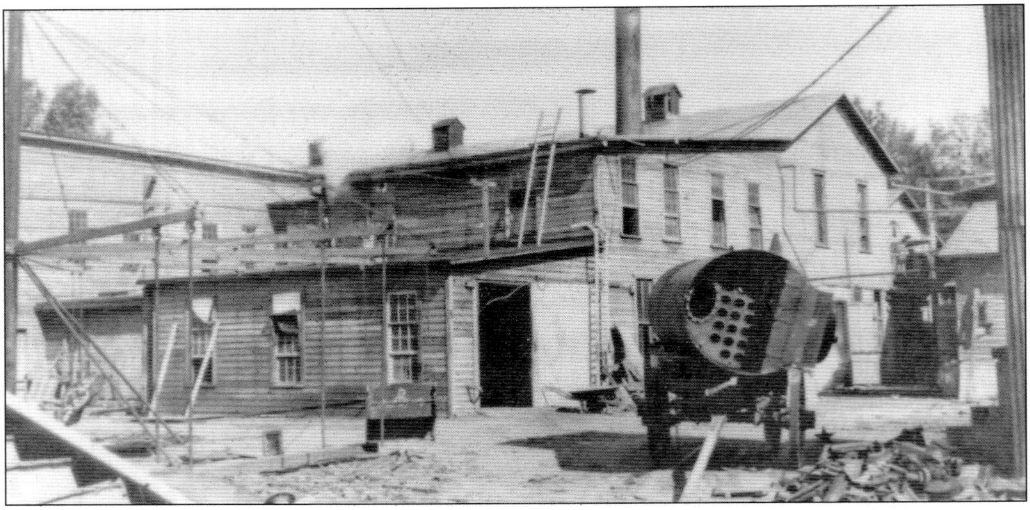

Parker built his first carousel in 1896. His first factory was at 2679 Parker Street in Abilene, Kansas. Eventually, he had several building scattered throughout the Abilene business district.

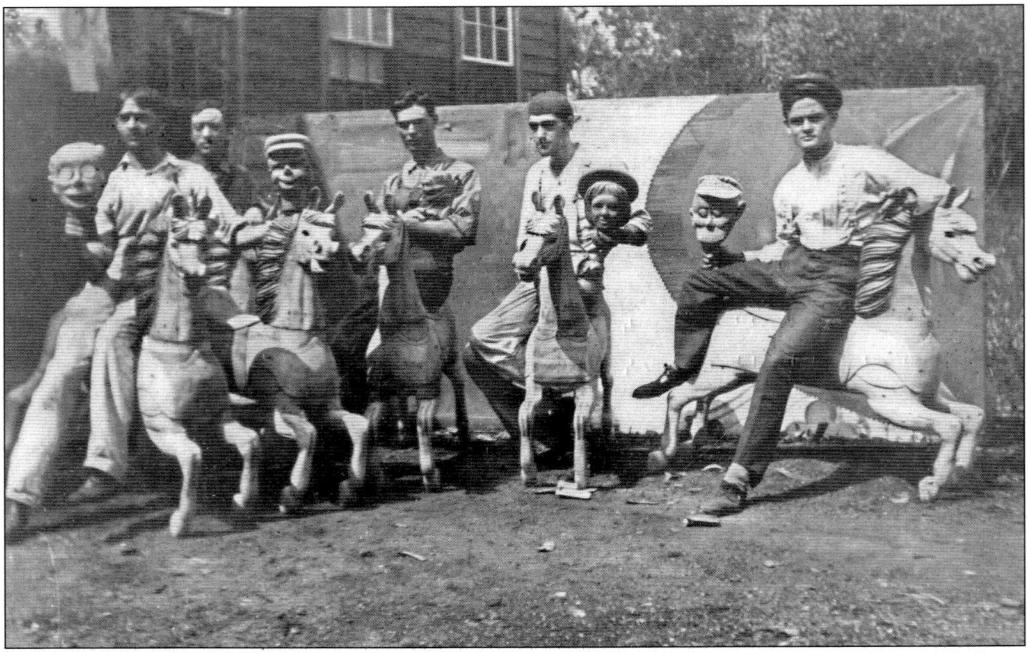

Parker and his team of young workers created brightly colored, fanciful carousels that delighted people at carnivals and fairs.

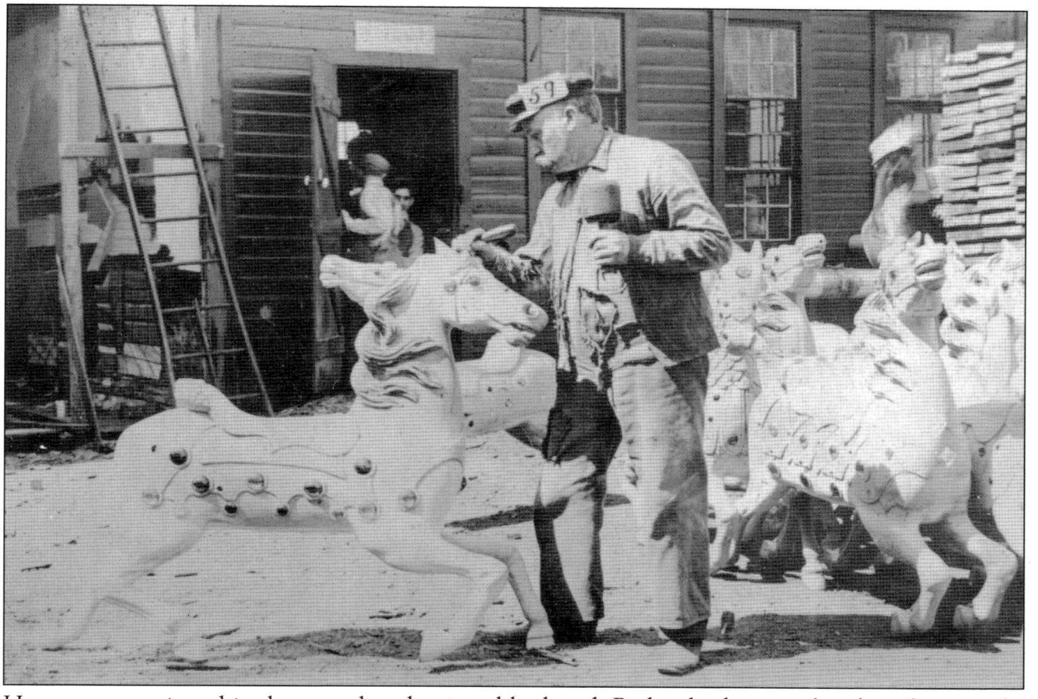

Horses were painstakingly carved and painted by hand. Parker built several styles of carousels, including machines that ran on a track and carousels that had jumping horses.

Parker dubbed his rides the "Parker Carry-us-all" as a play on the word *carousel*. The beautiful hand-carved horses were a part of a portable carousel system that could be set up on any site and quickly torn down after the fair or carnival. The horses and their mechanical parts were shipped by rail, and Parker bragged that his machines could be up and making money one hour after arriving.

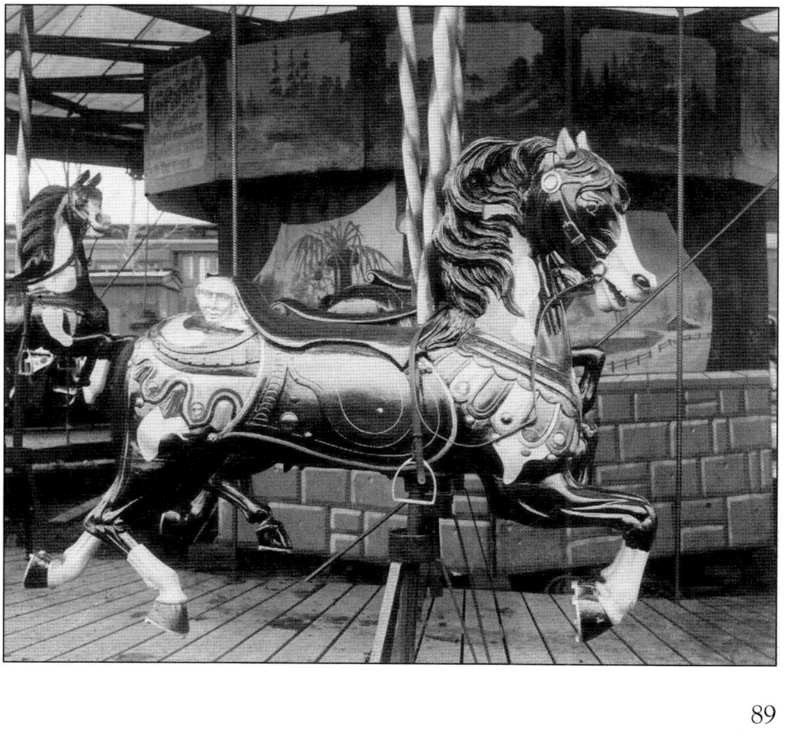

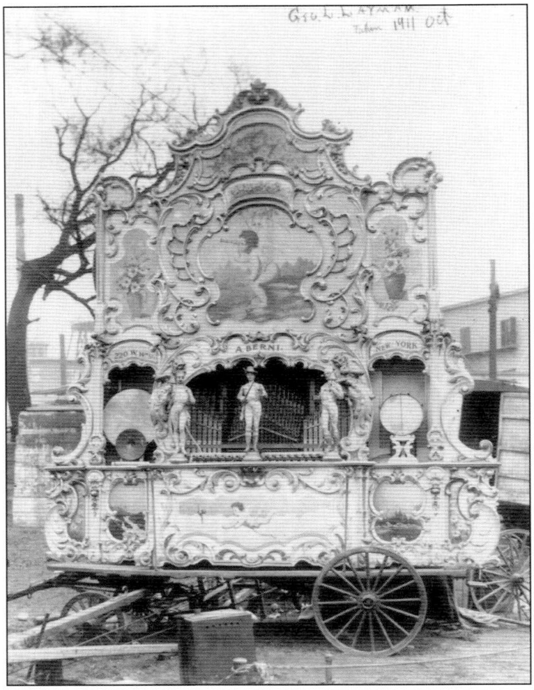

Parker and his team also created carnival pipe organs. The organs often had mechanical moving parts that whirled and twirled to the rhythm of the song.

Parker sponsored his own bands to travel and promote his carnival. Bands played in parades, gave concerts, and provided welcome entertainment across the country.

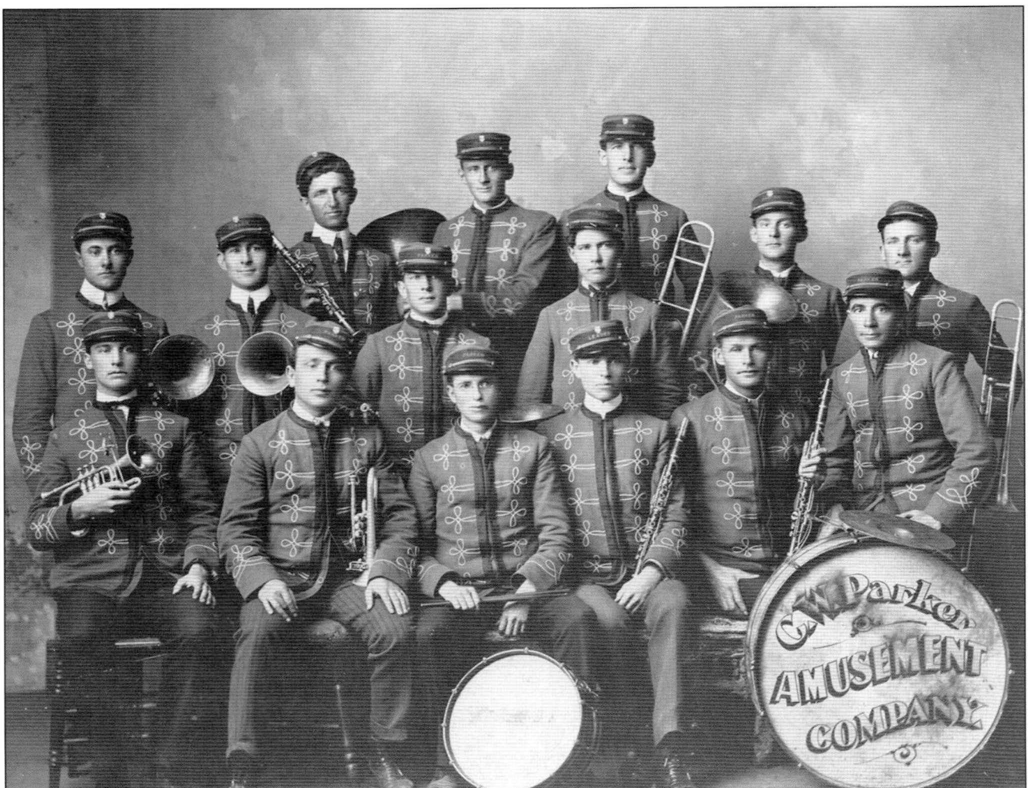

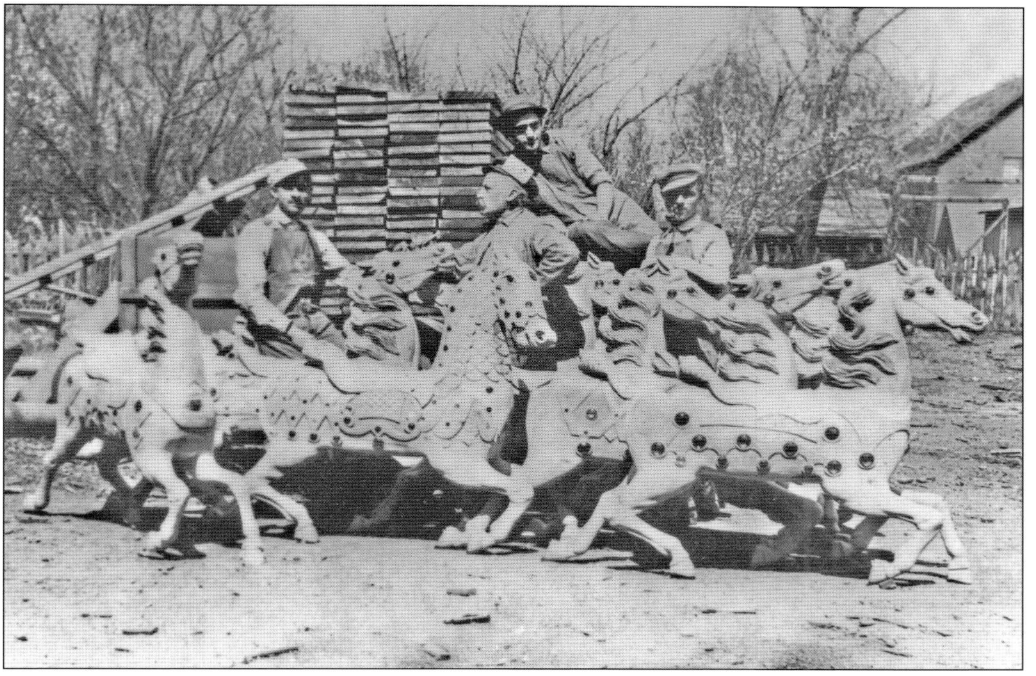

By 1905, C.W. Parker Amusements had four full-sized carnivals on tour throughout the United States. He owned multiple small buildings in Abilene but felt the need to expand to a larger area.

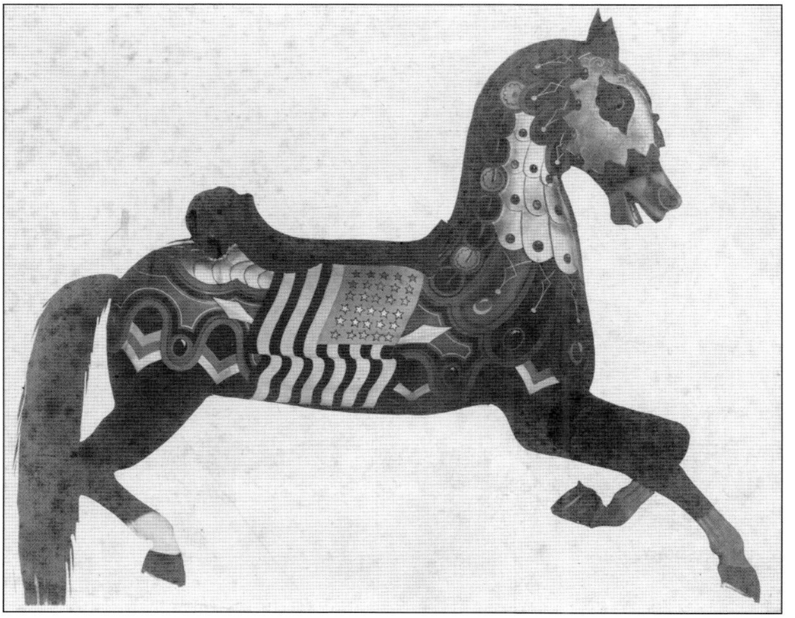

In 1911, Parker moved his business to Leavenworth, Kansas. From there, his designs and carnivals expanded until Parker was one of the largest manufacturers of carnival equipment in the world.

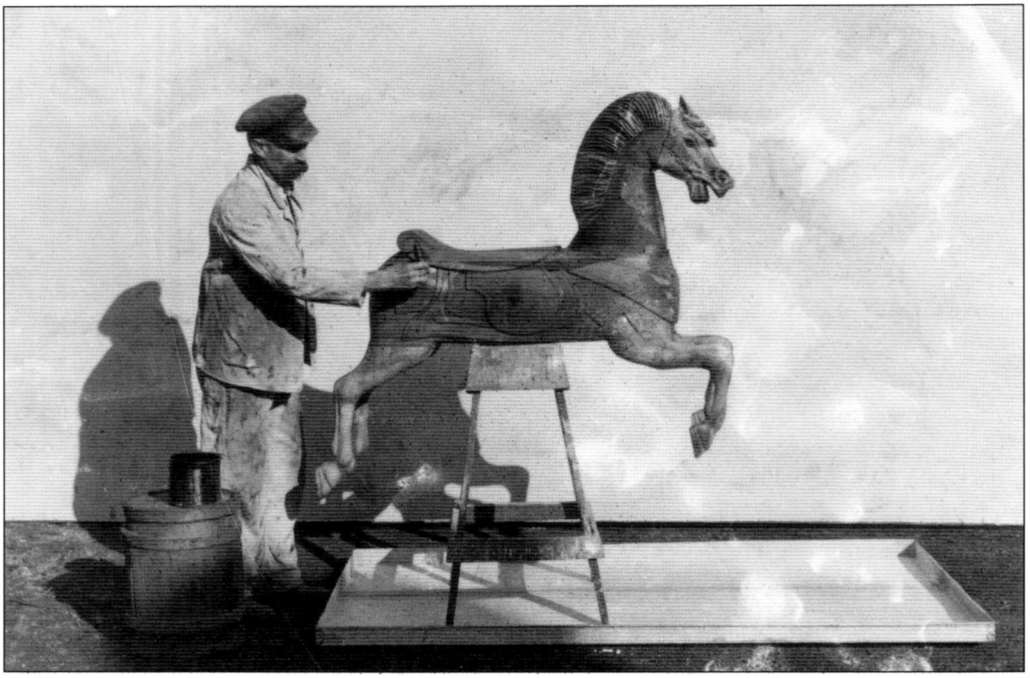

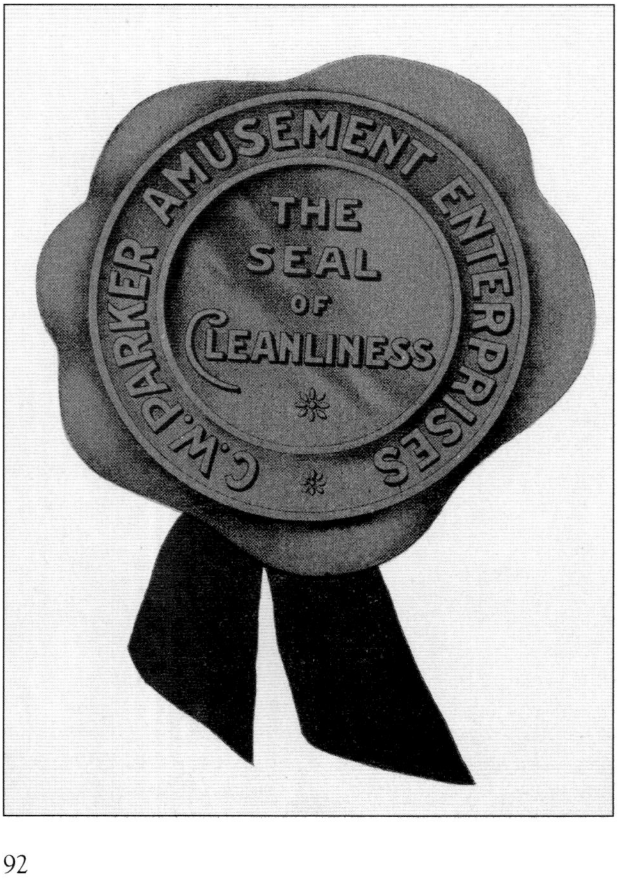

Parker continued to design and create carousels and amusement-park rides until his death in 1932. He was buried in a family plot in Abilene. His business was continued by his family until the 1950s.

The C.W. Parker seal of cleanliness set a high standard for amusement-park rides and attractions. Parker led the industry in innovation by creating rides that were colorful and mechanically safe and stable.

Six

Defying Disaster

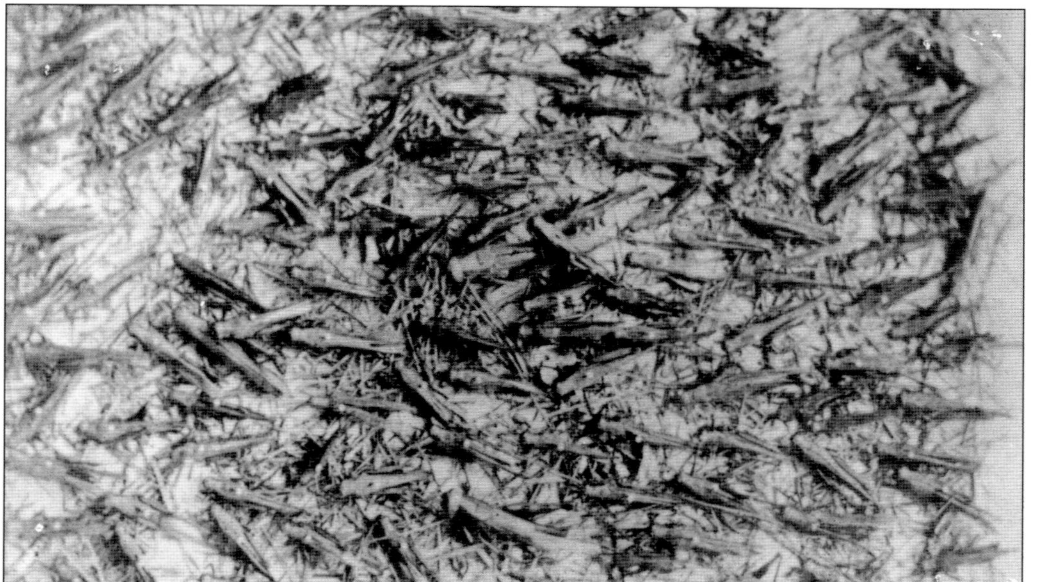

Life on the plains of the Kansas was not always easy. The summers could be sweltering hot, with temperatures often reaching triple digits. The winters were frigid and harsh. Added to the weather extremes were the hazards of fire, tornado, and pestilence. Periodic grasshopper infestations were commonplace during the early days of prairie farming. The grasshoppers would arrive in a swarm and eat until all the vegetation was gone. A grasshopper plague meant the total loss of a year's harvest.

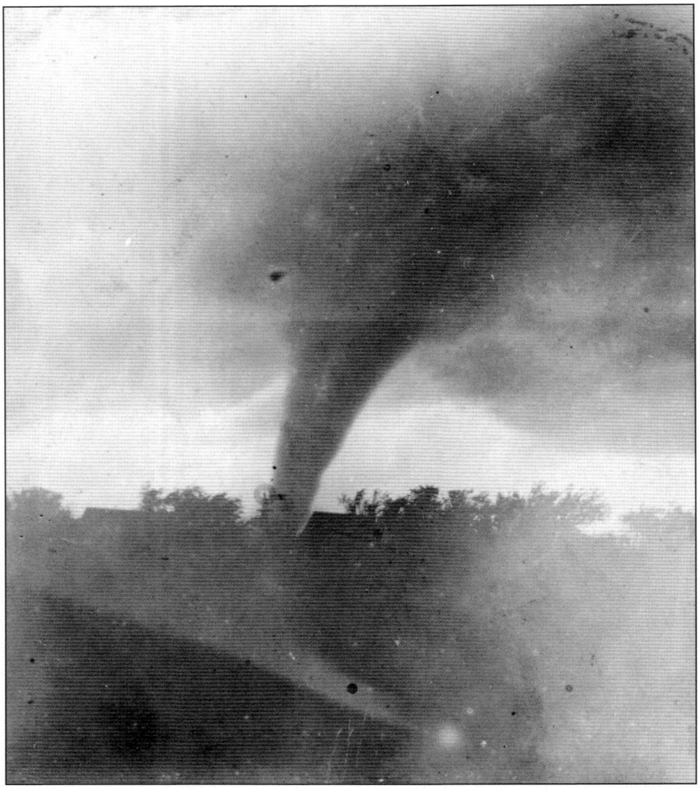

Tornadoes were another threat of Mother Nature. The swirling funnel cloud could travel at speeds over 70 miles per hour, destroying all crops and property in its path.

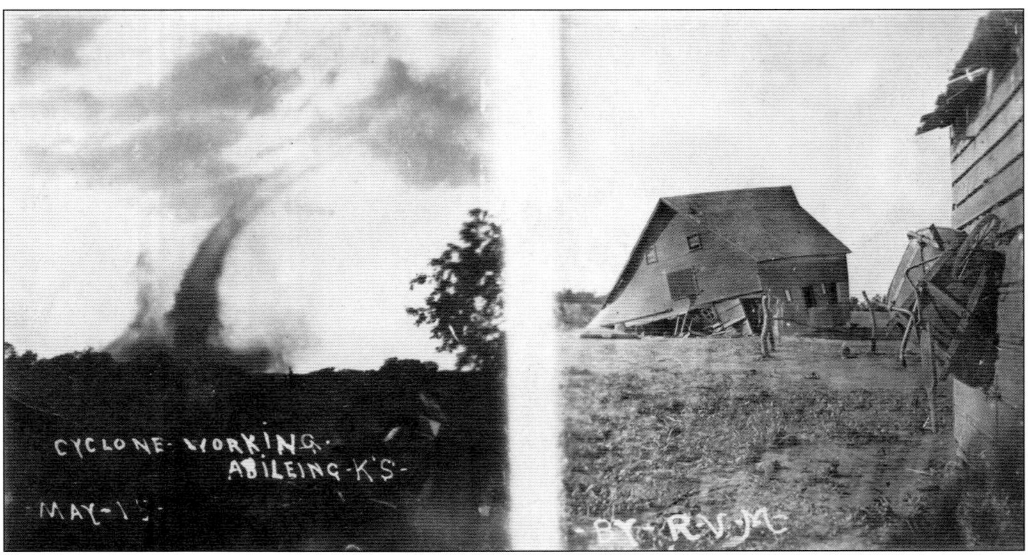

This double-frame postcard shows a cyclone that hit near Abilene on May 14, 1913, causing extensive damage to local farms.

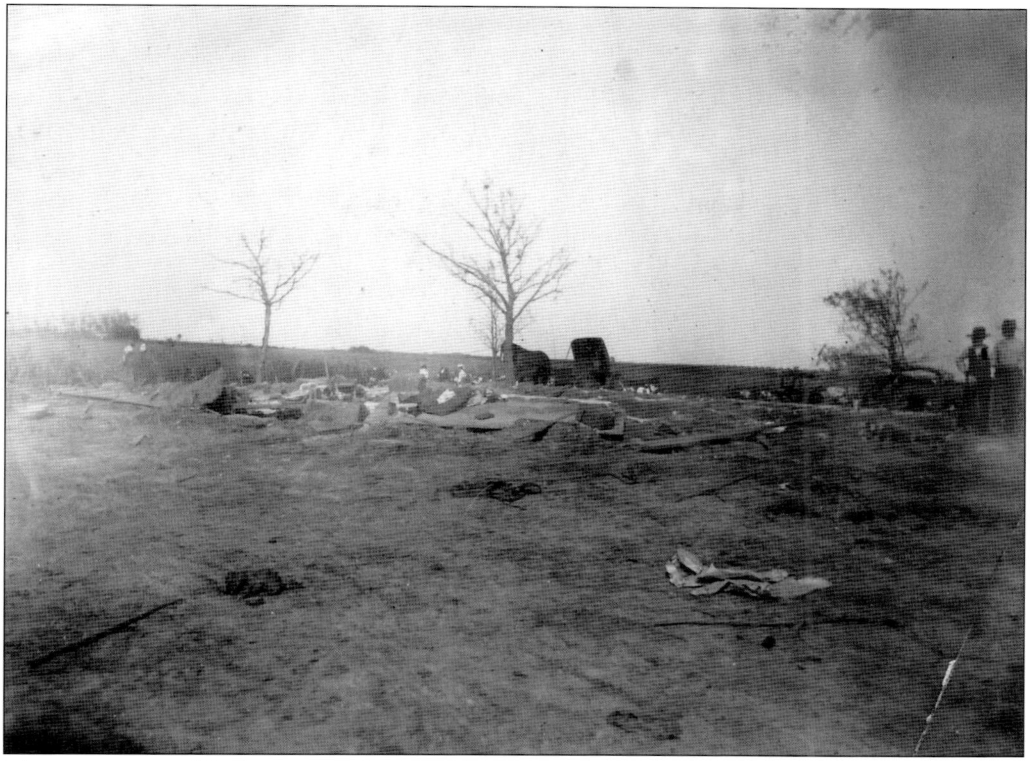

The Lawrence Kehler home was destroyed by a tornado in 1903. The debris from the home was scattered for miles.

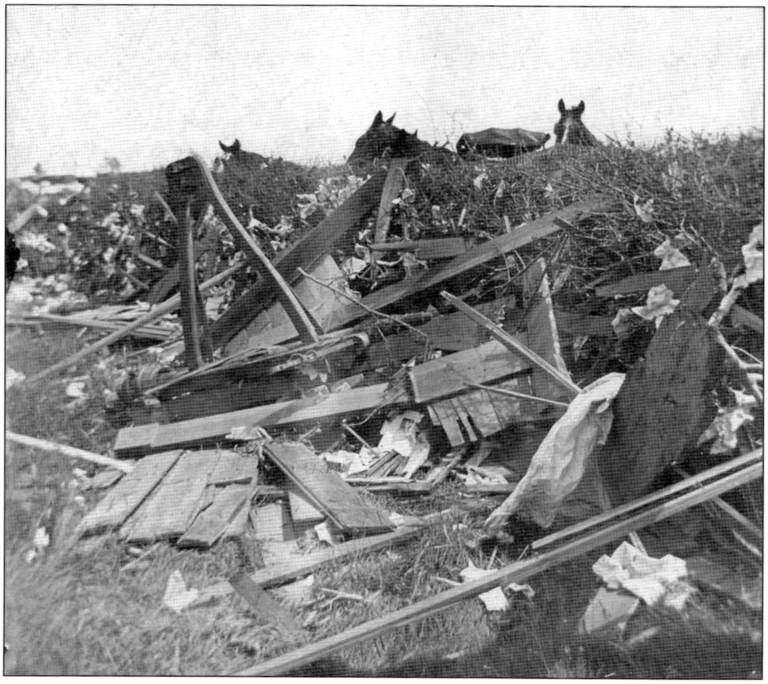

Tornadoes often left homes and barns in unrecognizable piles of rubbish. Insurance was not common, and a tornado could mean financial devastation for a family.

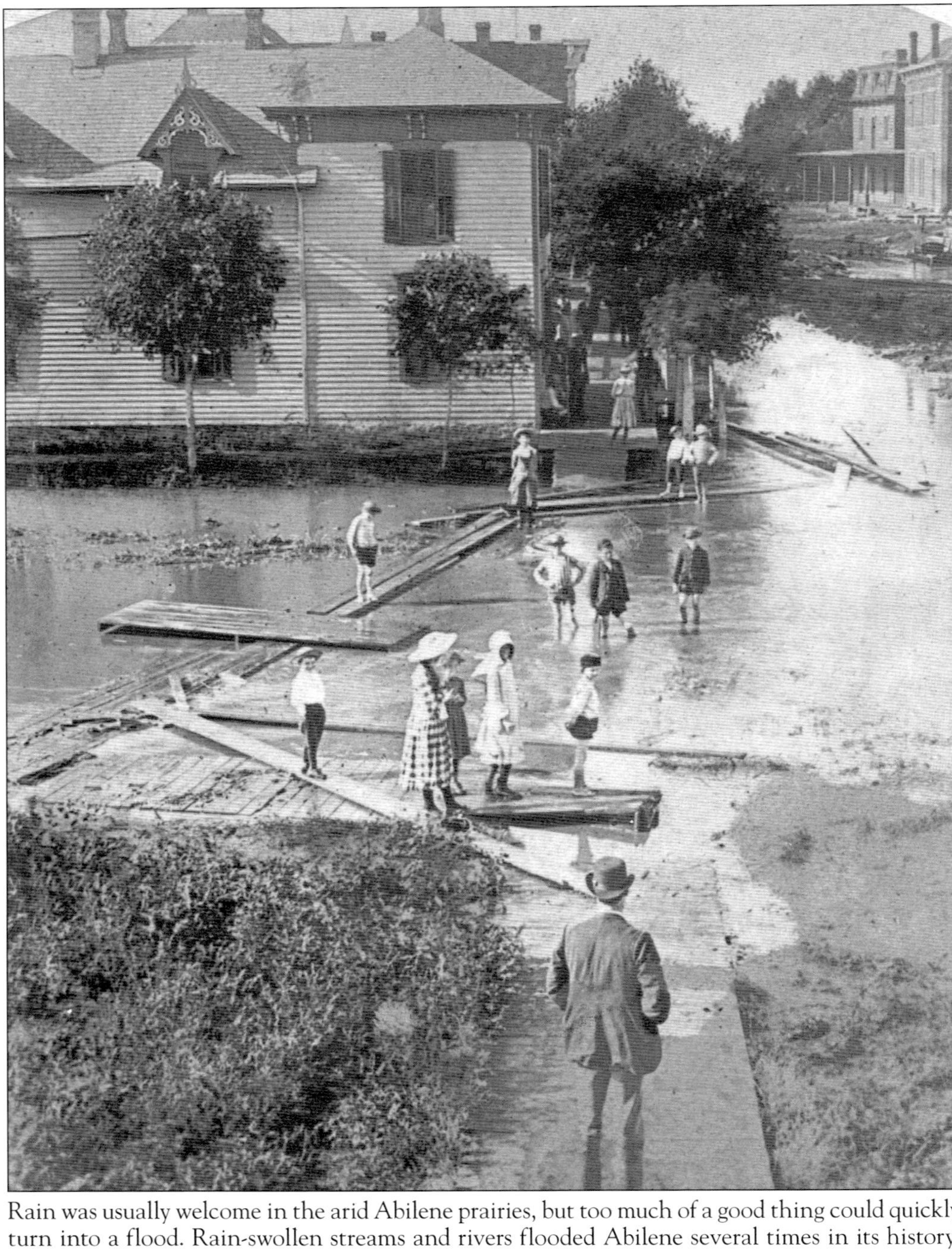

Rain was usually welcome in the arid Abilene prairies, but too much of a good thing could quickly turn into a flood. Rain-swollen streams and rivers flooded Abilene several times in its history. The flood of 1886 washed out boardwalks and streets.

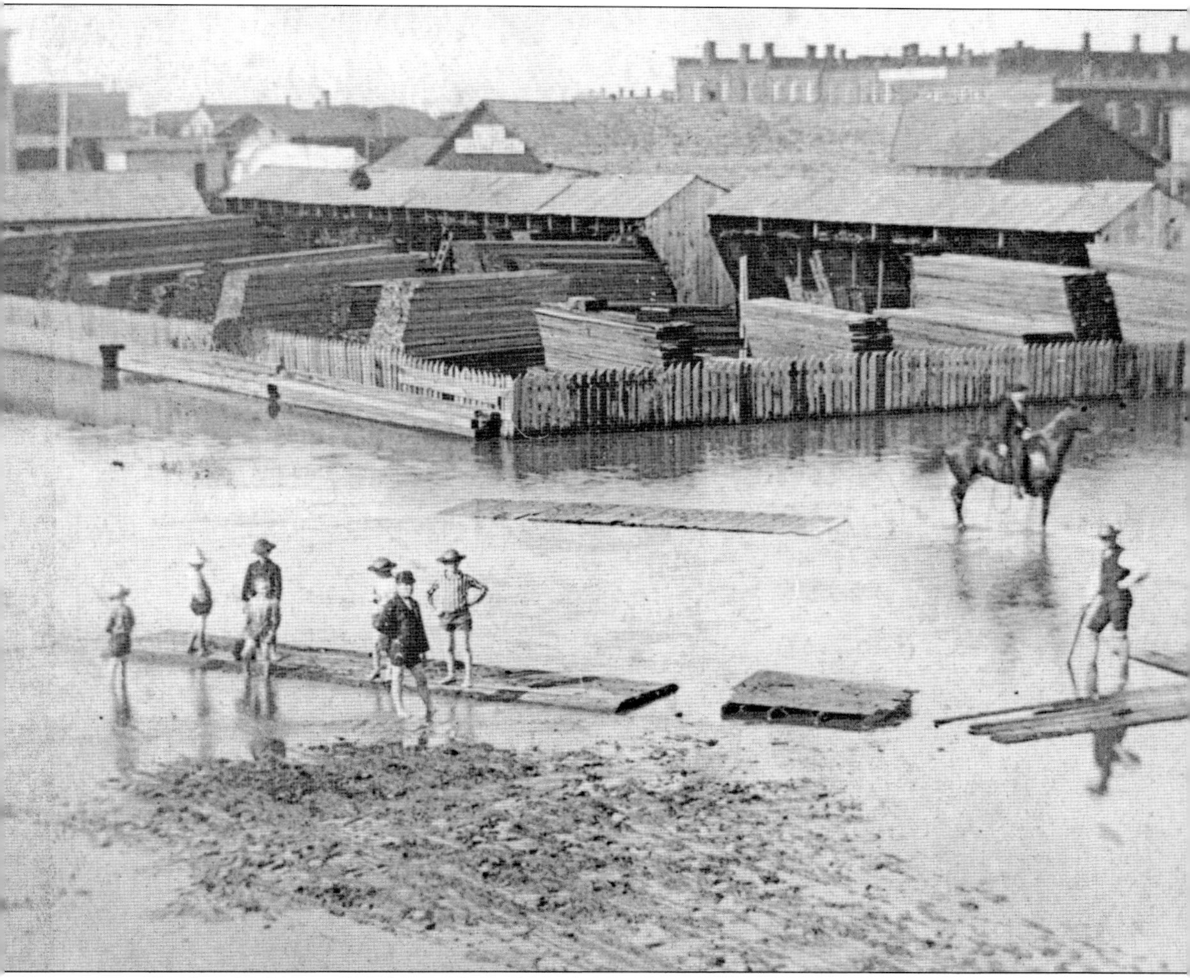

During the flood of 1886, local boys hiked up their pants and waded through the waters. The lumberyard looked like a fortress with a moat.

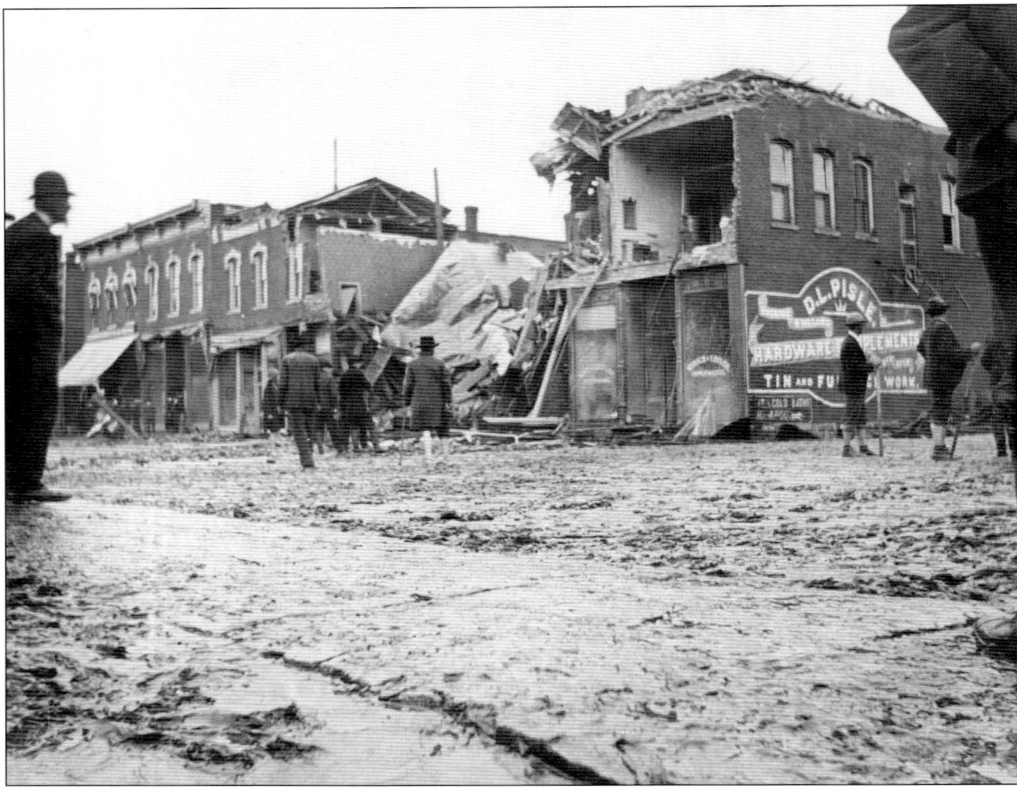

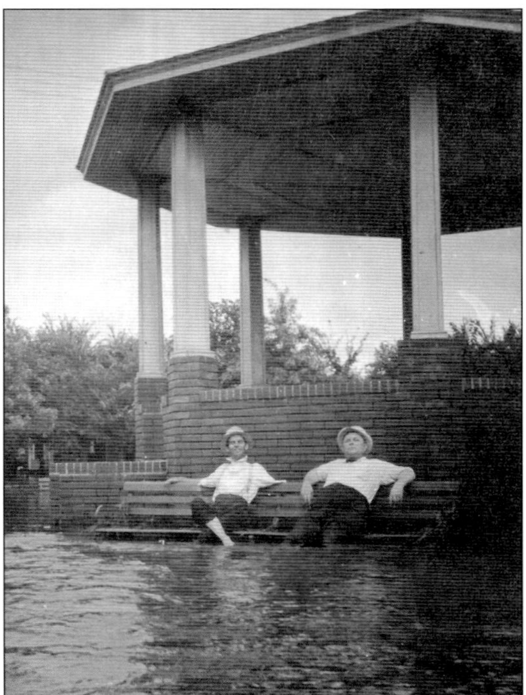

The flood of 1903 roared through the streets of Abilene, undercutting foundations and causing the collapse of buildings. After the waters receded, it took months to clean up.

Some residents of Abilene tried to take the floods in stride. Two local men are pictured here relaxing in the floodwaters at the local bandstand.

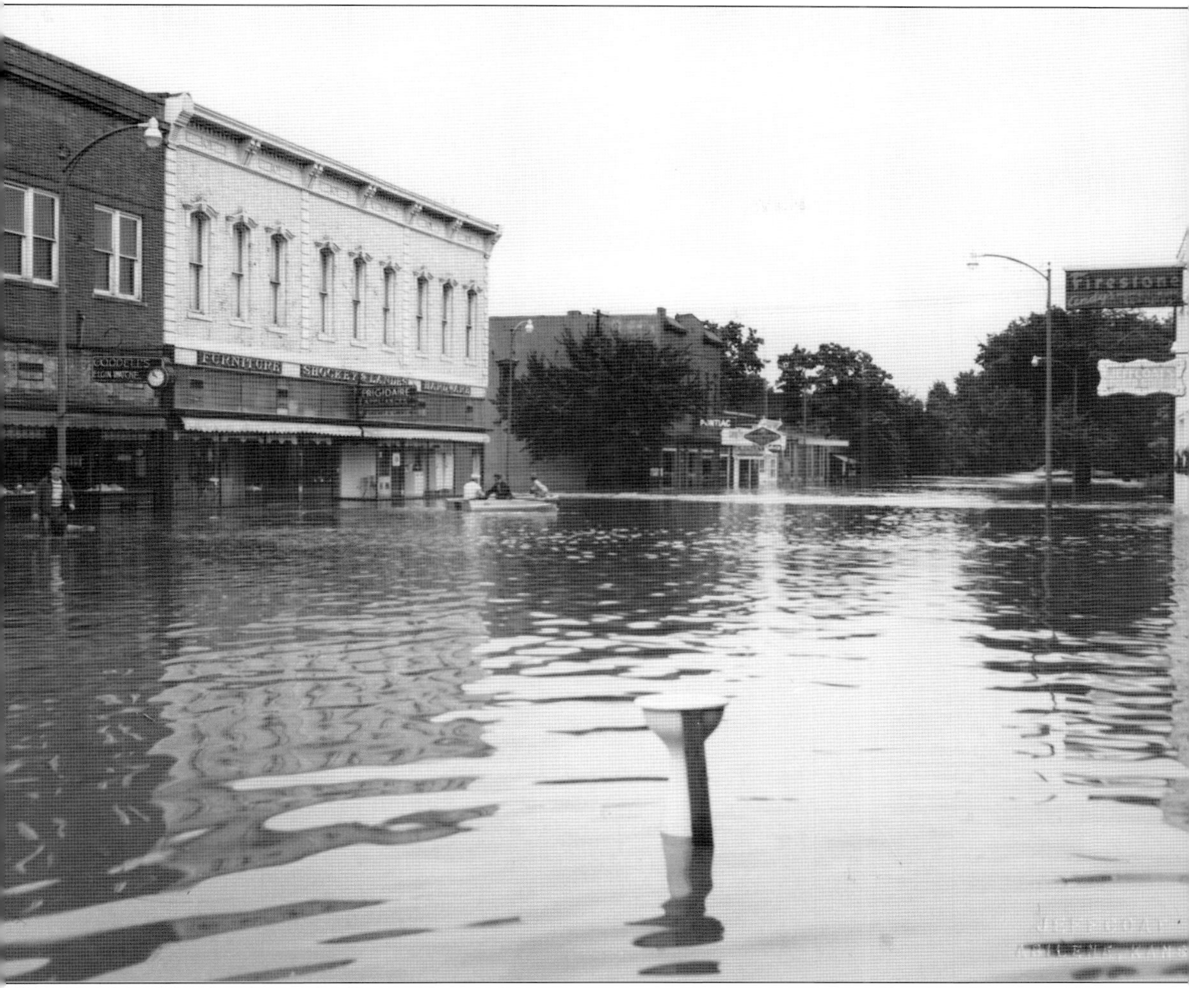

Flooding continued into the 1950s. The flood of 1951 covered the streets and storefronts. Federal reservoirs built in the 1950s and 1960s eventually controlled flooding in eastern Kansas.

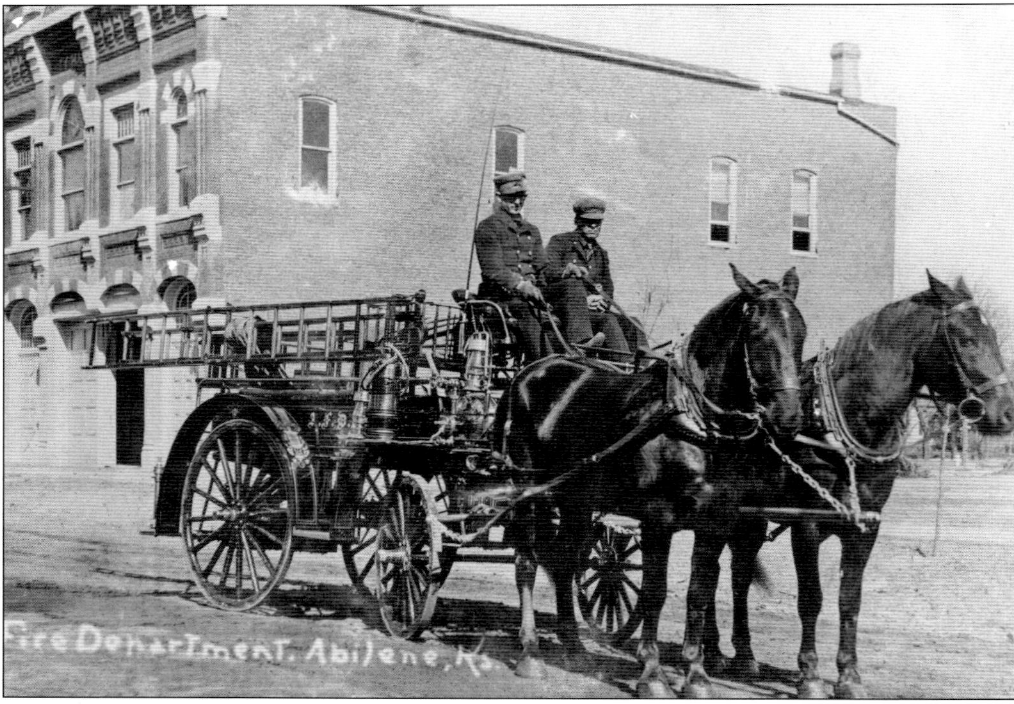

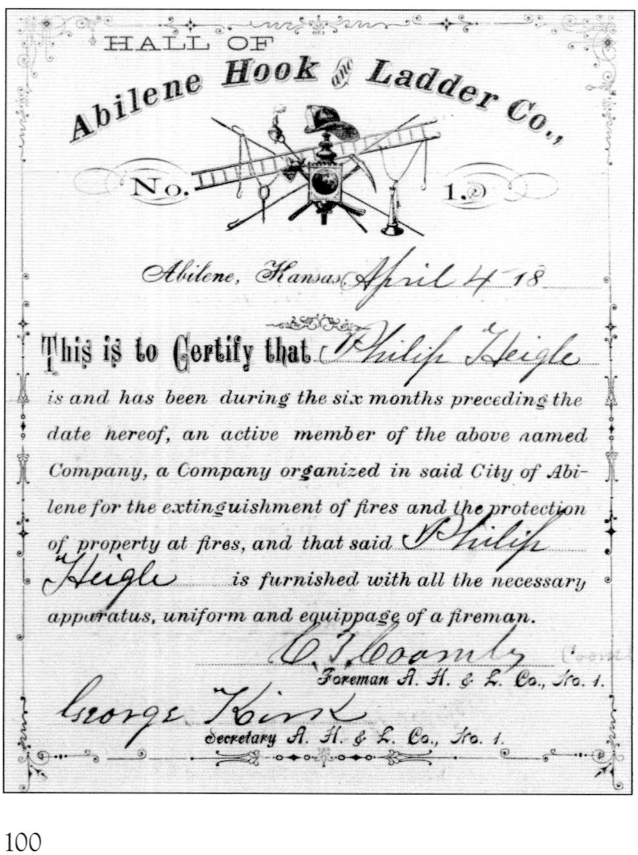

HALL OF

Abilene Hook & Ladder Co.,

No. 1.

Abilene, Kansas, April 4 18

This is to Certify that Philip Heigle is and has been during the six months preceding the date hereof, an active member of the above named Company, a Company organized in said City of Abilene for the extinguishment of fires and the protection of property at fires, and that said Philip Heigle is furnished with all the necessary apparatus, uniform and equippage of a fireman.

Foreman A. H. & L. Co., No. 1.

George Kirk

Secretary A. H. & L. Co., No. 1.

A good fire department was critical in early towns like Abilene. Many buildings were made of wood, and limited water supplies could mean disaster.

This certificate, presented to Philip Heigle, declared him a member of the Abilene Hook & Ladder Co. No. 1.

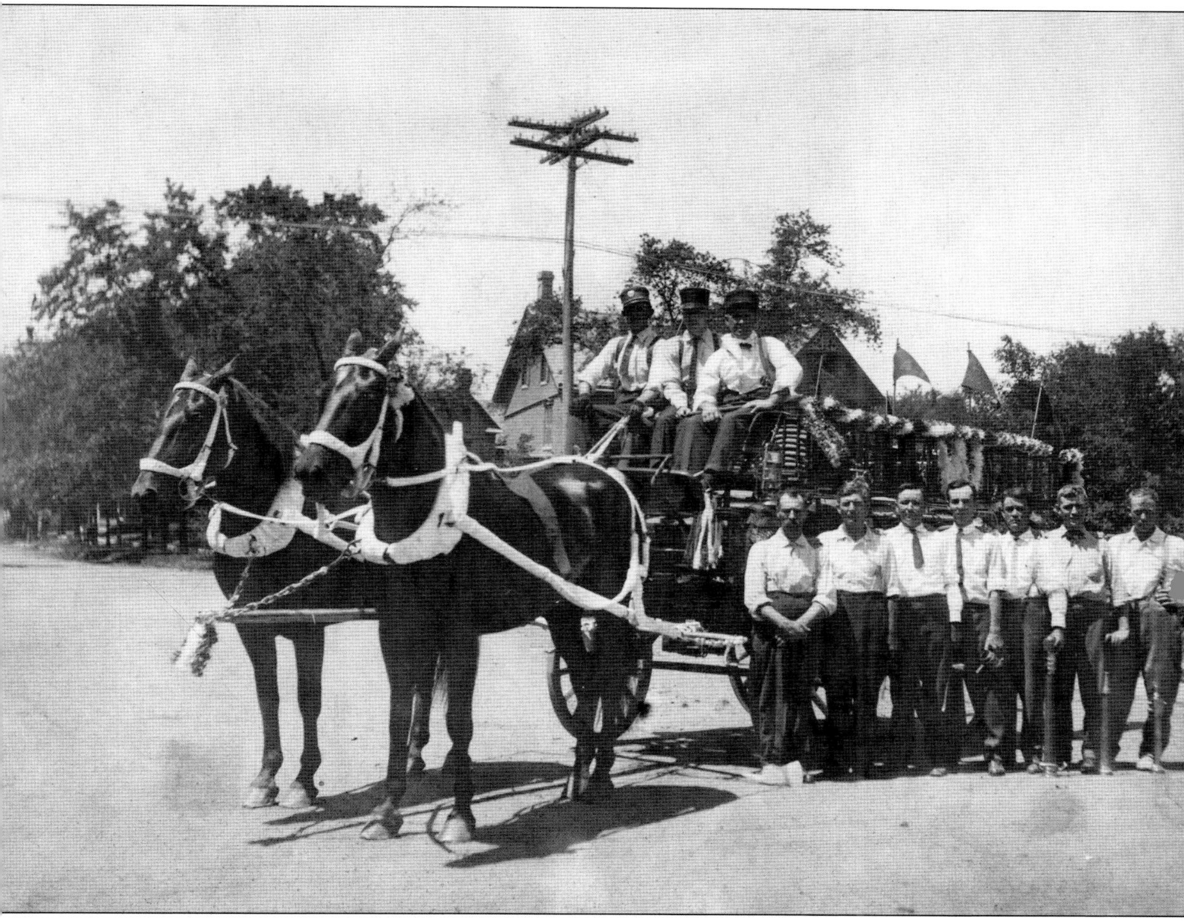

Members of the 1911 fire department pose for their picture during a parade. The two horses were named Nip and Tuck.

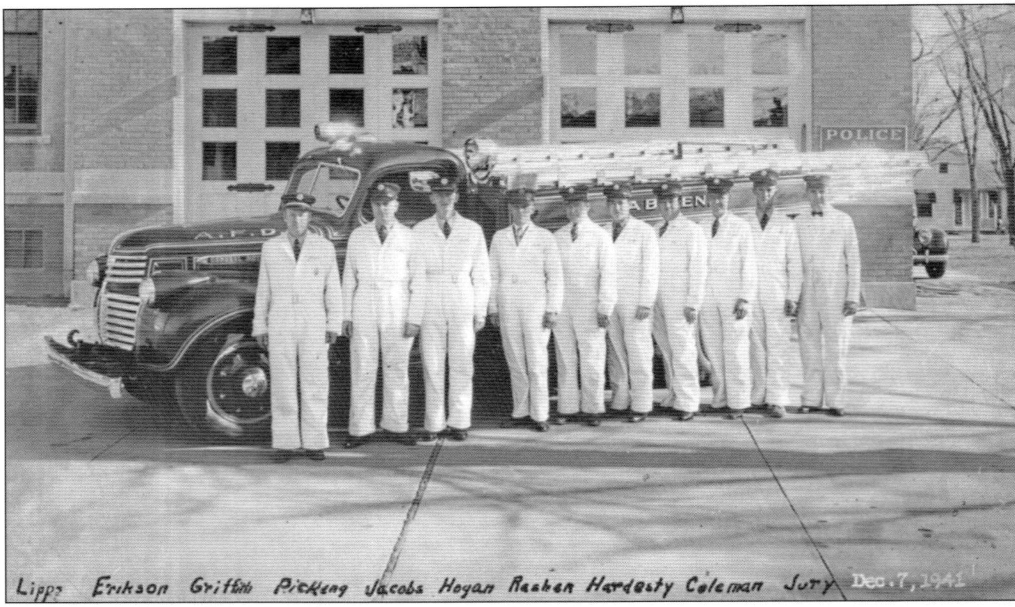

The 1941 Abilene Fire Department stands in front of a modern fire truck, complete with sirens. The white uniforms were for dress occasions like city parades and promotional events.

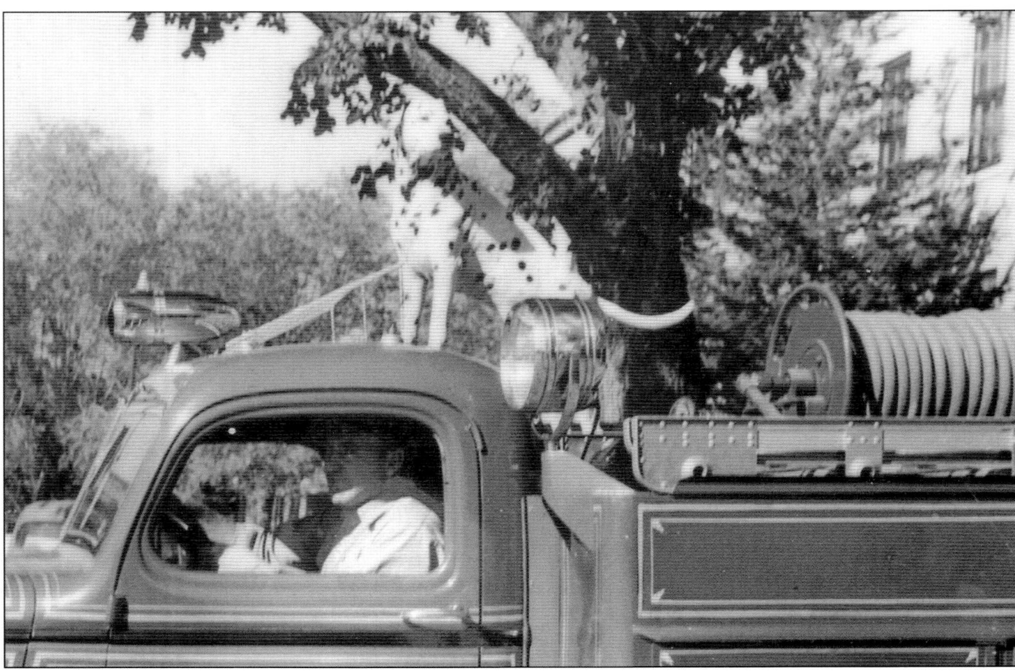

No upstanding fire department was complete without a Dalmatian leading the way. This 1940s photograph shows Abilene's four-footed mascot; his name was Ike.

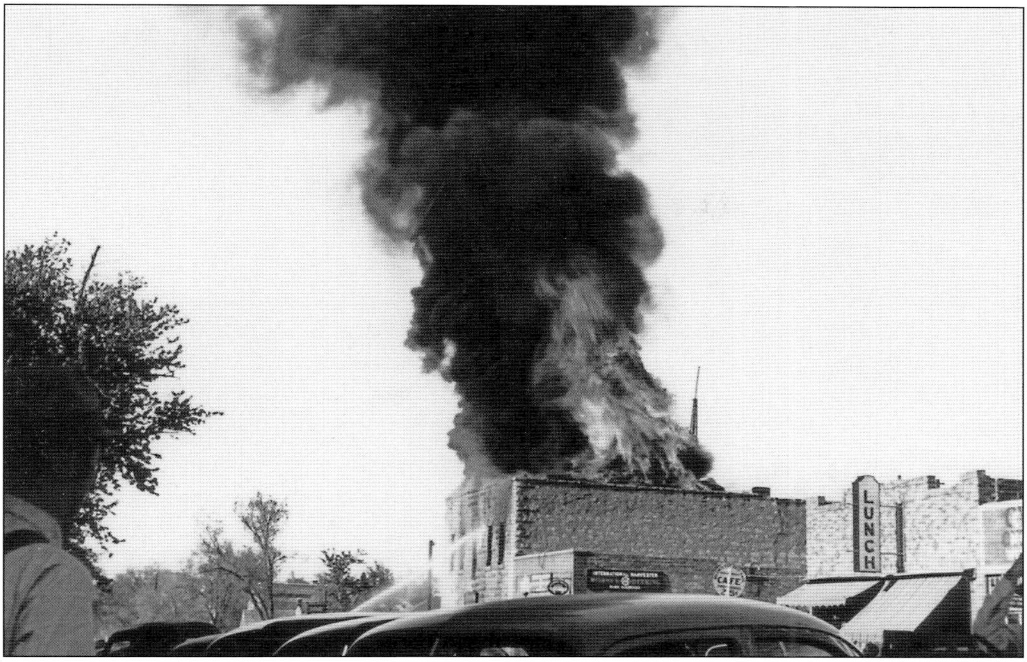

Even with a well-equipped fire department, fire could still take its toll. This 1940s fire destroyed the building before firefighters could get enough water on the blaze to gain control.

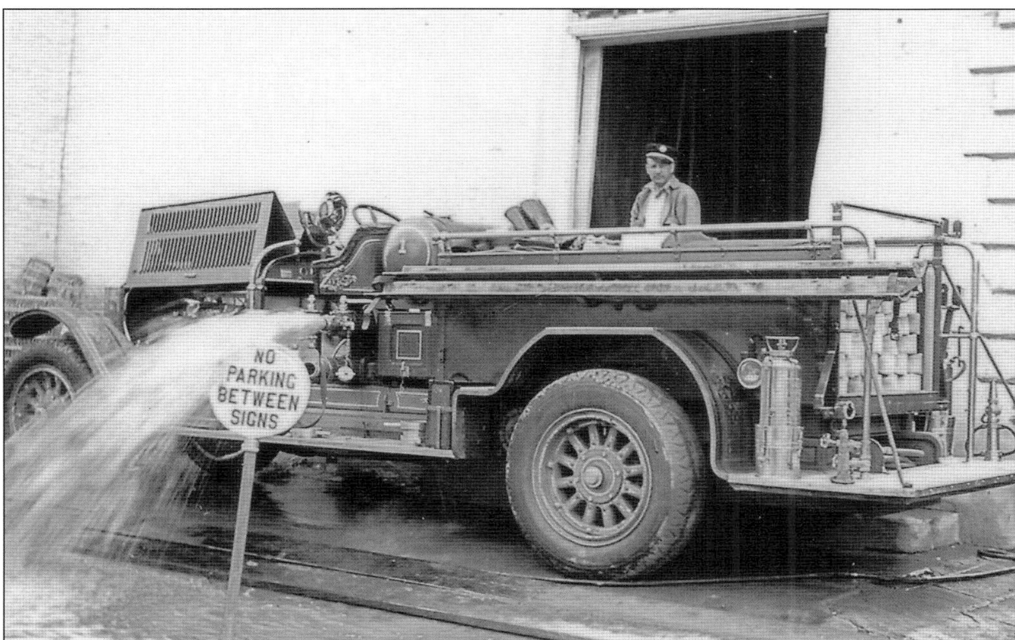

Maintenance of fire equipment was important and included checking tanks and hoses. Area children enjoyed the by-product of cold water on hot days.

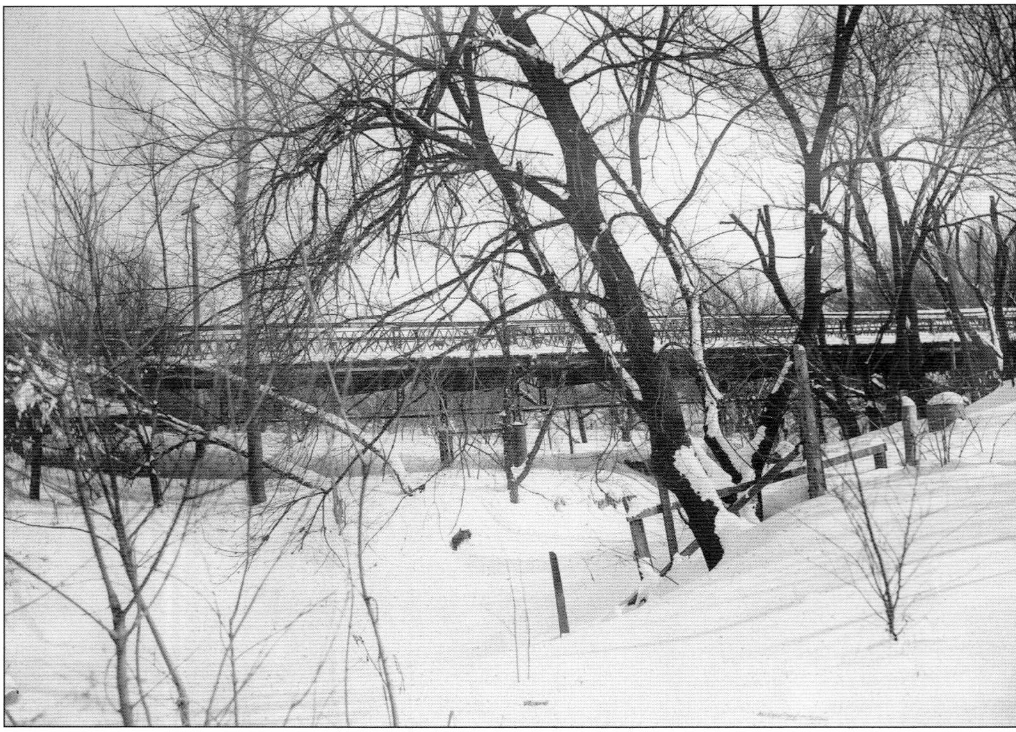

Winters on the Plains could bring heavy snow as late as March or even April, which blocked roads and stranded travelers. This image looks north toward the Third Street Bridge after a March 1900 snowfall.

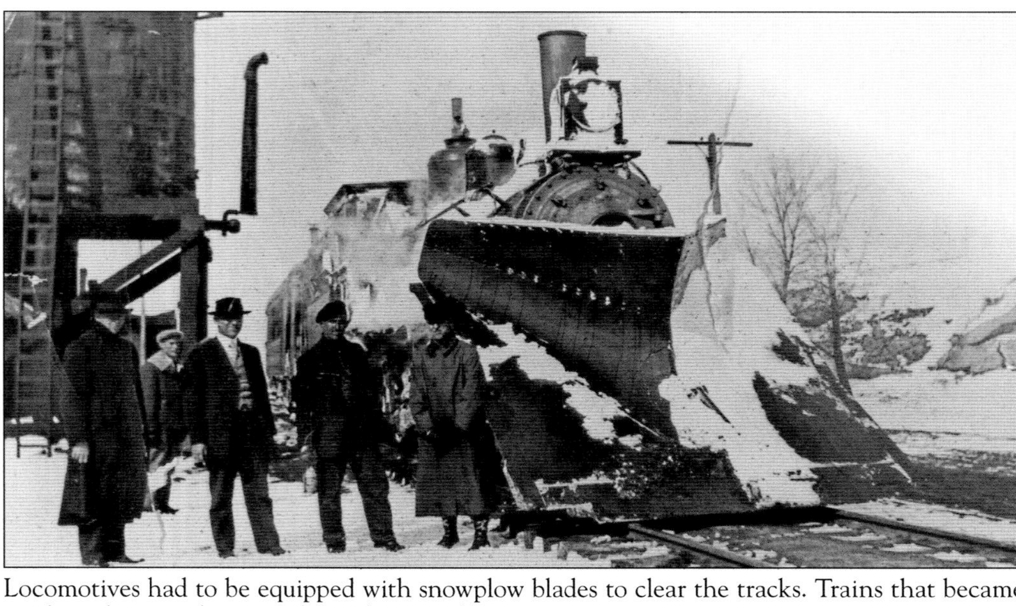

Locomotives had to be equipped with snowplow blades to clear the tracks. Trains that became stuck in the snow hampered travel across the entire country.

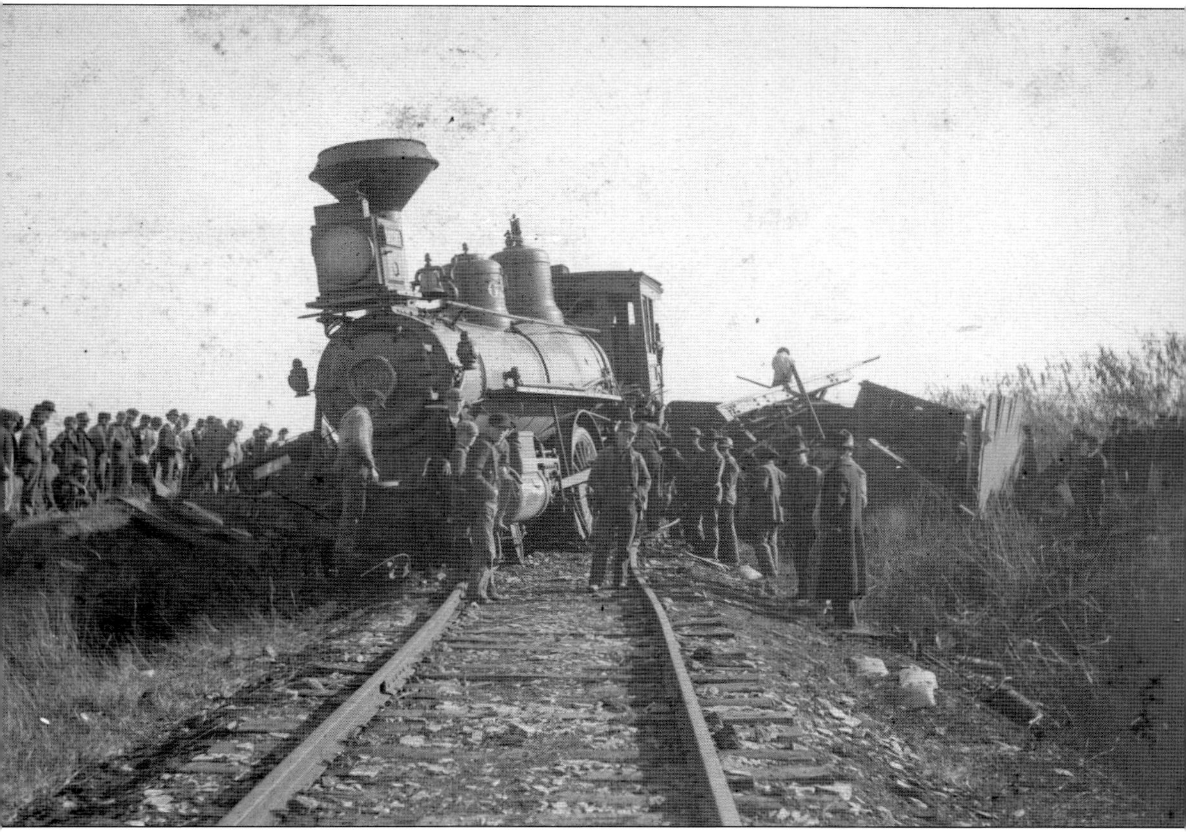

Train wrecks were a rare disaster and attracted large audiences. Here, onlookers view the damage of a train wreck near Abilene.

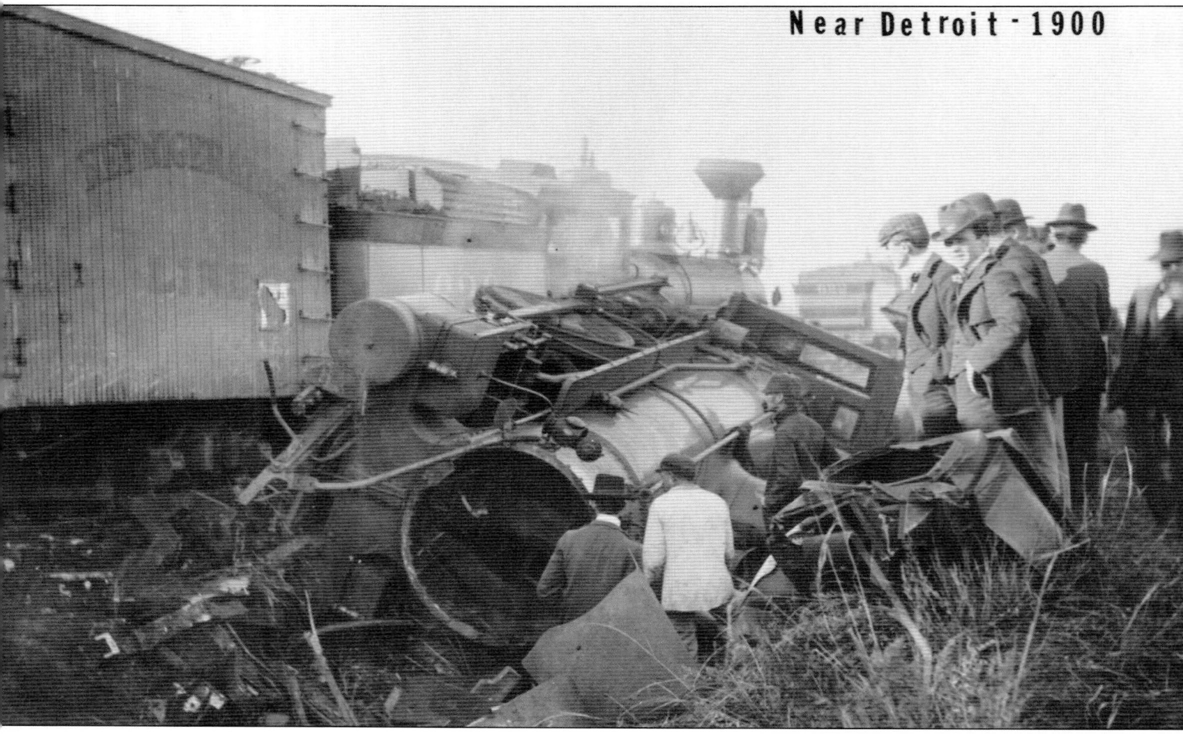

In 1900, an overturned locomotive halted train traffic near Abilene. A new one had to be brought in to carry out the trainload.

Seven

Politics and Presidents

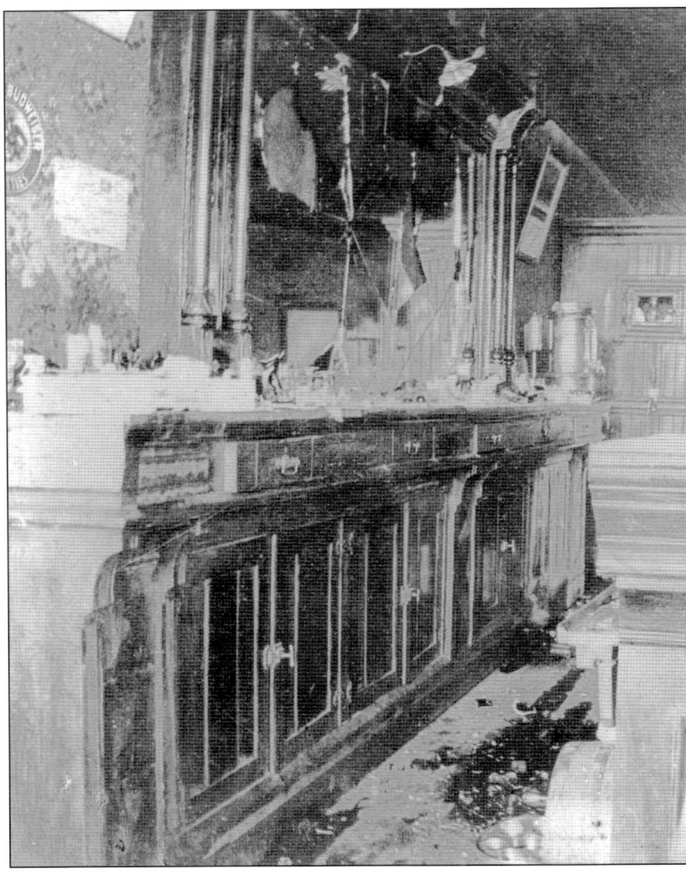

Carrie Nation paid an unwelcome visit to Dickinson County in 1901 and left her mark upon Enterprise Saloon. She smashed up the bar and declared alcohol to be the work of the devil.

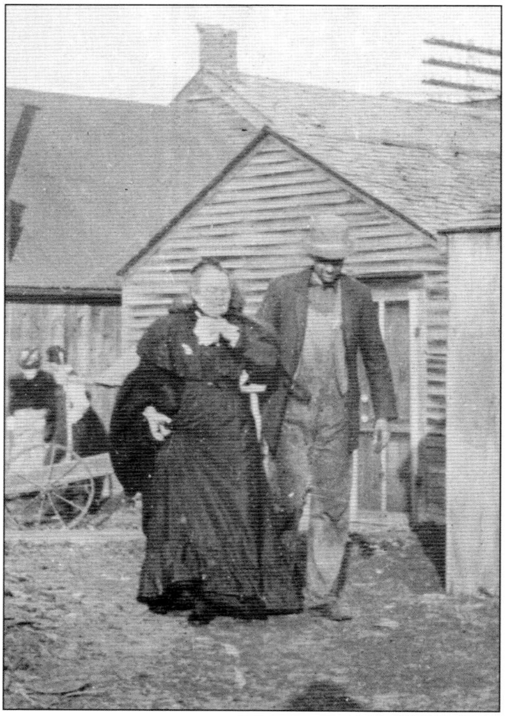

Nation was arrested for vandalism and ordered out of the county, but her message had reached the ears of temperance organizations—a war had been declared on alcohol. The politics of temperance began in Kansas and spread throughout the country.

In 1920, nine years after Nation's death, Prohibition was passed as the 18th Amendment to the US Constitution. The once-wild cow town of Abilene joined the ranks of "dry" towns.

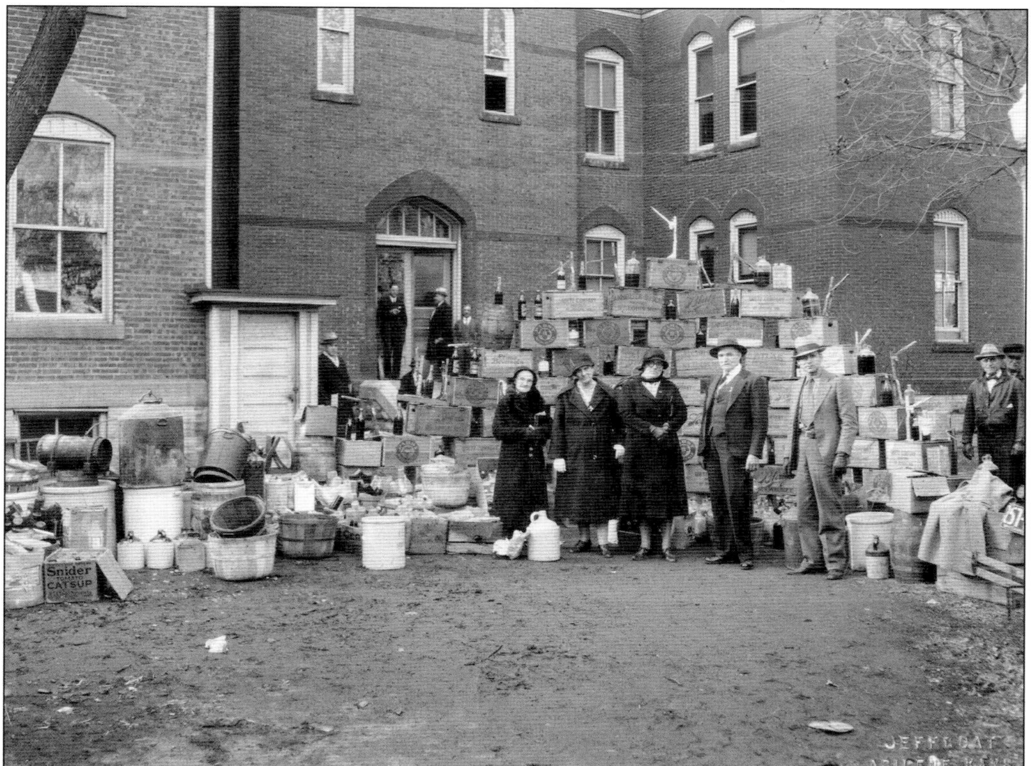

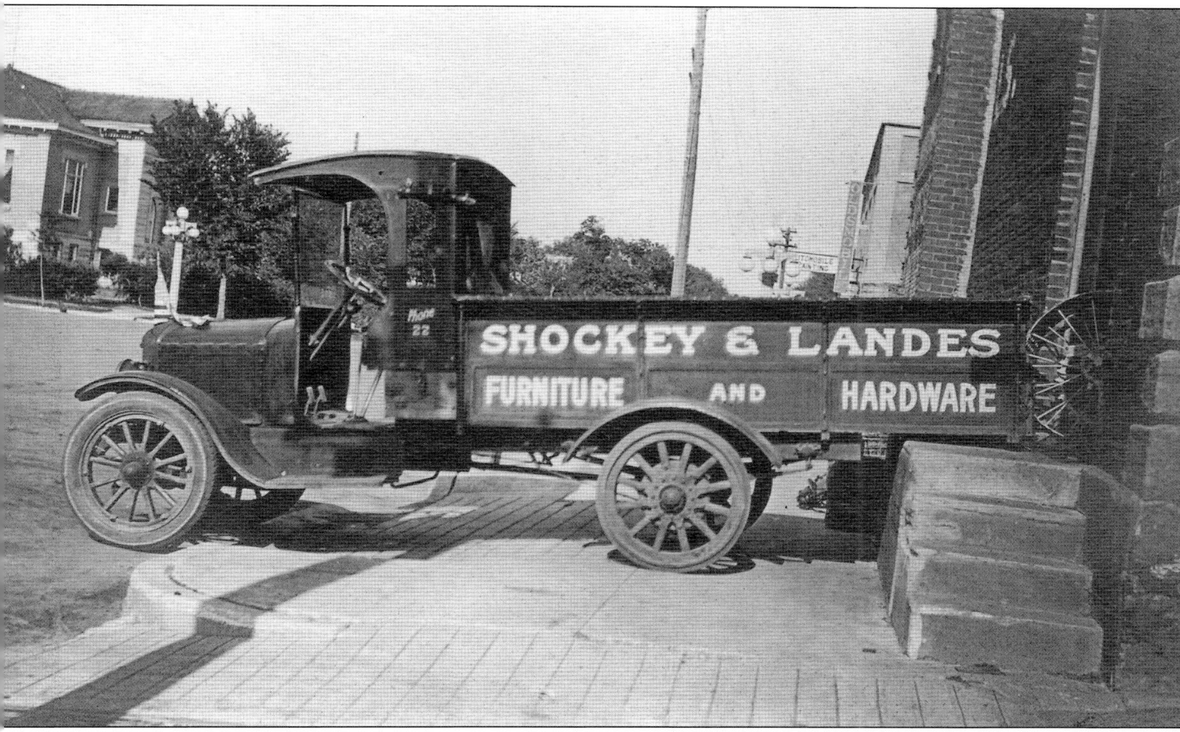

Other changes came to Abilene in the form of transportation. Automobiles and trucks rapidly replaced the horse and buggy as preferred forms of transportation. With the increase in automobiles came the demand for paved roads.

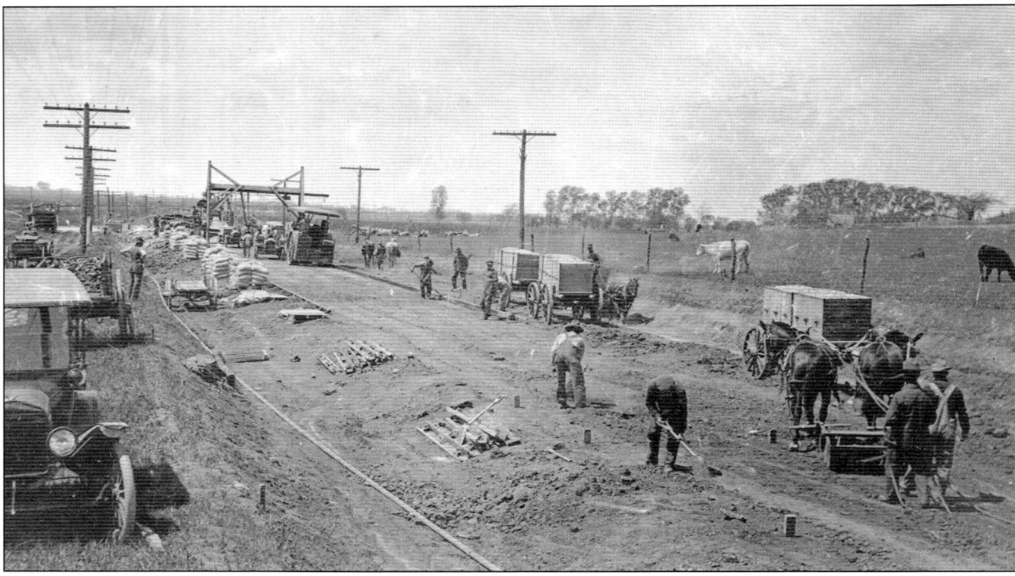

In 1921, construction on a fully paved, east–west interstate Highway 40 arrived in Abilene. The road gangs smoothed dirt, poured pavement, and still used the help of several horses.

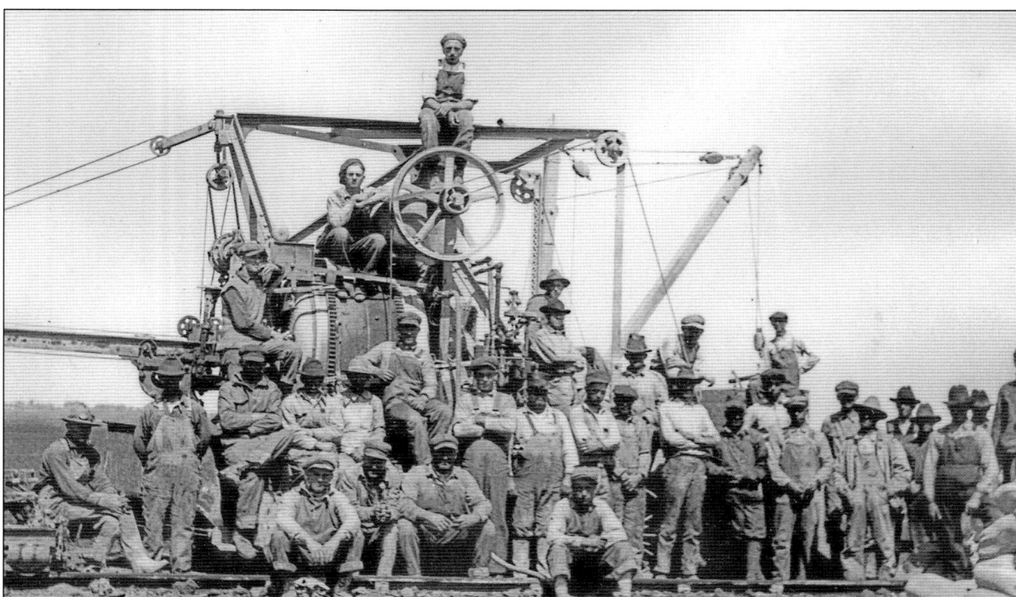

Road workers take a break to pose for a formal photograph. Highway 40 ran east to west from Atlantic City, New Jersey, to San Francisco, California.

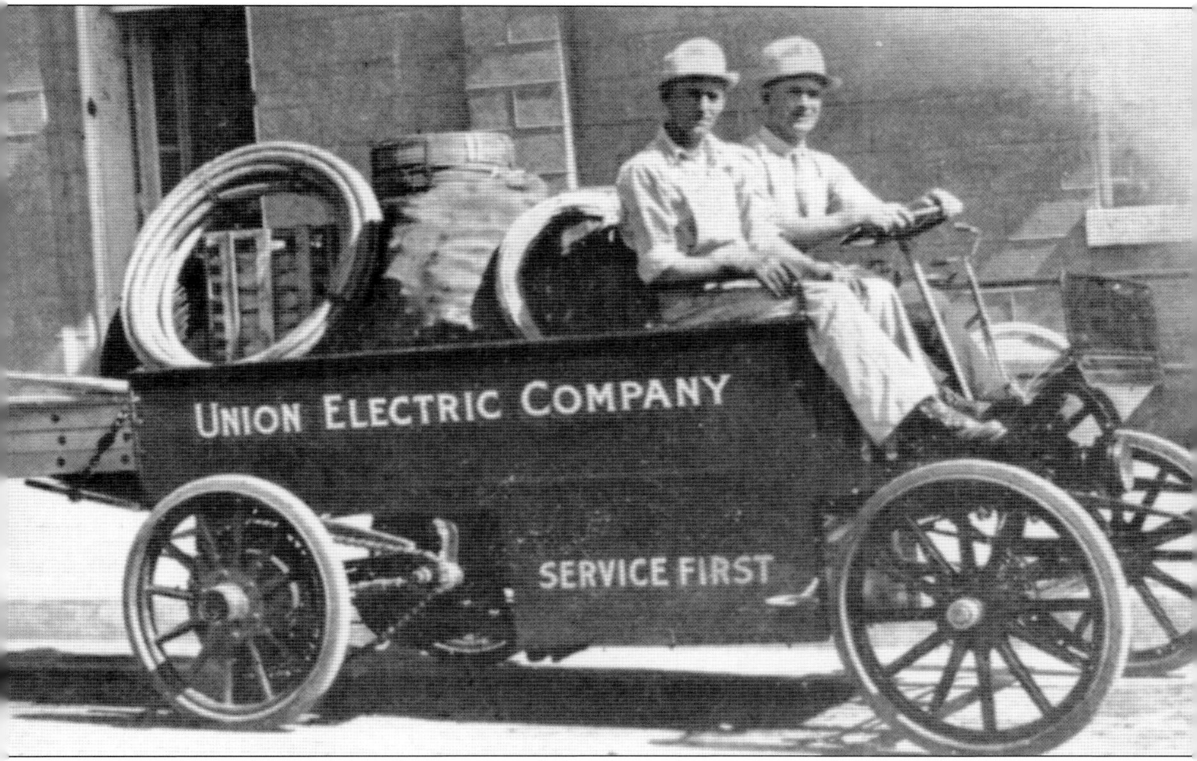

In 1910, Abilene boasted that the city provided 24-hour electric service for its residents. By 1920, almost every home had electric lights. The city was proud of its modern facilities, and employees worked hard to keep constant service to homes and businesses.

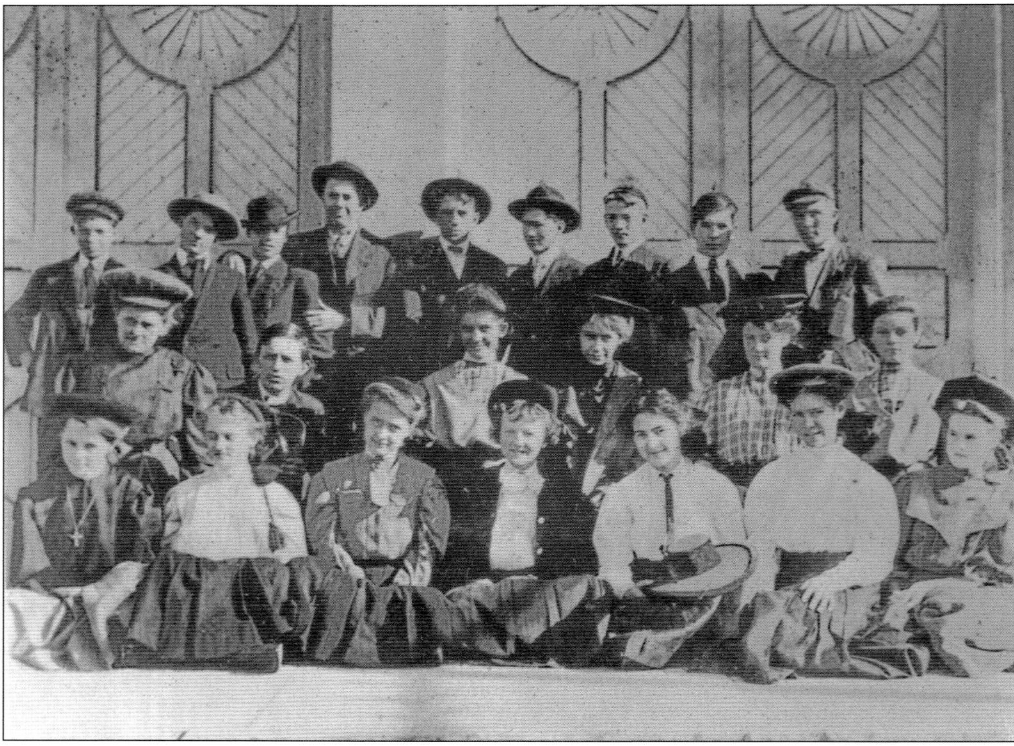

Abilene also took pride in its students, but when the 1904 freshman class posed for a photograph, no one suspected that one of the pupils would become president. Dwight D. Eisenhower is on the far left in the top row.

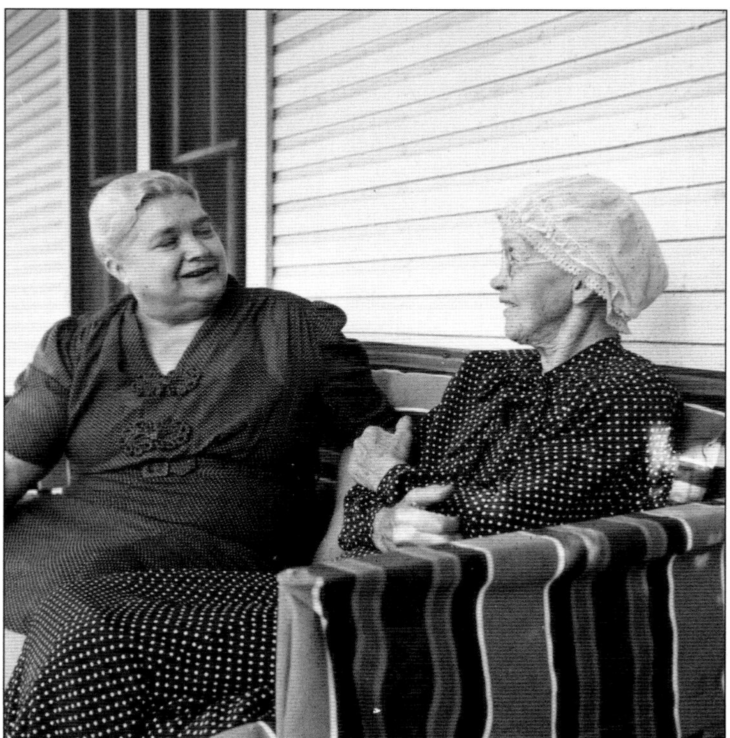

During high school, Dwight Eisenhower enjoyed playing sports and studying history. He loved reading history so much that his mother had to hide his books until his chores were done. Ida Eisenhower was a strong influence in Dwight's life. She is pictured on her front porch (left) talking with a friend.

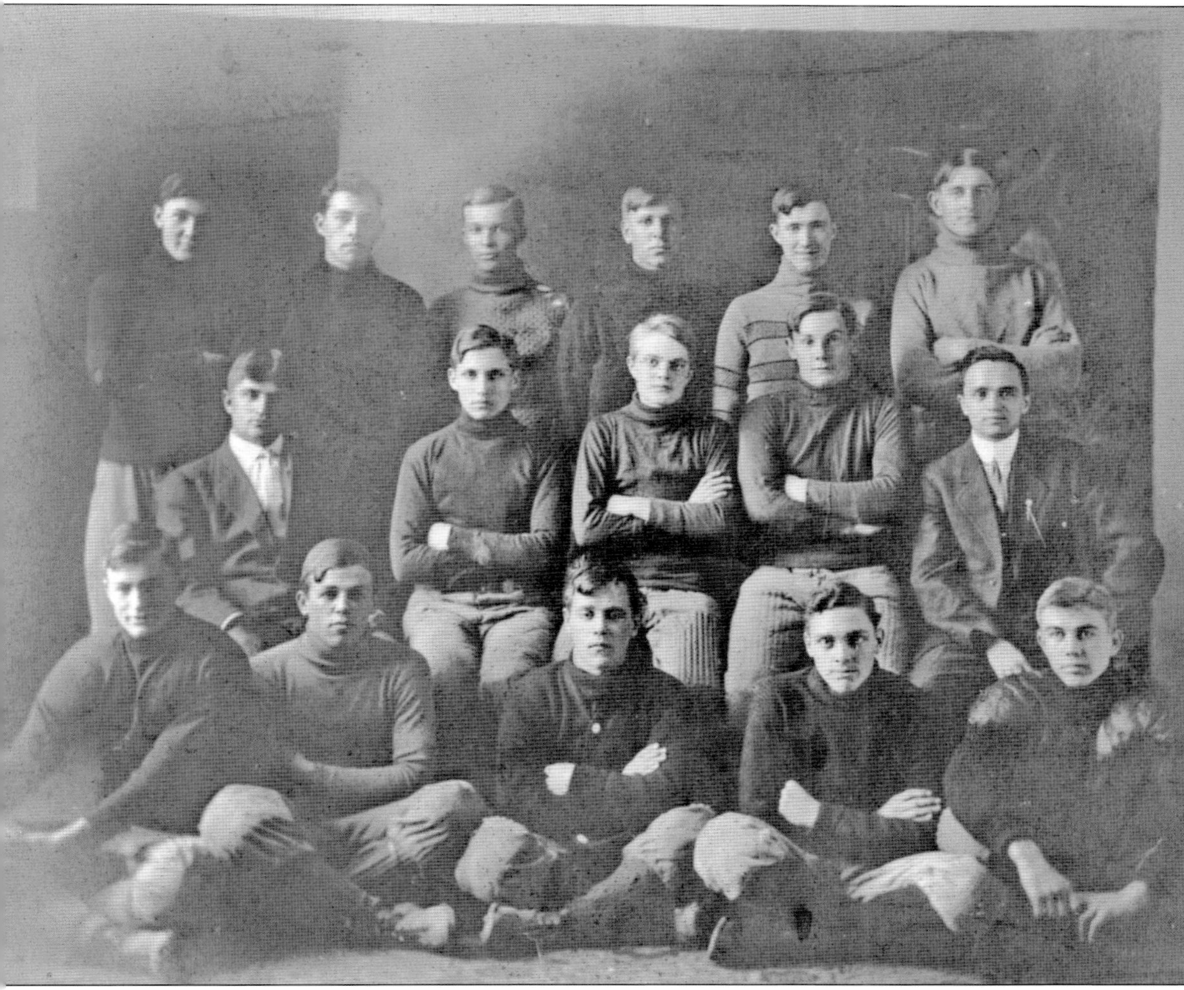

Eisenhower was also an enthusiastic athlete and played both football and baseball. He is pictured here third from the left in the top row.

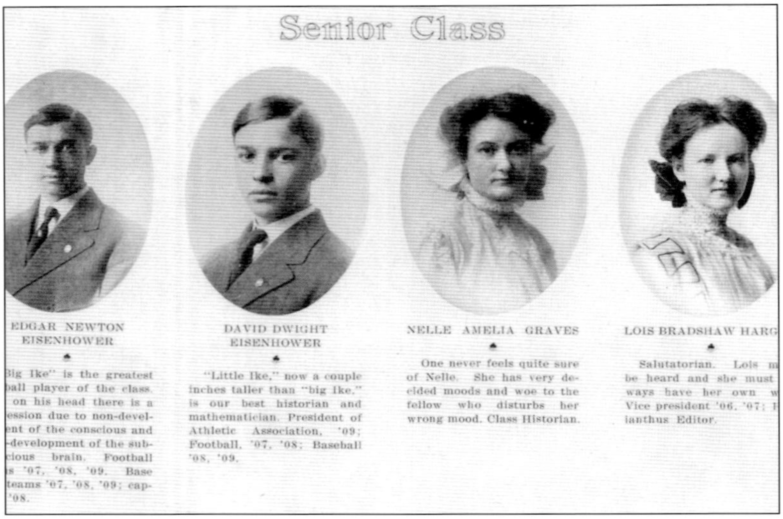

Dwight Eisenhower was one of seven sons born to David and Ida Eisenhower; one son died in infancy. Edgar and Dwight both graduated from high school in 1909. The class predictions saw Edgar as being president of the United States. Dwight was predicted to become a Yale history professor.

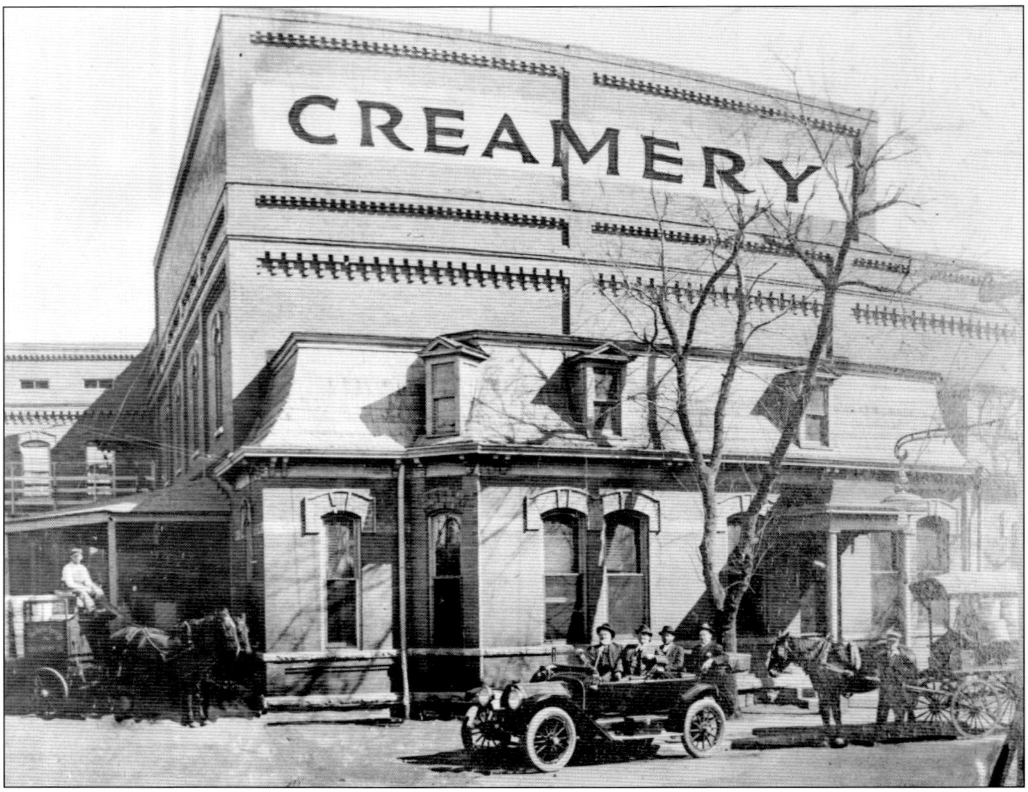

After graduation, Dwight went to work at Belle Springs Creamery, where his father worked as a maintenance man. Edgar and Dwight had made a pact that Dwight would work to help put Edgar through school, and Edgar would then do the same for Dwight.

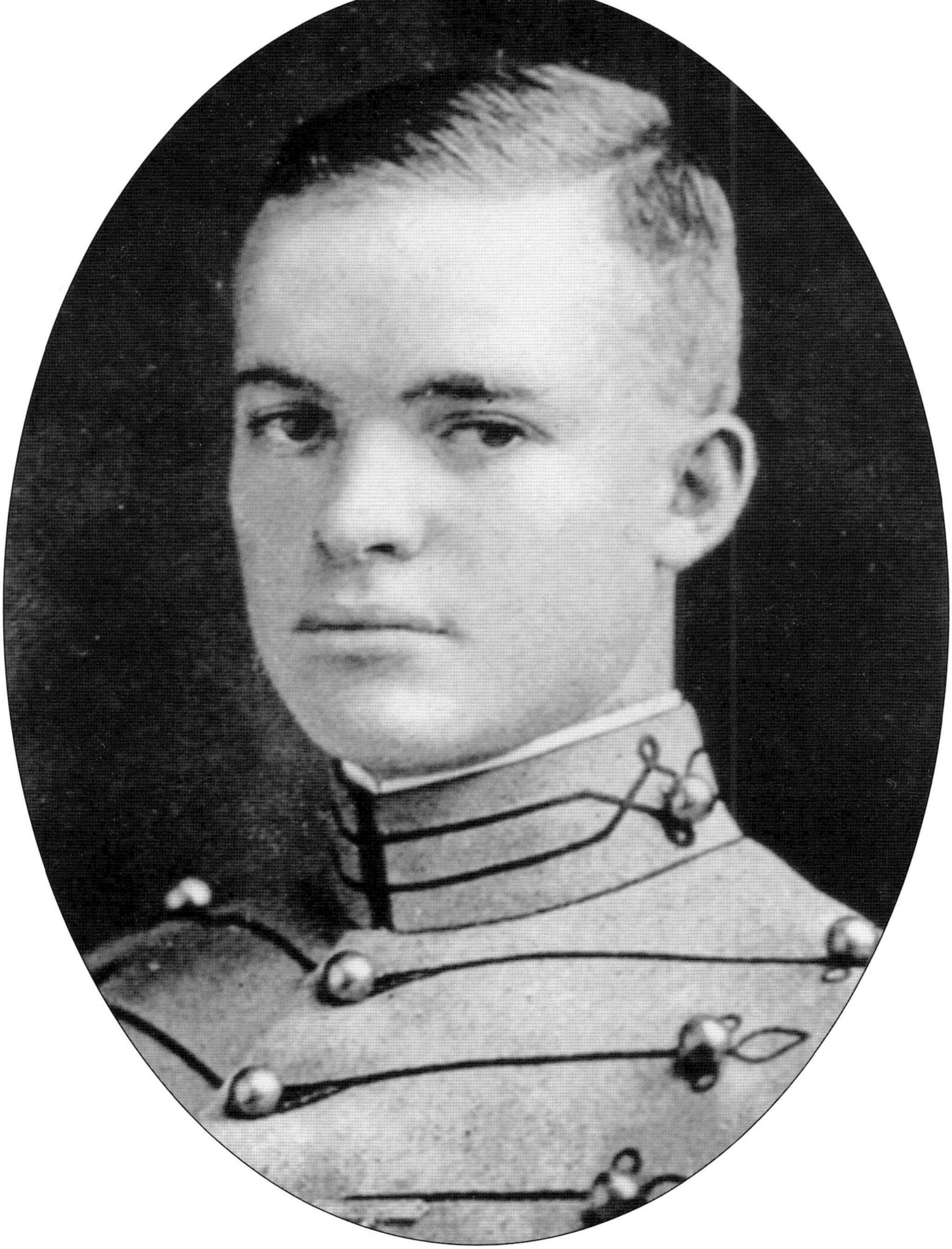

Dwight Eisenhower was selected as a cadet for West Point in 1911. He received a full scholarship and received his lieutenant commission in 1915. Edgar never had to pay a dime for Dwight's tuition.

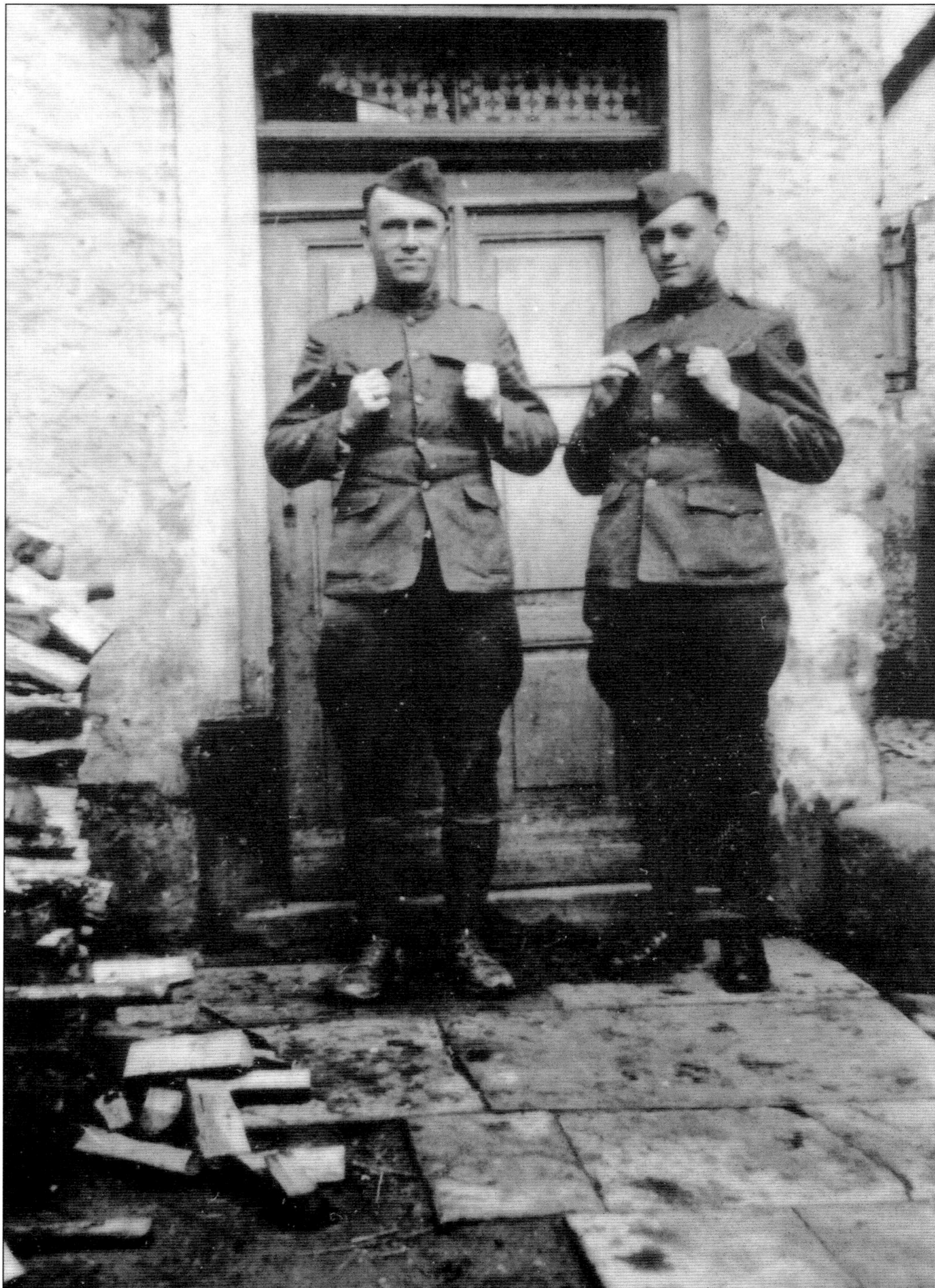

On June 28, 1914, Archduke Franz Ferdinand of Austria was assassinated. This event, thousands of miles from Abilene, was the start of World War I. By 1917, young men from Abilene were training to enter the war.

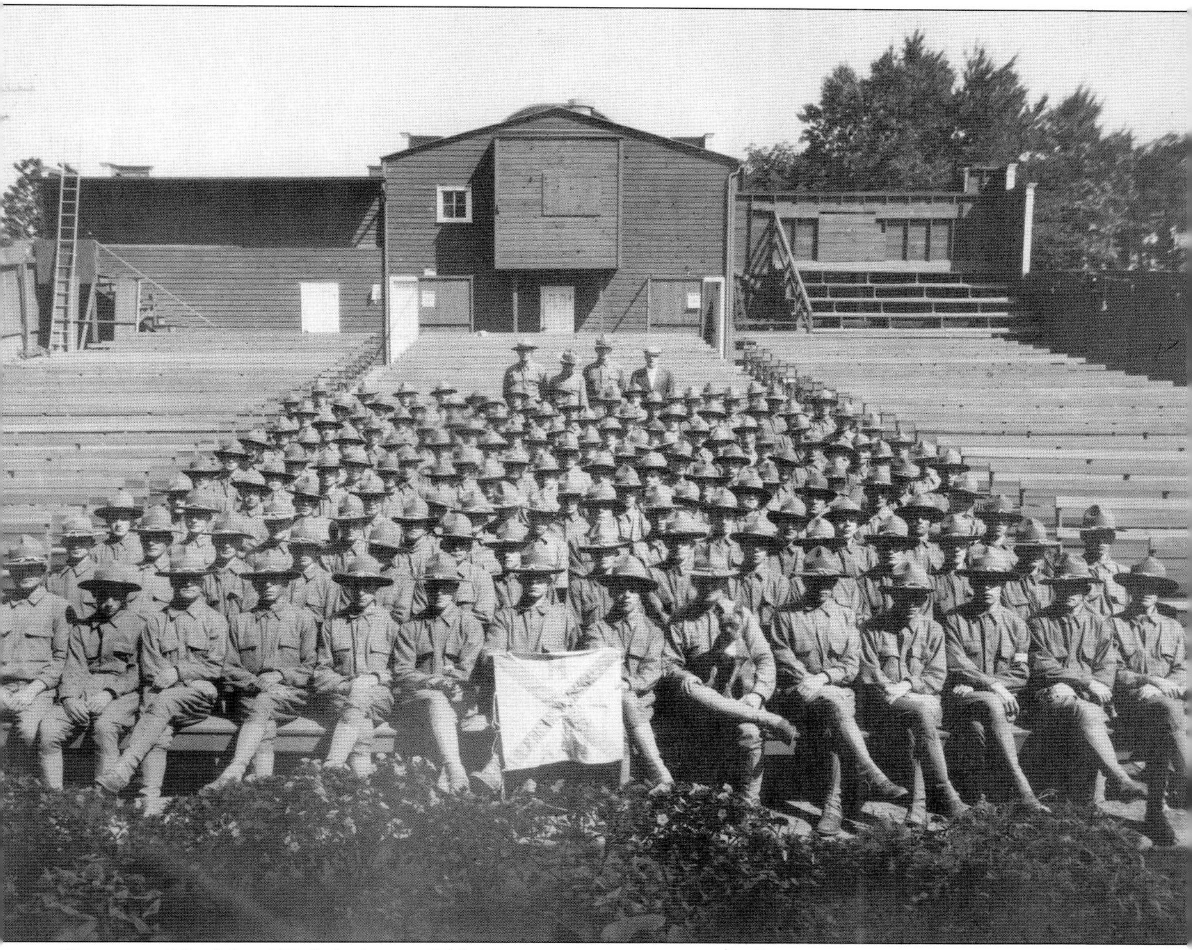

Company H of the 139th Infantry 35th Division was comprised of young men from Abilene and Dickinson County. The site of their military training was in Abilene.

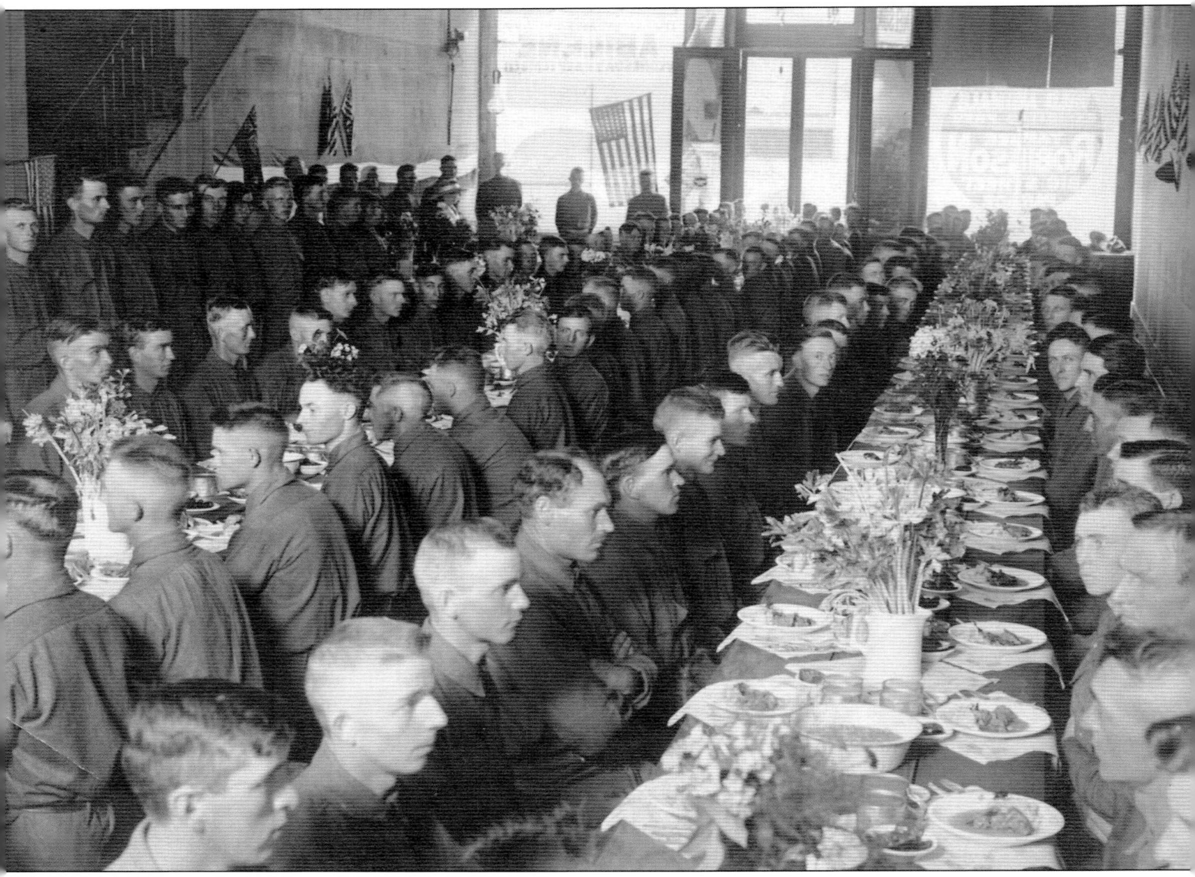

Members of Company H are seated in the mess hall before a meal. Note the bouquets of flowers provided by area ladies for table decorations.

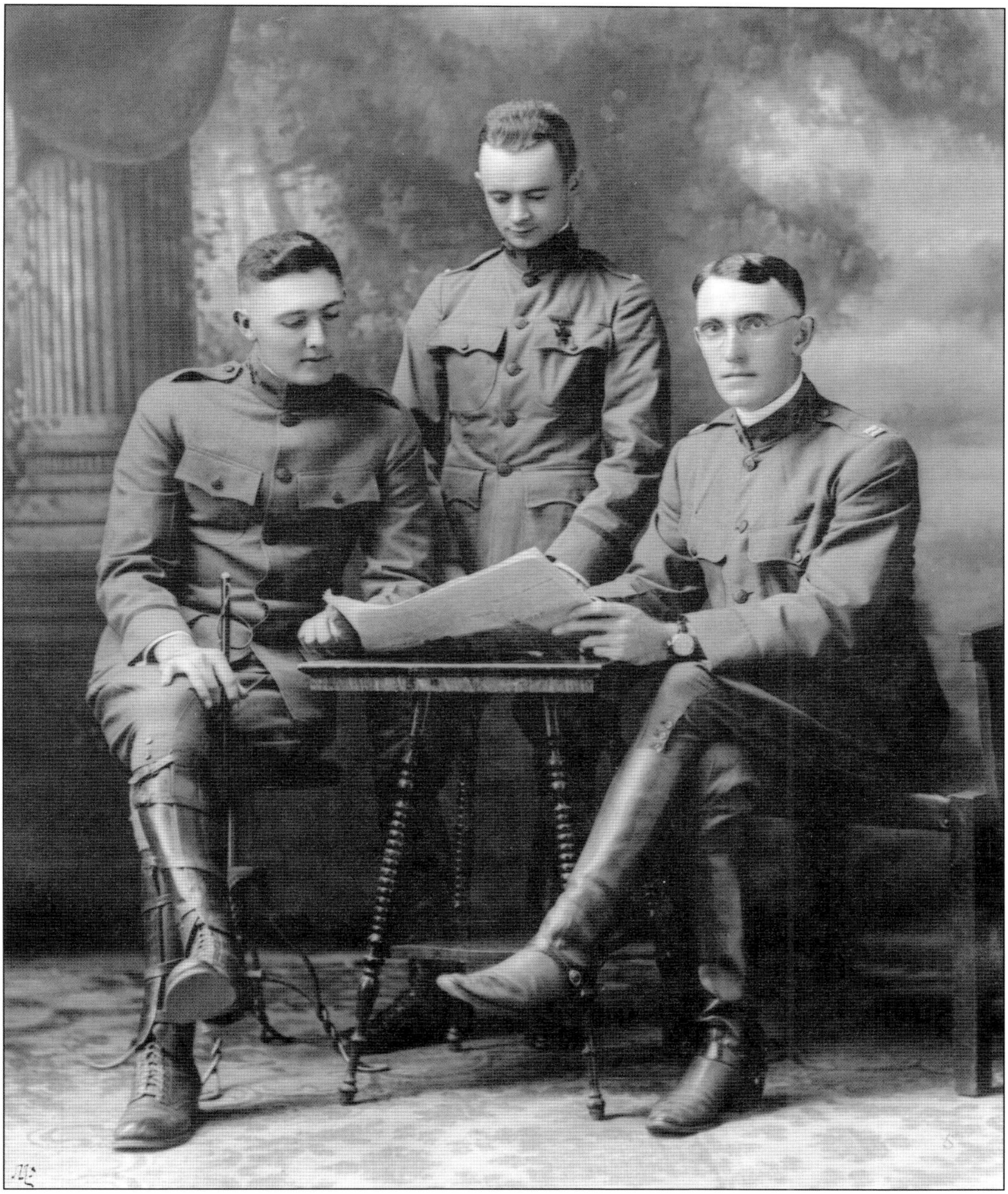

The commanding officers of Company H pose for the camera. From left to right they are Lt. Ralph Lucier, Lt. Jack McManigal, and Capt. C.H. Brown—all three were Abilene natives.

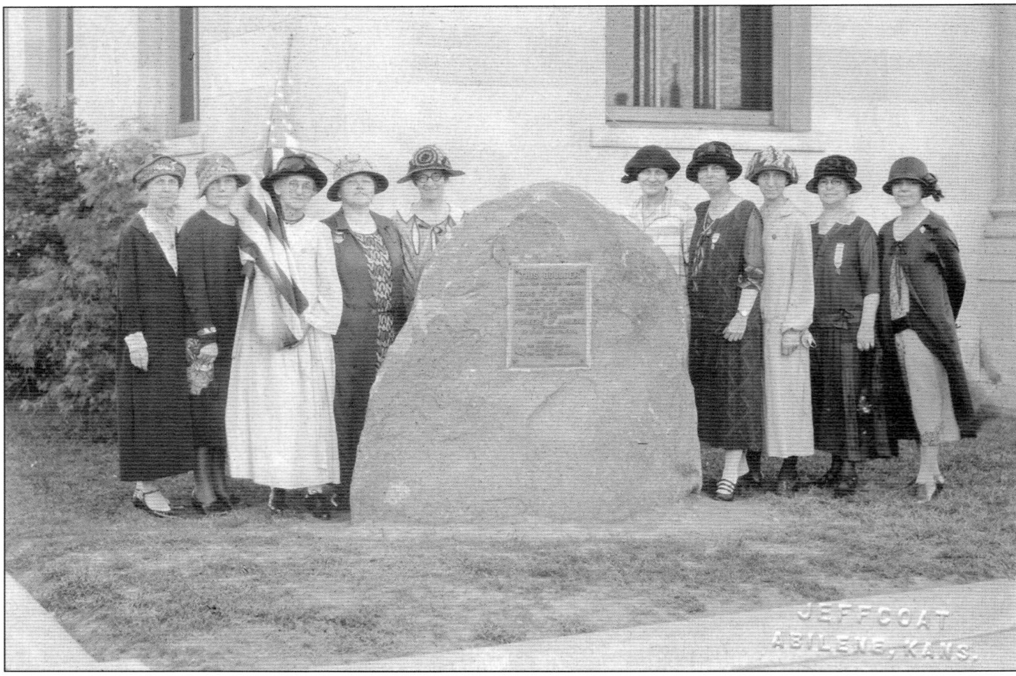

The end of the Great War brought a desire for peace and nostalgia for the "good old days." In 1926, the Abilene chapter of the Daughters of the American Revolution dedicated the "Texas Cattle Trail" boulder.

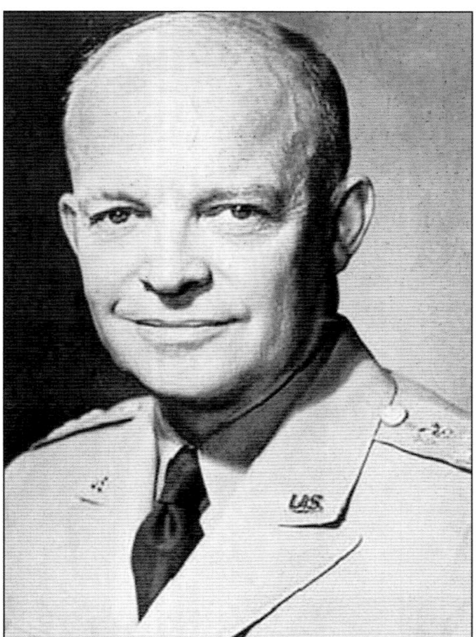

Peace was shattered again on December 7, 1941, when Japan attacked Pearl Harbor. The United States was thus hurled into World War II. Hometown boy Dwight Eisenhower was named supreme commander of the allied forces in Europe.

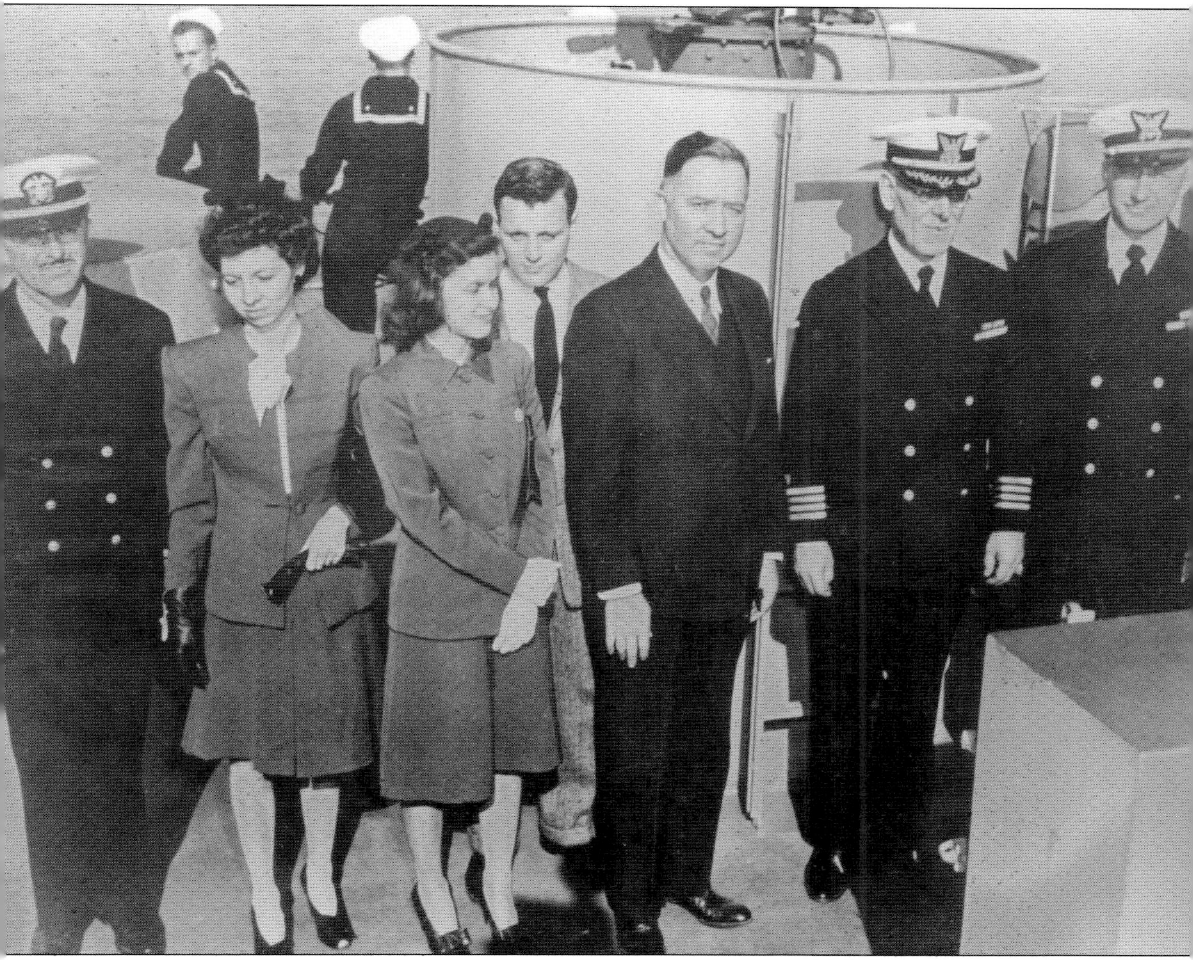

Eisenhower's hometown was honored with the Navy naming a ship the USS *Abilene*. The PF-58 Tacoma-class frigate was launched on May 6, 1943.

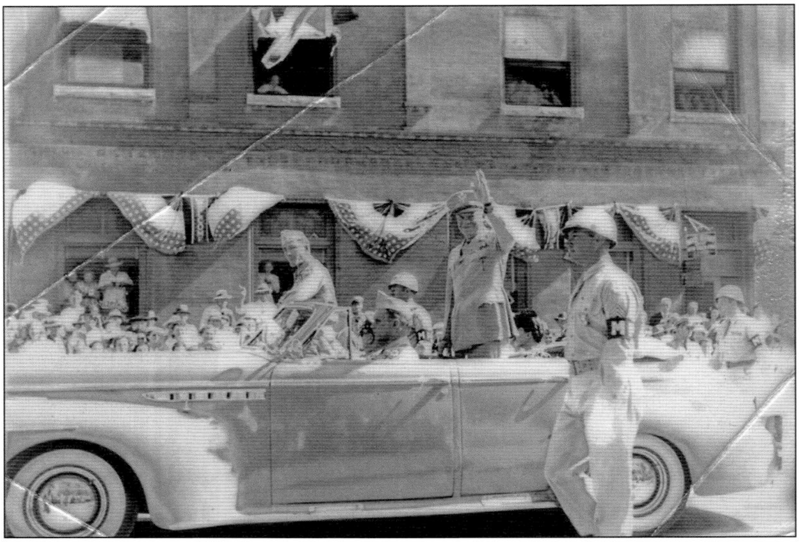

At the end of World War II, Dwight Eisenhower visited Abilene. He had been promoted to a five-star general, and Eisenhower was a household name around the world.

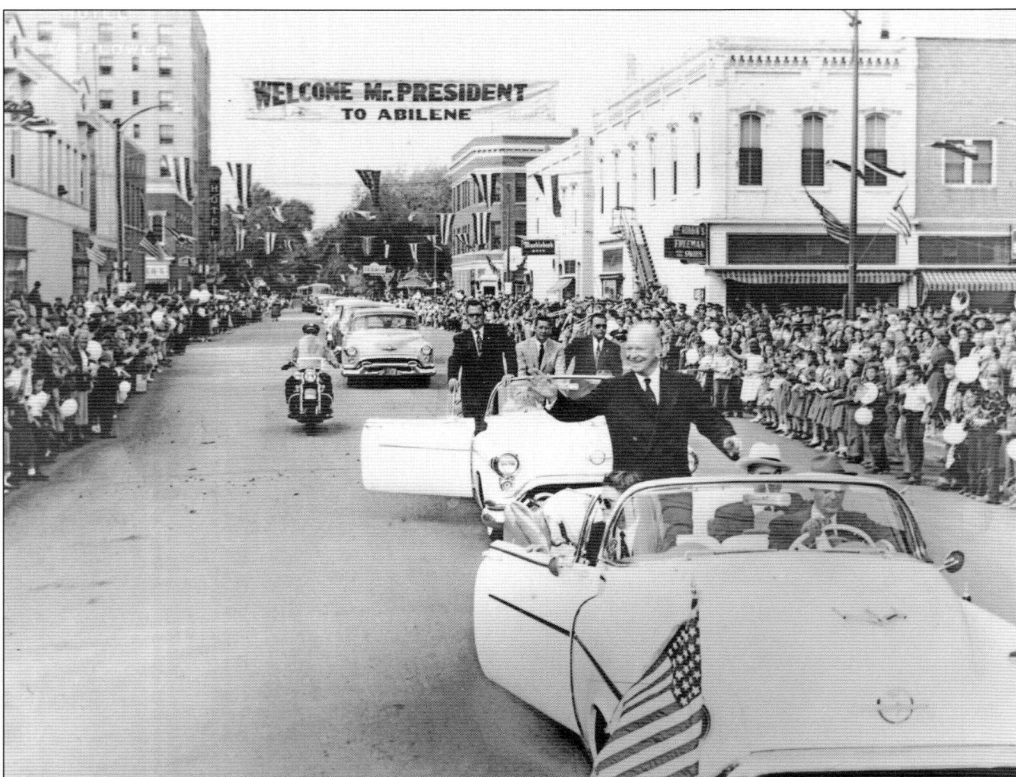

The entire town turned out for Eisenhower's homecoming. A parade was held in his honor, and the hometown boy received the praise of loyal admirers.

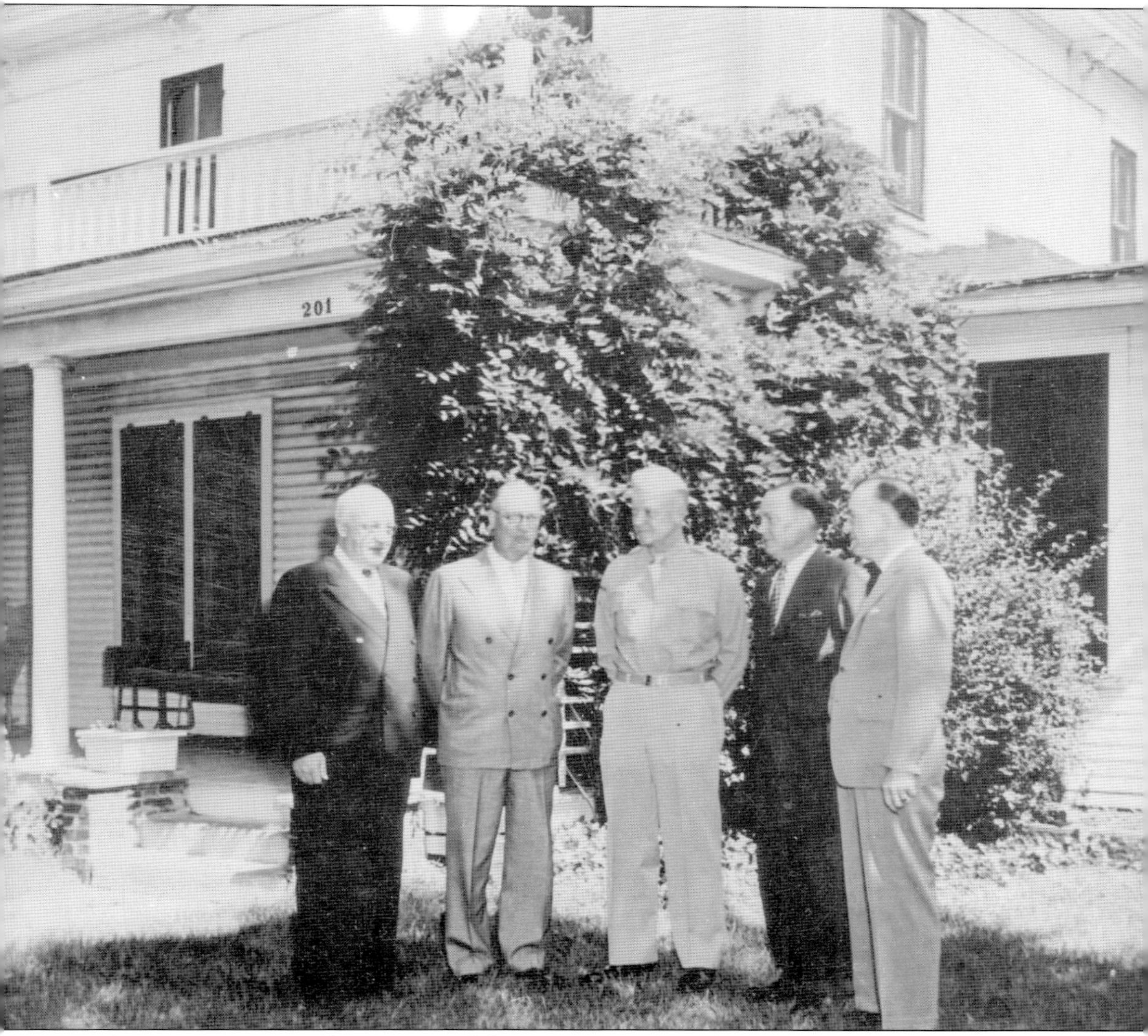

Eisenhower spent some of his time in Abilene visiting with his brothers. All of the Eisenhower "boys" did well in life: standing on the left is Arthur, who became a bank vice president; second to the left is Edgar, a lawyer; Dwight is in the center; second from the right is Roy, a pharmacist; and on the far right is Milton, who was at various times the president of Kansas State University, Pennsylvania State University, and Johns Hopkins University.

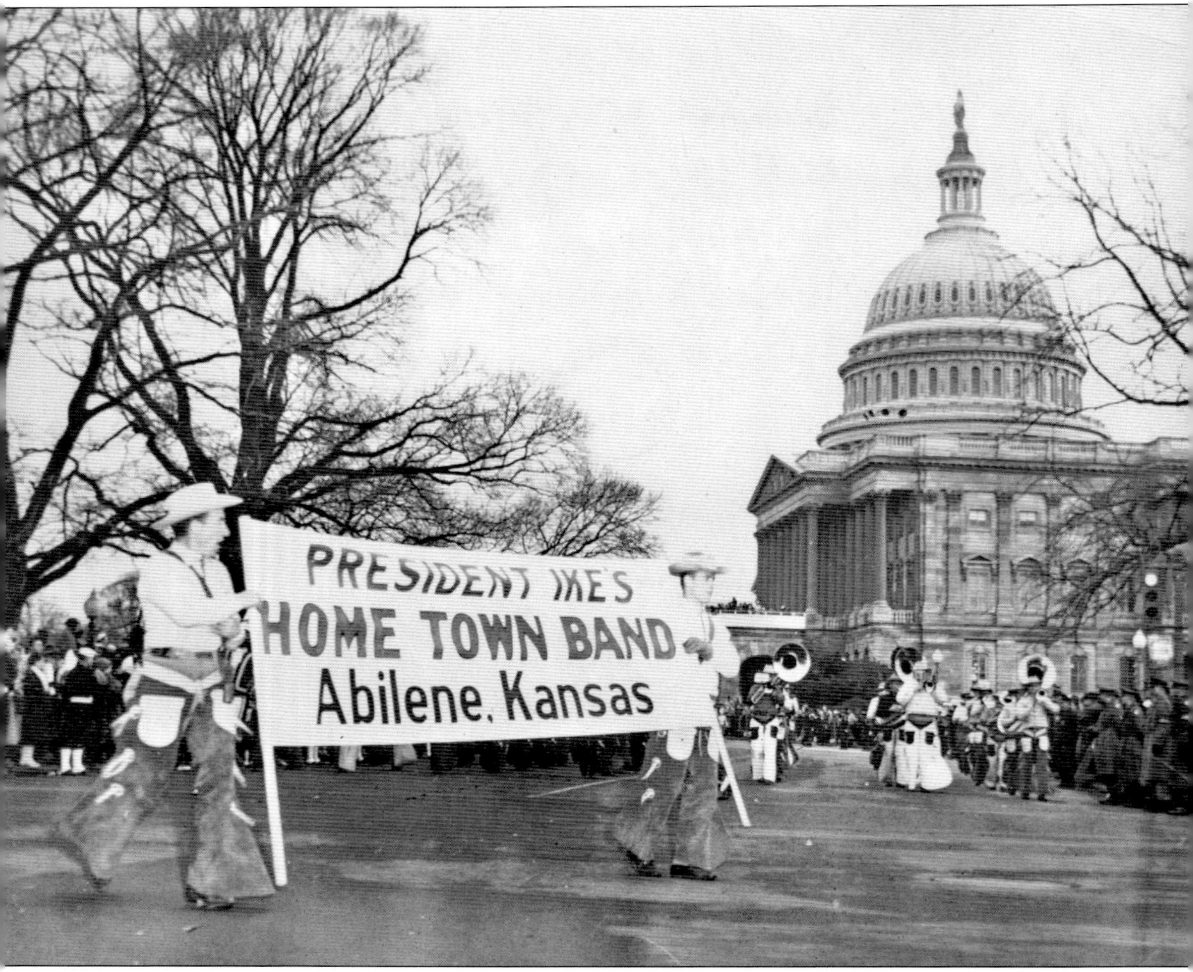

Eisenhower received the Republican nomination for president in 1952. He won by a landslide, defeating Democratic candidate Adlai Stevenson. The Abilene Band was invited to Washington, DC, to play in the inauguration parade.

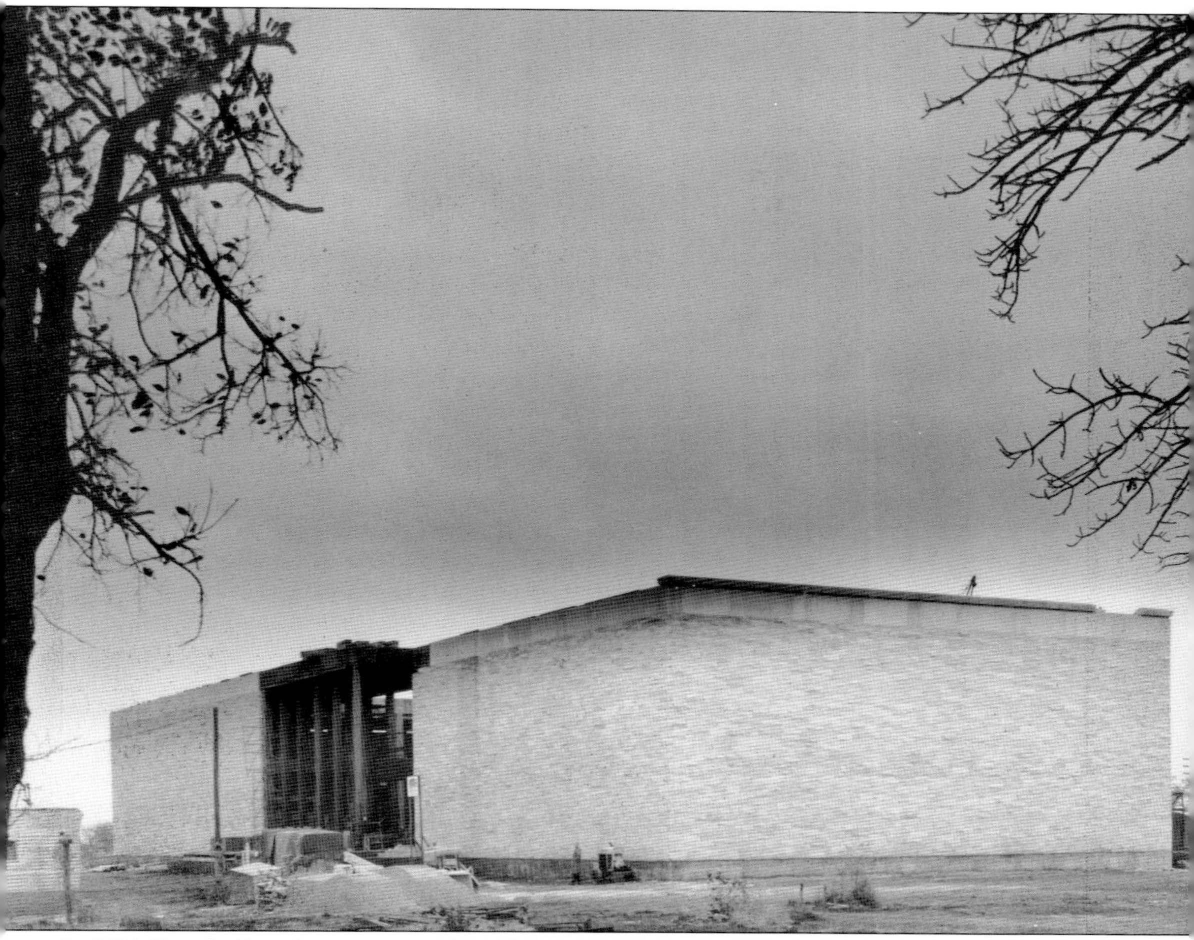

In 1954, Dwight Eisenhower returned to Abilene to dedicate his presidential library and museum. Eisenhower considered Abilene his hometown, and he was proud of where he came from. As President Eisenhower said, "The proudest thing I can claim is that I came from Abilene." The Eisenhower Presidential Library and Museum houses presidential papers and numerous artifacts from Eisenhower's eight years in office. Thousands of tourists visit the site each year.

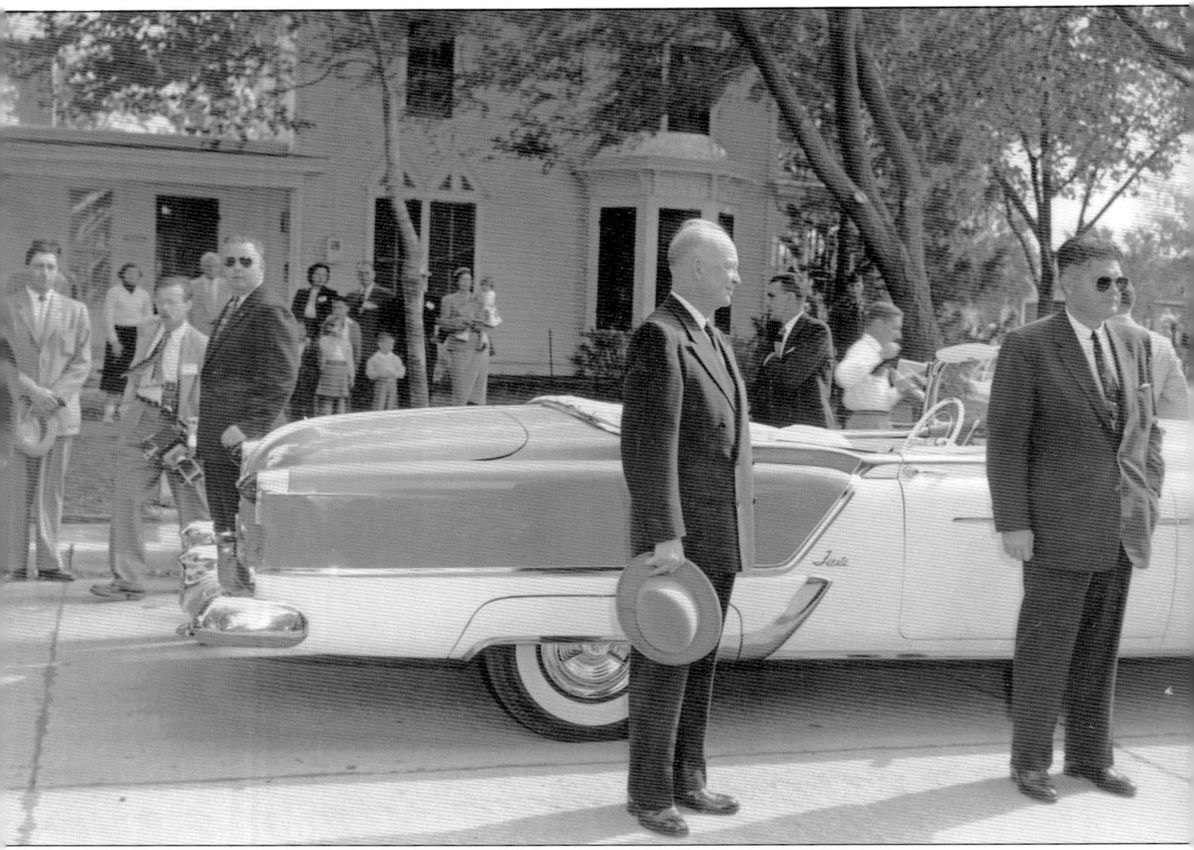

During Eisenhower's trip to Abilene, he visited the home where he grew up. The house was eventually incorporated into the museum site and is open to visitors.

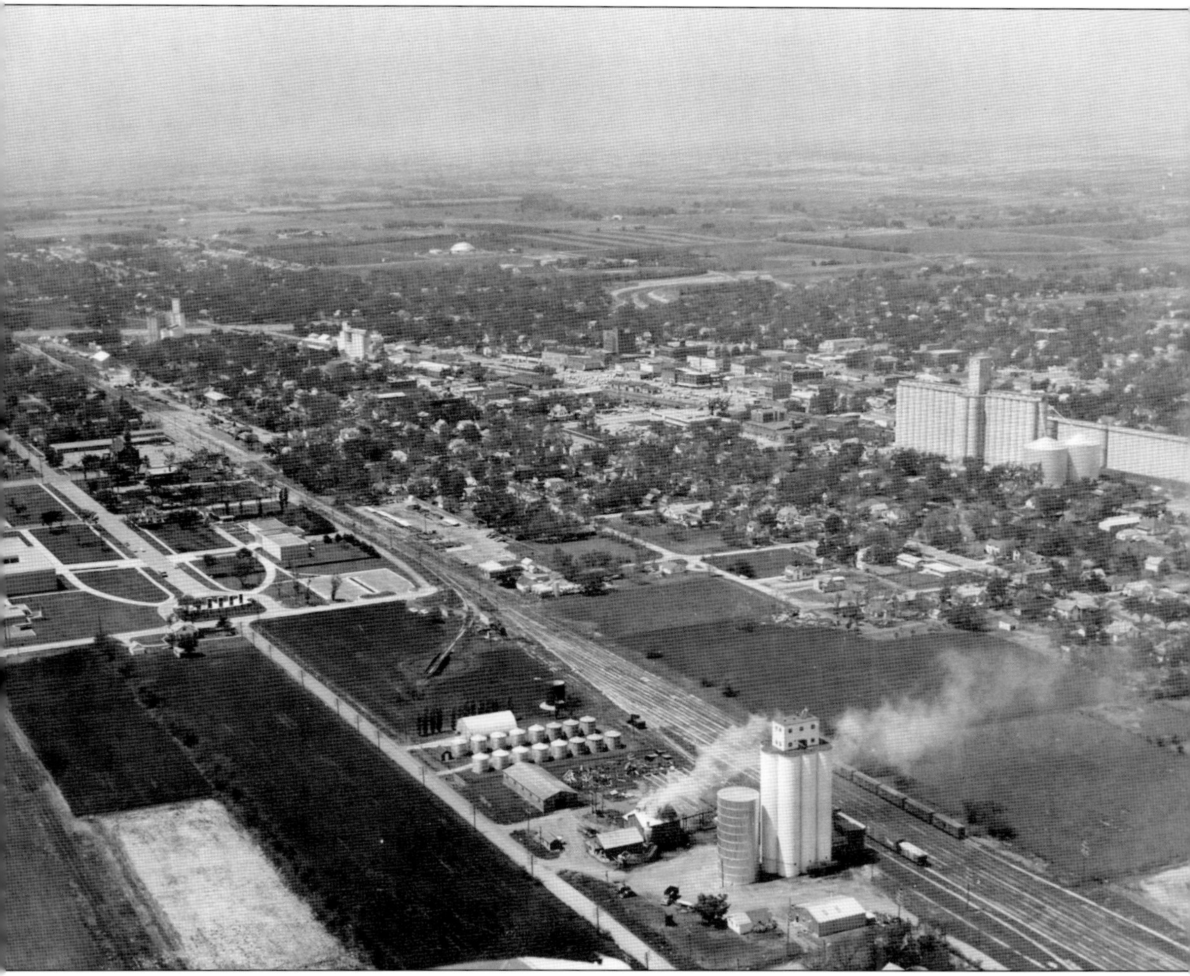

By the 1960s, Abilene had grown into a town that was home to three railroads, a presidential museum, and a vibrant farming community. Eliza Hersey's name is appropriate—Abilene is a "city of the plains."

Consistent with our mission to preserve history on a local level, this book was printed in South Carolina on American-made paper and manufactured entirely in the United States. Products carrying the accredited Forest Stewardship Council (FSC) label are printed on 100 percent FSC-certified paper.

MADE IN THE USA